CW01083899

THE MASTER MUSICIANS

TALLIS

SERIES EDITED BY R. LARRY TODD

THE MASTER MUSICIANS

Titles Available in Paperback

Bach • Malcolm Boyd

Bartók • Malcolm Gillies

Berlioz • Hugh Macdonald

Beethoven • Barry Cooper

Brahms • Malcolm MacDonald

Britten • Michael Kennedy

Bruckner • Derek Watson

Chopin • Jim Samson

Grieg • John Horton

Handel • Donald Burrows

Liszt • Derek Watson

Mahler • Michael Kennedy

Mendelssohn • Philip Radcliffe

Monteverdi • Denis Arnold

Mozart • Julian Rushton

Musorgsky • David Brown

Puccini • Julian Budden

Purcell • J. A. Westrup

Rachmaninoff • Geoffrey Norris

Rossini • Richard Osborne

Schoenberg • Malcolm MacDonald

Schubert • John Reed

Schumann • Eric Frederick Jensen

Sibelius • Robert Layton

Richard Strauss • Michael Kennedy

Tchaikovsky • Edward Garden

Vaughan Williams • James Day

Verdi • Julian Budden

Vivaldi • Michael Talbot

Wagner • Barry Millington

Titles Available in Hardcover

Beethoven • Barry Cooper

Byrd • Kerry McCarthy

Carter • David Schiff

Chopin • Jim Samson

Debussy • Eric Frederick Jensen

Elgar • Robert Anderson

Handel • Donald Burrows

Liszt • Derek Watson

MacDowell • E. Douglas Bomberger

Mozart • Julian Rushton

Musorgsky • David Brown

Puccini • Julian Budden

Rossini • Richard Osborne

Schoenberg • Malcolm MacDonald

Schubert • John Reed

Schumann • Eric Frederick Jensen

Schütz • Basil Smallman

Richard Strauss • Michael Kennedy

Strauss • Laurenz Lütteken

Stravinsky • Paul Griffiths

Tallis • Kerry McCarthy

Tchaikovsky • Roland John Wiley

Verdi • Julian Budden

THE MASTER MUSICIANS

TALLIS

KERRY McCARTHY

OXFORD
UNIVERSITY PRESS

OXFORD
UNIVERSITY PRESS

Oxford University Press is a department of the University of Oxford. It furthers
the University's objective of excellence in research, scholarship, and education
by publishing worldwide. Oxford is a registered trade mark of Oxford University
Press in the UK and certain other countries.

Published in the United States of America by Oxford University Press
198 Madison Avenue, New York, NY 10016, United States of America.

© Oxford University Press 2020

Library of Congress Cataloging-in-Publication Data
Names: McCarthy, Kerry Robin, author.
Title: Tallis / Kerry McCarthy.
Description: New York : Oxford University Press, 2020. |
Series: Master musicians series | Includes bibliographical references and index.
Identifiers: LCCN 2020014351 (print) | LCCN 2020014352 (ebook) |
ISBN 9780190635213 (hardback) | ISBN 9780190635237 (epub) |
ISBN 9780190635244 | ISBN 9780197533871
Subjects: LCSH: Tallis, Thomas, approximately 1505-1585. |
Composers—England—Biography.
Classification: LCC ML410.T147 M33 2020 (print) |
LCC ML410.T147 (ebook) | DDC 780.92 [B]—dc23
LC record available at https://lccn.loc.gov/2020014351
LC ebook record available at https://lccn.loc.gov/2020014352

3 5 7 9 8 6 4
Printed by Sheridan Books, Inc., United States of America

Contents

Preface

THOMAS TALLIS LIVED THROUGH (AND HELPED TO CREATE) A MORE radical transformation in musical style than any composer before him, in any era or any country. His long career, spanning much of the sixteenth century, also encompassed vast changes in English culture, religion, politics, literature, and visual art. The modern eye can capture something of this journey by visiting two adjoining rooms in the National Portrait Gallery in London. Passing from the rich, formal, subdued portraits of the early Tudor room into the rogues' gallery of Elizabethan courtiers and explorers and poets, flamboyant against plain dark backdrops, the viewer is left with the sense that something has shifted on a fundamental level. (There is no portrait of Tallis in either room; the familiar image of the long-haired man with quill pen in hand is, as far as we know, pure eighteenth-century fantasy.)[1]

The hand on the cover of this book does not belong to Tallis, but it belongs to a man who may well have met Tallis in passing. The French diplomat Georges de Selve was depicted by Henry VIII's court painter Hans Holbein during a visit to England in 1533. Tallis himself was employed in the early 1530s as an organist (see Chapter 1) in the town of Dover, the chief gateway to the English Channel, at a monastic house which received a constant onslaught of diplomats and other foreign guests. Two years after de Selve's journey, the head of the monastery complained about the damage wrought by the "strange ambassadors" who passed through.[2] Because this particular ambassador carried out his mission with great discretion, there is no evidence of the actual route he took. He was a young Catholic cleric with reformist sympathies who was summoned as part of a last-ditch diplomatic effort to avoid a break between England and Rome. According to the inscribed book on which his elbow rests, he was "in the 25th year of his age": born in 1508, of the same generation as Tallis.

Figure 0.1   Hans Holbein the Younger, Jean de Dinteville and Georges de Selve ("The Ambassadors"). © The National Gallery, London. Reproduced by permission.

The cover image is a detail from a larger work by Holbein, his famous double portrait (Figure 0.1) of *The Ambassadors*.[3] This life-size painting captures many of the beauties and preoccupations of Tallis's day. The table between Georges de Selve and his colleague is covered with elaborate scientific instruments built to measure the globe and scan the heavens. On the lower shelf, there are also instruments of music: a lute, a set of flutes, and a collection of devotional songs and hymns printed in Wittenberg nine years earlier. The book is open to a setting of *Komm Heiliger Geist*, a German translation of *Veni Sancte Spiritus*, the traditional prayer to the Holy Spirit for light and unity. The painting is full of unusual and complex textures, from the rich carpet and the inlaid marble pavement (recalling the priceless medieval Cosmati floor in the sanctuary of Westminster Abbey) to de Selve's thick silk damask robe. Holbein completes the tableau at floor level with a giant skull, a grotesquely distorted but unmistakable death's head. The whole thing is a powerful evocation of the English Renaissance in which Tallis lived and worked: the fascination with rich detail, learning and power and cosmopolitan exchange, the passage of time, and the ever-present specter of death, just on the edge of vision.

Tallis had the good fortune to enjoy a long working life in a range of cultural and musical circumstances. He spent time in nearly every environment typical for a church musician of his generation: a small priory (Dover), an urban parish (St. Mary-at-Hill), a large wealthy abbey (Waltham), a cathedral (Canterbury), and finally the private household of the English monarchs, whom he served for his last forty years. His career developed in close entanglement with the political upheavals of his day. He was sent away from the very last monastery dissolved in the English Reformation and was promptly appointed as one of the very first cathedral lay clerks in the newly reorganized Church of England.

Tallis's admirers and biographers, beginning in the late sixteenth century with the music scribe Robert Dow and the Elizabethan poet who wrote the composer's epitaph (see Chapter 17), have made much of the fact that he served in the Chapel Royal under four sovereigns. This has often been used as a kind of metaphor or shorthand for the vast liturgical changes he lived through. It is important to remember that he lived through them all in one secure post that was guaranteed for life. Public worship in England did not begin to change—give or take a few minor exceptions, mostly having to do with the Pope and politically volatile saints—until Tallis was safely ensconced in the royal household in the mid-1540s. Within five years, it was unrecognizable. Tallis was at the center of the musical Reformation as it happened, and he was lucky enough to experience it from an almost unique position of stability and power. Where other mid-century English composers reacted to events going on around them, he often seems to have taken the initiative in forging new musical ideas and styles.

Not all of the changes in Tallis's music were directly linked to religious reforms and counter-reforms. In his lifetime, he also saw a massive influx of new musical practices from outside England. He saw the birth of the music publishing industry in London. He saw the creation of new genres and the transformation of old genres beyond all recognition. It is no great surprise that he had a lifelong habit of revising and reworking his own material, sometimes at considerable length.[4] Through all this, he managed to keep his powerful musical personality and establish himself as a beloved elder statesman of English music. As Dow wrote in the early 1580s beneath a copy of Tallis's motet O *sacrum convivium*:

> Such and so great a musician are you, Tallis, that if the Fates carried you off in your old age, Music would be mute.[5]

There are many books to be written about Tallis. This is only one of them. After writing a biography of Byrd, I turned to his older colleague and found myself alarmed at first by the relative lack of documentation. We have evidence—sometimes just a few words of evidence—that Tallis made music in half a dozen different situations between 1530 and 1585. Unlike the well-published and litigious Byrd, he did not leave much of a paper trail. What remains is little more than a light scattering of fragments. It is often difficult, and in many cases impossible, to arrange his surviving musical works into any sort of timeline. After some reflection and a few false starts, I decided to build this book around what we still have, rather than lamenting or trying to extrapolate what we no longer have. The individual chapters are all focused on original documents of Tallis's life or on handwritten or printed sources of his music. (The one exception is Chapter 6, which is written as a journey down the River Thames, exploring the sites used by the musicians of the itinerant Chapel Royal.) These materials are limited, eclectic, and occasionally exasperating, but they give us the best chance we will ever have to meet Tallis on something like his own terms.

The first six chapters trace Tallis's career from his youthful appointment at Dover Priory to his years as a senior member of the Chapel Royal. The final chapter is a reflection on his epitaph and other postmortem remembrances, along with his will and the will of his wife Joan, two rare glimpses into the daily life of a Tudor composer's household. The rest of the book is built around a group of important musical documents which between them include all but a few of Tallis's known works. The scene is set with the *Antiphonale* of 1519–20, a monumental collection of chant containing two dozen plainsong melodies Tallis used in his own music and a thousand more he would have known as a young musician. The remaining materials are arranged roughly by date, from a handful of demonstrably early works through the developments of the Reformation years and the memorable "sacred songs" he published in 1575. This sort of chronology is not an exact science. In fact some of Tallis's best-known music survives exclusively in posthumous sources. Pieces as different as the forty-voice motet *Spem in alium*, the spartan Short Service (or "Dorian Service"), and the intricately wrought *Puer natus* mass have come down to us only through copies made in the early seventeenth century, a full generation after Tallis's death.

This focus on raw musical documents is not a conventional way to write about a composer's work. It may seem eccentric or tedious at times. Some readers will simply stop—or will at least want to stop—somewhere around Chapter 8 or 9. I cannot promise enlightenment to those who persevere, but I hope to bring them closer, in some small ways, to the everyday realities of Tallis's musical life. He did not work in isolation. He was part of a large and constantly shifting musical constellation that included several generations of composers, complex networks of performers, and the often anonymous figures who were responsible for the physical production and dissemination of music in sixteenth-century England, sometimes in quite challenging circumstances. His music did not appear in tidy collected editions with TALLIS printed on the cover—at least not until the publication of the *Cantiones sacrae* near the end of his life. It is almost always found side by side with the work of many other composers, subject to the tastes, whims, and mistakes of the people who copied and performed it. By taking a new look at the sources, it is possible to catch at least a hint of how Tallis's contemporaries would have experienced his art.

Readers who are interested in particular pieces of music may wish to consult the index first. Some of Tallis's works are taken as case studies and discussed in detail; some appear only in passing. I have not mentioned every individual piece in a systematic way, as John Harley has done in his recent book on Tallis, but I hope I have not neglected anyone's favorites.[6] Supplementary materials include a timeline of Tallis's life in documents and a series of short biographies of people who were significant to his career, as well as a website (see p. xvii) with a wide variety of audio samples. Footnotes refer readers to the sources of quotations and to other materials I have used in the making of this book. Digressions, reflections, and speculations of my own have been strictly excluded from the footnotes and confined to the main body of each chapter. All sixteenth-century texts in English are given in modernized spelling and punctuation.

Acknowledgments

FIRST OF ALL, MY SINCERE THANKS TO EVERY ONE OF THE PERFORM-
ers whose sound samples I have used to build the companion
website to this book. Their singing and playing has brought Tallis's
music alive for my readers in ways that the written word alone could
never accomplish. The *Journal of the Royal Musical Association* gave me
permission to reuse and adapt material from my 2010 review-article
on the Gyffard partbooks. In some ways that brief study was the origin of this entire project. I am grateful to John Milsom, who invited
me to write the article, and who has done many things since then
to make this a better book. Alan Howard at *Early Music* was also
generous in letting me use material from my 2019 article on Tallis's
epitaph. Peter Phillips has provided a refreshing dose of common
sense at various junctures. David Skinner has offered hospitality on
many visits to Cambridge and a keen eye for the latest developments
in Tallis's life story. David Mateer pointed me to the Windsor document naming a young "Byrd" as a chorister in 1548. The staff of the
modern Chapel(s) Royal have been generous in showing me around
their buildings: I am grateful to Paul Wright at St. James's, Colm
Carey at the Tower, and James Harris and Sophie Baylis at Hampton
Court Palace. David Allinson has been inspiring me to study and love
Tallis's music for almost twenty-five years now. John Harley has once
again been a delightful person to share a composer with. He read
every page of the draft and rescued me from a number of infelicities and absurdities. Magnus Williamson has given practical help all
along the way, including a shared Leverhulme research fellowship in
2017 and a long-term association with the Tudor Partbooks project.
Without his resourcefulness and kindness, this book would have taken

much longer to write. I also owe a great debt to the editorial team at Oxford University Press, especially to Suzanne Ryan, who has tolerated a repeat offender in the Master Musicians series.

Kerry McCarthy
May 2020

Photographic Acknowledgments

Permission to reproduce the following items is gratefully acknowledged: Cover image and Figure 0.1, National Gallery, London; Figures 1.1, 3.3, 3.4, 8.1, 8.2, 9.1, and 11.1, The British Library Board (with special thanks to Richard Chesser and Nicolas Bell); Figure 2.1, Ashmolean Museum; Figure 3.1, National Archives, Kew; Figure 3.2, Godfrey Bartlett, Essex Walks; Figure 4.1, Canterbury Cathedral; Figure 5.1, St. George's Chapel Archives, by permission of the Dean and Canons of Windsor; Figures 7.1, 7.2, 9.2, 14.2, 15.1, and 17.1, Christ Church, Oxford (with special thanks to Alina Nachescu); Figure 10.1, The Master and Fellows of Peterhouse, Cambridge; Figure 12.1, Bodleian Library; Figure 13.1, Princeton Theological Seminary; Figure 13.2, National Trust; Figure 14.1, The Board of Trinity College, Dublin; Figure 16.1, Royal Collection Trust; Figure 16.3, Victoria and Albert Museum, London.

About the Companion Website

www.oup.com/us/tallis

The volume you are now reading is only part of the *Master Musicians* book on Tallis. The other part is a website that is hosted (and will be permanently maintained) by Oxford University Press, with sixty brief audio clips chosen to illustrate specific points in the musical discussion. Each audio excerpt on the website includes a page reference to the book, a descriptive caption, and the information needed to find and purchase the whole track or indeed the whole CD. My hope is that readers will find these recordings to be a useful portal into Tallis's sound-world.

DOCUMENTS OF TALLIS'S LIFE

CHAPTER ONE

Dover Priory (1530–31)

THE ELIZABETHAN COURTIER AND EXPLORER SIR WALTER RALEIGH
wrote a letter to the Queen in the 1580s, praising the port of Dover
in extravagant terms: "No promontory, town, or haven of Christendom
is so placed by nature and situation, both to gratify friends and annoy
enemies, as this your Majesty's town of Dover."[1] The earliest surviving
record of Tallis's life shows him in this fortunate place, employed as
the organist at Dover Priory from September 1530 through September
1531.[2] (Monasteries, like modern-day universities, kept their records
from one autumn to the next.) We are lucky to have this document at
all. It is a handwritten booklet of sixteen pages, the only survivor from
what must have been a series of carefully kept annual accounts. It gives
us a snapshot of a single year in a small but busy monastic house.[3]

Tallis was not a monk himself. He was one of fifteen laymen
employed as "servants of the guesthouse," outsiders who played their
part in the complex task of running a Benedictine monastery. He is
listed between the brewer and the bell ringer, all three of them indis-
pensable to the daily routine of life. (The importance of these duties
is clear in an early-sixteenth-century report from the nearby priory of
St. Gregory in Canterbury, where the brothers were often absent from
services because there was no bell ringer to keep time, vexed by a cantor who did not know how to sing, and disgusted at the poor quality of
beer they were served.[4]) Tallis was among the best-paid lay employees

Tallis. Kerry McCarthy, Oxford University Press (2020). © Oxford University Press.
DOI: 10.1093/oso/9780190635213.001.0001.

at Dover Priory, receiving the same salary as the bailiff (legal steward) of the house, who held an equally specialized and demanding post.

The priory's records were kept in Latin, and the title given to Tallis was *joculator organorum*, player of the organs.[5] *Joculator* means "player" in the most literal sense—it is cognate with the French *jongleur* and the English *juggler*—and the accounts of 1530–31 used the same word for the minstrels and entertainers who arrived at Dover in the entourage of visiting dignitaries: twenty pence paid by the monks as a gratuity to the *joculator* of the Lord Warden of the Cinque Ports, overseer of trade and defense across the English Channel; twenty pence to the *joculator* of George Nevill, future Lord Warden, whose dyspeptic scowl was immortalized in a sketch by Holbein; four shillings to the stage magician and brilliant showman Thomas Brandon, the *joculator* of "our Lord the King," Henry VIII.[6] All of those performers were received as guests at Dover Priory while Tallis was there.

There was certainly no lack of visitors at the priory. Raleigh said in his note to Queen Elizabeth that anyone who made the journey from "any parts of the Low Countries . . . or of Spain, Portugal, France, or Italy, bound northward either to London or to any of the northern provinces . . . must of necessity touch, as it were, upon this promontory." This was only a mild exaggeration. As a primary gateway to the English Channel, Dover attracted thousands of European visitors and departing English travelers every year. In the earlier part of the sixteenth century, a considerable number of them found their way to the priory, which functioned as a sort of hotel for the retinue of politically important figures. Hospitality was an important part of the Benedictine tradition, but it seems to have been a mixed blessing from the perspective of the monks. Their prior, John Folkestone, complained bitterly in 1535 that vandalism and looting by outsiders led to chaos in his community:

> the strangers resorting [foreigners visiting] be such wasteful destroyers that it is not possible to keep any good stuff long in good order . . . especially strange ambassadors have such noxious and hurtful followers that have packed up tablecloths, napkins, sheets, coverpanes [bedspreads], with other such things as they could get.[7]

Tallis lived and worked in the midst of all this activity. As a "servant of the guesthouse," he was part of the public face of the priory, adding to its prestige with his skill. There are some hints of additional musical practices beyond his organ playing and the everyday singing of the monks. We find new shoes being purchased for an unspecified number of "boys of the choir," and, in an inventory drawn up a few years later, a salary paid to an unnamed "master of the song school."[8] It was common for monasteries to operate a school where children were taught liturgical chant and engaged to sing in services.[9] Dover Priory, despite its small size, appears to have maintained such a school. At one point in 1530–31 the community also hosted what seems to have been an extended visit by the boy choristers of the private chapel of William Warham, the Archbishop of Canterbury.[10] Even secular instrumental music had its place at the priory: the records during the year of Tallis's residency include payment to the waits of Canterbury, the city musicians who played for ceremonial occasions.

The surviving priory accounts also offer a glimpse into some other details of Tallis's everyday life in the early 1530s. Professional musicians in monasteries, like other lay staff, generally collected part of their pay in the form of food and accommodation. (One unusual exception was the composer and organist John Tyes, who a few generations earlier had turned down Westminster Abbey's standard offer of room, board, and clothing in favor of a more generous cash salary.)[11] The refectory (dining hall) at Dover was large enough to accommodate the staff as well as the monks and their numerous guests; the building, which still stands today, is an imposing hall over a hundred feet long, with eight high windows on each side and a faded fresco of the Last Supper at the east end. The diet at the monastery was far from austere during Tallis's time there, although imported luxuries such as ginger, saffron, and fifty pounds of "Greek raisins" may have been bought for the sake of distinguished visitors rather than the everyday needs of the brethren. Archbishop Warham was treated to a dish of prawns during Lent. Provisions for the house included eggs, butter, oatmeal, Suffolk cheese, a suckling pig at Christmas, leeks in early spring, and vast quantities of fish on just about every possible occasion.

The daily life of a Benedictine monk included a formidable routine of sung services, eight during the day and one during the night. Lay musicians employed by English monasteries were not normally expected to take part in this full round of worship. Their primary duty was most often to provide special music for Sundays, feast days, and, above all, devotions to the Virgin Mary. (It is no surprise that all of Tallis's apparently earliest polyphonic works are settings of Marian texts, even though such texts represented only a small percentage of the daily liturgy at Dover Priory or any other English church.) By the early sixteenth century, many of the wealthier monasteries in England employed full ensembles of professional musicians to adorn their most important services. One of the most vivid accounts of this practice comes from the Renaissance humanist author Desiderius Erasmus. During the years he spent in England, he visited many monastic churches, including the rich and powerful Benedictine monastery at Canterbury, of which Dover Priory (barely twenty miles away) was a dependent house. Shortly before leaving the country for the last time in 1515, he interrupted his scholarly annotations on St. Paul's first letter to the Corinthians to deliver a lengthy polemic on the decadence of contemporary church music. He singled out the English for special abuse.

> These things [elaborate musical practices] are so satisfying that monks do nothing else, especially among the English: and men who should be singing lamentations think they are pleasing God with lascivious neighing and agile throats. In the Benedictine monasteries in England, adolescents, young boys, and expert singers are even maintained, who sing the morning service to the Virgin Mother with the most melodious vocal chattering and organ music.[12]

Erasmus obviously took a dim view of English monks and their taste for chattering young musicians. Of course he was not an impartial observer: he was deeply disillusioned with monastic life after having been forced into an Augustinian priory as a destitute orphan in his late teens. His earliest musical experiences also seem to have been unhappy; his friend and biographer Beatus Rhenanus recalls his stint as a boy chorister, "usually undertaking small singing duties on account of his very feeble voice."[13] Although Erasmus had his own prejudices, his diatribe tells us something about the typical situation in the larger English monasteries. The collaboration of lay musicians was not only tolerated but expected, most of all (as he correctly observed) at the daily Lady Mass.

Dover Priory, with its dozen monks and its rather precarious finances, was not equipped to support a full-scale ensemble of professional singers, and there is no evidence that it ever did. If Tallis was already composing elaborate vocal polyphony around 1530, it was quite likely being sung somewhere else, or by visiting musicians not consistently employed by the priory. It is telling that his job description was "organ player" rather than "cantor" or "master of the choristers." Although we have no trace of his original contract, we can discover something about the duties of monastery organists from other musicians who were specifically employed as such. When John Smythe was hired in 1534 as organist of Sempringham Priory, he agreed to "serve the choir with the organs" on the twelve "principal feasts" of the year at matins, mass, vespers, and compline (about five hours of service in total); to play at mass and vespers on regular Sundays and lesser feasts; and to perform lighter duties on various other occasions.[14] Many organists were primarily engaged to play for Marian devotions. Some were expected to give keyboard training to young choristers or even to musically-inclined monks.[15]

The hiring of a professional musician such as Tallis had become a mark of monastic prestige by 1530. It would have been especially desirable in a place such as Dover, with its rich diplomatic and social life. For just a few pounds a year, and some maintenance of instruments and manuscripts, monks could share in the musical tradition of great churches and great households. These choices were fueled by ambition as well as piety, and it is no surprise that Dover Priory recruited an organist of unusual talent. Given Tallis's relatively generous pay (at least in comparison to the pittance given some other employees) and his prominent place among the full-time "servants of the guesthouse," he seems to have been accepted to some extent as a member of the community. Such acceptance was frowned upon in stricter circles. After a visitation and inspection of the Cistercian abbey of Thame in 1526, the monks were warned against frivolity in music-making and worship; they were allowed to hear "organ playing by a brother, or by an honest secular man," as long as he "does not have too great a familiarity with the brothers."[16] We know nothing about Tallis's familiarity with the brothers at Dover, although the Thame visitors might have raised an eyebrow at the blatantly secular title they gave their *joculator*—a term that one prominent sixteenth-century Latin-English dictionary defined simply as "jester."[17]

The duty of lay organist or lay choirmaster in a monastery seems often to have been a task for young people. Twelve different laymen served as director of the Lady Chapel choir at Westminster Abbey in the six decades before the Reformation, starting with William Cornysh when the post was established in 1480, and not a single one of them is known to have held any position of authority elsewhere before coming to the abbey.[18] In other words, it was always someone's first job, a dozen times in a row. Westminster was a large, prestigious, well-placed monastery, one of the richest in England, but its highest-ranking lay musicians all appear to have been rather young and inexperienced. John Smythe, the organist at Sempringham, was given a month's vacation each year "to sport him among his friends": this does not suggest a grave middle-aged householder.

Although it is dangerous to assume anything about Tallis's age from evidence of this sort, we can hazard a guess that he was still relatively young when he was employed at Dover. If it was his first serious musical post, it was not a bad start. Raleigh wrote half a century later in his letter to the Queen that "no place or town of Christendom is so settled to receive and deliver intelligence for all matters and actions in Europe"; he was of course speaking about political intelligence, but his point also applies to musical intelligence. In the everyday round of hospitality and exchange, Tallis may well have found opportunities to see or discuss (or indeed hear) various forms of music from other countries. Dover was a place where English culture and foreign culture met and mingled, and sometimes clashed. This environment must have made an impression on a composer who would go on to adopt a number of up-to-date Continental techniques in his own music.

The records of 1530–31 show the monks of Dover working on long-term maintenance of their property: "repair of the water conduit," "painting various images in the church," "making new vessels in the brewhouse." They could hardly have known that their community would survive for only four more years. Dover Priory surrendered to the Crown in 1535, a casualty of the first round of Henry VIII's dissolution of the monasteries. The deed of surrender, dated 16 November, is a document of quiet resignation. There is none of the ideological bluster found in some other monastic deeds of surrender, renouncing "our pretended religion" or "dumb ceremonies." The monks simply say, after the usual legal formalities, that their monastery is in danger of falling into ruin "unless it is quickly aided by royal support," and that they willingly hand over the priory with its land, its buildings, and all its possessions.[19]

The situation at Dover Priory was not quite as dire as this final document suggests. (It is worth noting that suspiciously similar terms are found in the deeds of surrender by the neighboring priories of Langdon and Folkestone, also signed in mid-November 1535.)[20] The buildings were indeed in some disrepair, and money was short as always, but the monks could hardly have been living in squalor or extreme poverty when they offered hospitality to such a wide variety of visitors just a few years earlier, and there is no evidence that things were in radical decline. If anything, the priory seems to have been in a phase of quiet reform and renovation when Tallis was there. When Archbishop Warham had made an official visitation in 1511, he had interviewed the novices, discovered that they were not being taught to read Latin properly, and ordered an immediate change in their training.[21] By 1530–31, the annual accounts included a purchase of "grammatical books for the novices." One of Thomas Cromwell's agents was sent to the priory shortly before the dissolution to look for signs of decadence and corruption. This is the full report he made to Cromwell in October 1535: "The prior of Dover and his monks be even as others be, but he the worst; sodomites there is none, for they need not, they have no lack of women."[22] There were certainly a number of women on the payroll, including the woman who washed clothes and household linen, and a dairymaid with several female assistants. Given some of the lurid tales, both real and imagined, to come out of these monastic visitations, the tone of this short note is hardly surprising.

An inventory made in 1534, as the process of dissolution began, reveals a bit more about the physical circumstances in which Tallis worked.[23] This list was part of the national *Valor Ecclesiasticus* (church assessment) compiled by Henry's agents. It has little in common with the annual account drawn up a few years earlier: it is concerned with the valuable assets of the house rather than ephemera such as oatmeal, shoes, and musicians' fees. The inventory notes the presence of an organ in the priory church, which was presumably the instrument Tallis played during services. The organ is listed among the treasures of the choir and vestry, including a considerable hoard of gilded silver and a selection of vestments embroidered with roses, leaves, birds, and stars. It may well have been a very fine instrument. Tallis himself does not appear in any of the dissolution records; his name is absent as the monks and lay staff are pensioned off and sent away. There is also no positive evidence that he left Dover before November 1535, but so many documents were lost in those turbulent days that it is risky to argue from silence.

All that remains of Tallis's earliest known post is a brief note (Figure 1.1) in fading brown ink. It is not unhelpful as brief notes go, because it tells us something important about the trajectory of his career. He began his professional life at the very end of an era. The years around 1530 were a high-water mark of musical extravagance in English churches. Not long afterward, the whole edifice began to collapse. Henry and his reform-minded advisors wasted no time in dismantling the monasteries and all they stood for: prayer for the dead, devotion to the saints (Dover was the primary way-station for the crowds of Continental pilgrims who visited the shrine of Thomas Becket at Canterbury), and loyalty to a church whose leaders in Rome had little time or concern for the political demands of the English monarchy. While Tallis played the organ at Dover Priory, the earliest stage of the English Reformation was already in progress. Whether or not he was aware of it, some of the diplomats and scholars passing through Dover were working frantically to obtain an annulment of the King's ill-fated

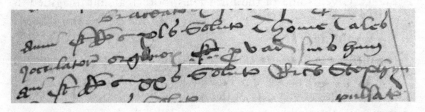

Figure 1.1   Tallis at Dover Priory: *xl s solut[um] Thome Tales Joculator[i] organor[um] p[ro] vad[iis] suis hui[us] ann[i].* (40 shillings paid to Thomas Tallis, player of the organs, for his salary this year.) © The British Library Board. Reproduced by permission.

marriage to Catherine of Aragon. By the time the priory was suppressed in 1535, England faced an extended period of political turmoil and musical upheaval. The next few chapters of this book are simply an account, as well as it can be traced, of how Tallis worked his way through those difficult years.

CHAPTER TWO

St. Mary-at-Hill (1536–38)

THE FLEMISH ARTIST ANTON VAN DEN WYNGAERDE CAME TO London around 1544 and sketched a detailed ten-foot-long panorama of the city.[1] His drawing is the closest we will ever come to seeing Tudor London, most of which was irreparably destroyed in the Great Fire of 1666. Wyngaerde's panorama shows a forest of tall narrow houses interspersed with church steeples. One of the churches (Figure 2.1), just north of the Thames and not far from London Bridge, is called St. Mary-at-Hill. In the late 1530s, Tallis is named twice in the roster of musicians employed there. This is the first time he appears in London.

Sixteenth-century London was a patchwork quilt of more than a hundred tiny parishes packed into one square mile. The parish of St. Mary-at-Hill was barely 200 feet across from east to west, just enough to span the church itself and a couple of adjoining streets. It was almost three times as long from north to south, because it extended all the way from the main thoroughfare of Eastcheap down to the river. True to its name, the parish was (and still is) on a rather steep hill. At the bottom of the hill, adjacent to the river, was the large and very busy Billingsgate Market, which can be seen at the lower edge of Figure 2.1. By the sixteenth century, Billingsgate had become a specialist market for seafood, where shipments of "fish, both fresh and salt, shell-fishes," and similar commodities were unloaded from boats and sold to buyers in the city.[2] Its name became a byword for rough language—a character in one Elizabethan retelling of the story of King Lear has "as bad

Tallis. Kerry McCarthy, Oxford University Press (2020). © Oxford University Press.
DOI: 10.1093/oso/9780190635213.001.0001.

Figure 2.1   Detail from Wyngaerde's panorama of London, ca. 1544. (Tallis's church of St. Mary-at-Hill is on the left side, halfway up. It has a row of five windows in the nave and, immediately to their left, a large bell tower with a pyramidal roof.) Ashmolean Museum. Reproduced by permission.

a tongue . . . as any oyster-wife at Billingsgate"—and the smell must have been pungent on hot summer days.[3] One later observer described this part of town with evident disgust: "The narrow streets and alleys, and their wet slippery foot-ways, will not bear description, or invite unnecessary visits."[4] The seafood business was lucrative, especially in pre-Reformation England, where meat was not eaten on more than one-third of the days in the year. Billingsgate may have had a rough reputation, but it was one of the economic centers of London, and St. Mary-at-Hill was a well-to-do parish. It also appears to have been one of the most musically active parishes in the city.[5]

We know a great deal about the everyday life of St. Mary-at-Hill during the reign of Henry VIII. Unlike most London churches, it has a well-preserved set of annual churchwardens' accounts which survive almost completely intact between 1500 and 1540. They show that Tallis was employed there for a total of one year. (He receives half a year's wages in two different annual accounts. One of those accounts runs from 29 September 1536 to 29 September 1537; the other runs from 29 September 1537 to 29 September 1538.[6]) These are physically more imposing documents than the financial records of Dover Priory. They are gathered in a large, formal, spacious ledger with a single entry on each line. Many of the entries have to do with musical expenses: payment of singers, organ repair, purchase of chant books, copying of polyphony, maintenance of the parish's choir school, and other related costs.

The choir of St. Mary-at-Hill was not a fixed entity with a set number of musicians. There were generally a couple of stalwarts each year who were paid a full year's wage and seem to have been in permanent residence, but most of the people who sang there with Tallis were present only part of the time.[7] Many singers were paid for one quarter, three quarters, or assorted fragments of the year. Roger Kenton, who would eventually follow Tallis into the Chapel Royal, was present for just a couple of months in 1537: "from the 24th day of February to our Lady's day the Annunciation" and "5 weeks and odd days after midsummer."[8] This is not a tidy annual payroll. Even if Tallis's two half-years at St. Mary-at-Hill were in fact one contiguous year, from March 1537 through March 1538, there is still a definite sense that he was one of many moving parts in a complex machine. There normally seem to have been somewhere between four and six paid musicians at work at any given moment. Other entries in the church accounts appear to confirm this. Several new sets of surplices were made for the singers during the 1530s, one set each of four, five, and six.[9] Payments were made in 1523–24 for "six round mats of wicker for the clerks," and again in 1531–32 "to a basket maker for five round mats for the clerks to stand upon."[10] Wicker mats would have offered welcome cushioning and warmth while standing on a stone floor during long services. Given what seems to have been the intensity of musical life there, it is no surprise that they wore out and had to be replaced in less than a decade.

The church also procured "two yards of wicker mat for the children's feet."[11] The young choristers did not get their own round mats. They are treated in the records, here and elsewhere, as an anonymous group. St. Mary's choir school seems to have been relatively small and unpretentious.[12] Its origins can be traced to the musically inclined rector Alan Percy, who was in charge of the church from 1521 to 1560. Shortly after Percy arrived there, he employed a professional organist, John Northfolke, who promptly made two major changes.[13] First, he had the organ repaired (a sum was paid "for mending the organs according to the mind of Mr. Northfolke and at his device") and engaged John Howe, London's most prestigious organ builder, to maintain the instrument year-round. Second, he began to teach a group of boy choristers, who at first were simply called "Northfolke's children." The choir school was set up next door to the church in a building known as Abbot's Inn, a property owned by Waltham Abbey, where Tallis would be employed a few years later. A number of other tenants also occupied Abbot's Inn, including Tallis's colleague Richard Wynslate, who rented a room there. The school itself was only a single room, which became more comfortable in 1536–37 when a chimney was installed.[14] The boys enjoyed seasonal festivities and a "playing week to make merry."[15] There are no direct reports of what they sang in church, but the presence of trained treble voices would have allowed the choir of St. Mary-at-Hill to perform the most ornate and wide-ranging vocal music of the day. Northfolke provided the church with new collections of five-part anthems and masses in 1529–30.[16] Two reform-minded men of the parish were reported in 1541 for "dispraising a certain anthem of our Lady, beginning 'Te matrem' etc., saying that there is heresy in the same."[17] This seems to be a description of Hugh Aston's popular five-part piece *Te matrem Dei laudamus*. If so, the choir was indeed singing difficult polyphony, and in a conspicuous enough way for people to complain about it.

It may seem surprising at first to see so much attention paid to music in such a small parish: no more than 400 people were living within the parish boundaries around 1550, although that number referred only to people who received communion and would thus have excluded young children.[18] The geographical territory Tallis served here may have been small, but it was far from insignificant. (It was also far from insular. Over ten percent of the taxpaying residents of the Billingsgate area at the time were foreigners.[19]) Music-making in English parish churches could and did reach a very high level of accomplishment, even equal in some cases to what was going on in the cathedrals.[20] This was also possible in the case of St. Mary-at-Hill because London was home to a large and complex musical network that transcended parish boundaries.[21] The presence of good musicians seems to have attracted other good musicians, whatever the size of the venue. In addition to its regular pool of singers, this particular parish had a long tradition of hiring extras from nearby churches on special days. They even borrowed voices from the Chapel Royal on occasion, although there is no evidence that this happened while Tallis was there.[22]

Professional singers in London, like members of other skilled trades, were organized into a guild which encouraged collaboration across parish lines.[23] This particular guild fulfilled the roles of both a traditional devotional brotherhood (it was known as the Fraternity of St. Nicholas) and a trade union (it was also known as the Company of Parish Clerks.) Members celebrated an annual evensong and feast at Guildhall, and received charitable assistance from their brethren when necessary. They were exhorted to pray for their deceased colleagues—the main reason why their names were so carefully written down over the years. They also imposed a strict set of rules about who could sing where and when. The clerks' guild held an official monopoly on singing for pay in London, although that restriction seems to have been hard to enforce and flouted to some extent. Tallis himself was quite likely a member, given his musical activity in the city; unfortunately the roster of the Company of Parish Clerks is lost after 1521, so it includes figures such as Cornysh, Fayrfax, and Ludford but excludes Tallis and his immediate contemporaries.[24] By the early sixteenth century, this system had already produced a community of insiders who were closely tied to a shared professional identity as well as to their particular geographical locations within London.

During Tallis's relatively short time at St. Mary-at-Hill, between September 1536 and September 1538, the churchwardens' accounts show a wide range of expenses for all sorts of goods and services.[25] There are payments for "the making of the song book for the church"—its contents are unspecified—and for the copying of "carols for Christmas" and "five square books." "Square" had nothing to do with the dimensions of the books. It referred to the conventional melodies commonly called "squares" on which music was often improvised and composed; the Gyffard partbooks (see Chapter 11) contain several masses "upon the square," including two by William Mundy, who was employed by the parish not long after Tallis. There was "mending of the bellows of the organs" and hiring of a man to pump the bellows at two pence per week. Four new surplices were made for the young choristers, a modest number that matches well with the length of the wicker mat under their feet. The church was regularly adorned with seasonal decorations, including palms and flowers on Palm Sunday, garlands on Maundy Thursday and Corpus Christi, birch at midsummer, and holly and ivy at Christmas. There was also "ringing of the great bell six hours for Queen Jane": Henry's third queen, Jane Seymour, who died in October 1537 shortly after giving birth to the future Edward VI.

This last entry is a rare reminder of the political turmoil that was going on outside the church doors. By the time Tallis was employed there, St. Mary-at-Hill was already a parish subject to the royal supremacy over the Church of England, with no religious or administrative ties to Rome. Despite this new state of affairs, the elaborate Latin liturgy and the day-to-day activities of the parish seem to have continued with no visible change. Even a chapel dedicated to Thomas Becket, that most controversial of English saints, was still being mentioned in the accounts (on the same leaf as his namesake, Thomas the professional musician) without apparent unease.[26] Public religious unrest certainly made its way into this part of London while Tallis was there: in May 1538, a group of iconoclasts visited the neighboring church of St. Margaret Pattens at night and smashed the large crucifix that stood in the churchyard along with the shrine containing it.[27] Tallis's fellow-singer Richard Wynslate, who lived around the corner, would have heard the commotion. The late 1530s were a time of confusing and often contradictory developments as the national church tried to sort out its own identity. Several sets of doctrinal guidelines were published during these years, after rival emendations by various churchmen and by the king himself.[28] Most of these were rather mild documents with relatively little to offend traditional-minded readers. A more ominous tone can be heard in a proclamation of November 1538, which declares that the "ceremonies heretofore used in the Church of England, which as yet be not abolished nor taken away by the king's highness" are to be taken as "good and laudable . . . until such time as his majesty doth change or abrogate any of them."[29] The casual "as yet" speaks volumes about the situation. The English church of Henry's later years was quite conservative in its views and practices, but that conservatism was built on the personal whim of the monarch and could shift at any moment.

Tallis probably did not anticipate a much greater change in religious practice, because—as we will see in the next chapter—he left his London parish in 1538 and went back to work in a monastery. He may even have accepted a post at Waltham Abbey for what seemed at the time to be its stability. The smaller and less significant monasteries had been dispensed with, leaving the larger ones securely established; in fact the initial round of dissolutions in the mid-1530s, which Tallis may well have experienced first-hand at Dover Priory, was officially announced as a positive move that would strengthen the "great solemn monasteries of this realm wherein (thanks be to God) religion is right well kept and observed."[30] There were also long-standing connections between St. Mary-at-Hill and Waltham, not least because of the land and buildings they shared (amicably, it seems) at very close quarters in central London.

When Tallis disappeared from the payroll of St. Mary-at-Hill, he was following the same general path as many of his fellow-singers: fewer than one in ten stayed there for more than four years.[31] The parish seems often to have served as a springboard to more prominent musical positions. A number of Tallis's colleagues there were recruited by cathedrals, as he himself would be a few years later. Wynslate became master of the choristers at Winchester Cathedral. John Thorne became organist at York Minster. William Fox went to Westminster Abbey "to sing and serve in the choir daily." Several others eventually made their way into the Chapel Royal. Tallis's presence in London in the later 1530s reveals him as part of a close-knit and versatile group of urban musicians who were active during the last years before the Reformation severely limited the scope of parish music-making.

CHAPTER THREE

Waltham Abbey (1540)

THE NEXT DOCUMENT OF TALLIS'S LIFE IS A LESS HAPPY ONE. IT shows him being sent away from the last monastery in England on the day of its dissolution. Waltham Abbey was a distinguished house of Augustinian canons in Essex, fifteen miles northeast of central London. Generations of English royalty, including Henry VIII, had used the abbey as a hunting lodge and a convenient country retreat; the final inventory includes the richly furnished "King's chamber," with Turkish carpets and hangings of green silk.[1] Royal favor was not enough to save the abbey. It all ended on 23 March 1540, two weeks before Easter, with a note signed by the abbot and his seventeen brethren, declaring that they surrendered their monastery "by unanimous assent and consent and spontaneous will."[2] This small piece of folded-over parchment is marked with the very last imprint (Figure 3.1) of the seal of Waltham Abbey.

Tallis was a lay employee, not one of the canons of the abbey, so he did not sign the deed of surrender. His name is found in a separate and much larger document with all the financial details of the house.[3] Waltham seems to have had a healthy musical establishment until the end. Tallis is not given an official title here—organist, choirmaster, cantor, or otherwise—but he was the highest paid of more than sixty lay staff, which implies a position of some importance and authority. He had several organs at his disposal (one in the Lady Chapel, two in the

Tallis. Kerry McCarthy, Oxford University Press (2020). © Oxford University Press.
DOI: 10.1093/oso/9780190635213.001.0001.

Figure 3.1   Final impression of the seal of Waltham Abbey, attached to the document of surrender dated 23 March 1540. The National Archives, Kew. Reproduced by permission.

main choir area) and a group of "five children in the church" who were paid a modest stipend to serve as choristers.[4]

Unlike some English monasteries that were simply abandoned and left to fall into ruin, Waltham was strategically demolished after the dissolution. The entire east end of the church, which had been the exclusive province of the monks, was gone by the 1550s. The west end, the Norman nave with its massive round pillars, was the section of the church that had been frequented by the local laity, and it was kept for use as a parish church. This part of the building is still intact today. It includes the Lady Chapel, a Gothic addition to the south side which survived through post-Reformation use as a vestry and classroom. The Lady Chapel was where Tallis would have done much of his work. His five choristers almost certainly sang the Lady Mass there with him, and quite likely an evening votive antiphon as well. As in other abbey churches, it was a separate sphere from the monastic choir: a place where lay people were welcome, and where elaborate music and other displays of public devotion could be cultivated for a wider audience.

Modern visitors who step into the Lady Chapel at Waltham will find themselves standing underneath a large wall painting (Figure 3.2) that stretches across the east end of the room and reaches up to the ceiling. It is a fifteenth-century depiction of the Last Judgment, hidden for centuries and rediscovered during Victorian restoration work. Angels play curved trumpets while Christ, enthroned on a rainbow, judges a multitude of souls and sends them on their journey. Some go to his right, where St. Peter (with keys in hand) welcomes them into an elegant palace. Others go to his left, into the jaws of a grotesque beast, full of flames, sharp teeth, and little scrolls with the names of the deadly sins: the most clearly legible is *Invidia*, envy. Some monastic buildings in England had more arcane murals with various symbolic scenes from the Apocalypse, but straightforward Last Judgment paintings of this sort—Doom paintings, as they were often called—were a much more common sight in parish churches and other spaces open to the public.[5] Like the polyphonic music that was sung in so many Lady Chapels, they had a clear and unmistakable appeal to lay audiences. Tallis would have stood in front of this painting in the course of his everyday musical duties. In fact the raucous trumpeting of the seven angels is one visual depiction of music-making he definitely saw.

Figure 3.2 Doom painting in the Lady Chapel of Waltham Abbey. Godfrey Bartlett, *Essex Views*. Reproduced by permission.

When Waltham Abbey was dissolved, Tallis was sent away with a payment of 40 shillings, 20 in "wages" and 20 in "rewards." (This was not a permanent pension, and his wages were certainly not 20 *pounds*, as erroneously stated elsewhere: that would have placed him in more comfortable circumstances than the senior canons, not to mention almost every professional musician living in England at the time.)[6] Lay servants of abbeys were generally awarded a bonus of one quarter's pay at the dissolution.[7] The sum of 20 shillings was equivalent to one pound, so this would imply that Tallis's annual salary at Waltham had been £4. This seems like a significant step down from his salary of £8 at St. Mary-at-Hill, and a surprise given the relative prestige and wealth of the abbey. It makes more sense when we recall that a monastery was an all-encompassing institution in a way that even the most active parish was not. As at Dover Priory, Tallis would have enjoyed benefits such as food, drink, clothing, and quite likely accommodation as well. At Westminster Abbey around 1500, a situation for which unusually detailed records survive, the cash stipends given to lay employees made up no more than 21 percent of the full value of their earnings, sometimes as little as 6 percent.[8] In an urban parish such as St. Mary-at-Hill, a professional musician could expect a festive meal once in a while and new choir robes when his old ones were wearing out. An abbey could offer far more.

One of the last benefits that Tallis collected from Waltham Abbey was much less conventional: he took a large handwritten textbook of music theory with him when he left. The book had been compiled at Waltham around the middle of the fifteenth century—more or less contemporary with the imposing Last Judgment scene painted in the Lady Chapel—and signed by the scribe John Wylde, who identified himself in the book as precentor of Waltham, the person in charge of the singing at the abbey. The other name, added a few generations later, is Tallis's own. It appears twice at the end of the manuscript (Figure 3.3), once in a cursive signature and once in formal capital letters. (The second, more stylized inscription may have been added by someone else, although it is worth noting that the Elizabethan eccentric and polymath Simon Forman inscribed one of his own manuscripts with exactly the same type of capital lettering.)[9] This is the only surviving trace of Tallis's handwriting. Byrd left his signature in quite a few books

Figure 3.3 Tallis's name written twice in Lansdowne 763 (f. 124v), from Waltham Abbey. © The British Library Board. Reproduced by permission.

later on in the sixteenth century, but Tallis, as far as we know, only signed this one.[10]

The page with Tallis's name also includes a scrawled inventory of other books, all unnamed and now untraceable: "21 gilt books in quarto and octavo; 10 books in folio; 3 fair sets gilt books." It is unclear whether these were also musical books, although "sets" could imply groups of polyphonic partbooks. The abbey seems to have built up an impressive library by the early sixteenth century, including historical documents, theological works, and two "gospels in the Saxon tongue."[11] This whole collection was dispersed in 1540. Some former residents of other English monasteries purchased (or were given, or simply took) large numbers of books at the dissolution. William Brown, erstwhile prior of Monk Bretton, bought more than thirty with his own money; Richard Hart rescued a hundred and fifty from Llanthony Priory.[12] Tallis's book of music theory may or may not have been part of a larger hoard of music manuscripts—nothing else of the kind has survived from Waltham—but it is clearly an object that he valued and wanted to claim as his own at a moment of great instability.

This large manuscript, now held by the British Library as Lansdowne MS 763, is not a work by a single author. It is an anthology of twenty different treatises on music, almost all dating from the fourteenth and fifteenth centuries. Some are in Latin, others in English; some are substantial and others are very brief. These treatises were not state-of-the-art music theory by 1540, but they were also far from obsolete or useless. In fact they sum up much of the information that any English singer of Tallis's generation would have needed to ply his trade in most pre-Reformation musical venues. There are no instructions on composing elaborate "modern" polyphony of the sort Tallis cultivated in his own large works. Lansdowne 763 offers a different and broader set of musical skills: how to sight-read polyphonic notation, how to handle plainchant, how to improvise on pre-existing melodies, and how to compose simple everyday music in a pleasant, consonant style. There are also a few arcane chapters showing complex ratios between note values (some of them more bizarre than any performer was ever likely to need in real life) and esoteric theories about the nature and notation of music. Some monastic musicians certainly pursued the more difficult side of music theory. John Dygon, a Benedictine monk in Canterbury until 1538, was an accomplished composer and theorist who wrote a book drawing on the great Italian compendium *Practica musicae* by Franchino Gaffurio.[13] Dygon even recomposed Gaffurio's musical examples in an English style to illustrate his own work, showing the reader how to perform intimidating rhythmic feats such as 13 notes in the time of 9. The musical "proportions" in Lansdowne 763 are not quite as difficult, but they are very much present. In fact the only real sign of Tudor-era interest in this manuscript (other than Tallis's signature) is a set of additions to an incomplete table of musical ratios on folio 120r, with technical terms such as *sesquialtera* and *sesquioctava* written in what appears to be a hand from the first half of the sixteenth century. Someone of Tallis's generation was not only reading the book but going to the trouble of correcting and completing it.

The first chapter of Lansdowne 763 is by far the longest, covering almost fifty pages of the manuscript.[14] It is a detailed guide, written in Latin, on the theory and practice of Gregorian chant. It starts with a basic introduction to the musical scale and to the Guidonian hand (Figure 3.4), the ubiquitous mnemonic device used to teach sight-reading to children. The author says that the notes of the scale should be traced on the student's left hand if possible, since that hand "is more closely attached to the heart, and best makes an impression upon it." The chapter goes on to explain clefs, accidentals, and the art of solfege,

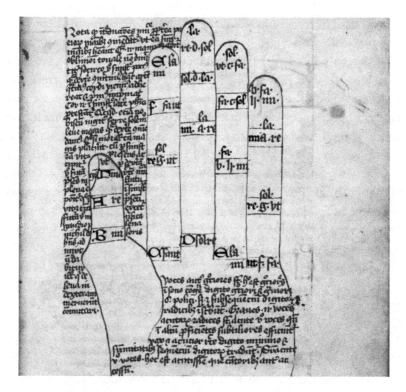

Figure 3.4 Guidonian hand in Lansdowne 763 (f. 6r), from Waltham Abbey. © The British Library Board. Reproduced by permission.

with a little jingle that teaches intervals from the semitone up through the octave. This is followed by a more complex exposition on the various genres of chant and the practicalities of the eight traditional modes. Anyone who studied this treatise well, and persevered to the end of it, would have become an accomplished and discerning singer of plainsong.

Another treatise, copied later in the manuscript, teaches an entirely different skill. It is written in English and has to do with simple polyphonic music created around a plainsong melody.[15] The author is Leonel Power, an early-fifteenth-century contemporary of Dunstable. This brief guide contains, among other things, the first known use of the word *counterpoint* in the English language. Power sets out his mission in clear terms: "This treatise is contrived upon the gamut for them that will be singers or makers [composers] or teachers." He promises

that the careful reader "may not fail of his counterpoint in short time."
His rules will still be familiar to any novice student of counterpoint: a
strict ban on parallel fifths and octaves, a call for proper observance of
vocal ranges, avoidance of unseemly gaps between voices, correct mix-
ing of perfect and imperfect consonances (and never more than three
parallel imperfect consonances in a row), and a number of other technical guidelines that have not changed all that much in the intervening
centuries. The music that resulted from this process had rather little
superficially in common with monumental pieces such as Tallis's votive
antiphons, but simple counterpoint was still a crucial part of everyday
music-making in church during the first half of the sixteenth century.
These were also the basic practices that laid the groundwork for more
florid composition. Tallis himself would have learned them thoroughly
and used them regularly.

This whole manuscript collection of music theory eventually ended
up far from the monastic library of Waltham, in the hands of Thomas
Morley, who appears to have drawn on it in the 1590s for some of
the more arcane points in his *Plain and Easy Introduction to Practical
Music.* When Tallis signed his name on its last page around 1540, it
was old-fashioned but still part of a living tradition. Half a century
later it was downright archaic. That was not necessarily considered a
fault in Morley's day. A number of Elizabethan authors and editors
had a marked taste for the archaic, even when they had to explain
terms such as *sesquioctava* to their uninitiated readers. When Morley
took the time to discuss obsolescent musical techniques in the *Plain
and Easy Introduction*, he had a great deal in common with his literary colleague Thomas Speght, whose edition of Chaucer, published in
1598, featured a convenient list of "old and obscure words explained"
for contemporary readers who might find them unfamiliar.[16] (A few of
these "old and obscure" Chaucerian terms even found their way back
into English usage in due time: *sentiment, ruthless, engine, phantom, nar-
cotics* . . .) Lansdowne 763 was a set of fascinating old texts that appealed
to educated Elizabethan audiences in much the same way that Chaucer
or Lydgate appealed to them. The manuscript was also a physical sou-
venir of a world that had met an unexpectedly quick demise.

It could be argued that medieval England ceased to exist on the
day when the last monastery was dissolved in March 1540. At least one

monastic choir, earlier that winter, had kept on singing until the bit-ter end. A handwritten note added to a Bible from Evesham Abbey in Worcestershire (along with some assorted mid-sixteenth-century musi-cal jottings) tells the story: "The monastery of Evesham was suppressed by King Henry VIII the 31st year of his reign, the 30th day of January, at evensong time, the convent being in the choir at this verse, *Deposuit potentes*, and would not suffer them to make an end."[17] The singers were forcibly stopped in the middle of the Magnificat, at the verse that declares "He hath put down the mighty from their seat." No such eye-witness account survives from Waltham. There are only a few scraps of evidence about what actually happened there in the final days, includ-ing a report that the local parishioners sent a petition to the king to buy and keep the five large bells in the tower of the abbey church; they obviously did not want to lose that part of their local soundscape.[18] The dissolution itself was overseen by the local magnate Sir William Petre, whose son John would become a great patron of Byrd's music and an advocate for beleaguered Catholics.

In some ways it is pure coincidence that Tallis happened to be employed at the one English monastery that managed to hold out the longest. In other ways it fits well with what is known of his increasingly close connections to the centers of power and patronage. He certainly seems to have been protected to some extent from the worst of the upheavals. The imperial ambassador Eustace Chapuys, a close observer of social change who spent almost two decades in England, was already writing during the first round of dissolutions in 1536 that between monks, nuns, and people who had been associated with former mon-asteries, there were now more than "twenty thousand who knew not how to live."[19] Tallis was fortunate enough not to lose his livelihood in any permanent way. In fact he resurfaced barely a year later in one of the most prestigious musical positions in England, at the head of a list of professional singers hand-picked for the newly reorganized Canterbury Cathedral.

CHAPTER FOUR

Canterbury Cathedral (1541)

ANTERBURY CATHEDRAL WAS FOUNDED AT THE END OF THE sixth century by Italian missionary monks, sent to Britain by St. Gregory the Great. It soon became the richest and most powerful church on the island. After the assassination of Thomas Becket in 1170 in the cathedral, and his almost immediate canonization as martyr and miracle-worker, it also became the most important pilgrimage site in England, immortalized in Chaucer's *Canterbury Tales*. By the late Middle Ages, the cathedral had built up a strong musical tradition. The fifteenth-century precentor John Borne was said to have had the best singing voice of any monk in the realm; his colleague John Stanys, who "arranged and directed all the polyphony in the church," was reportedly "the outstanding polyphonic singer of his time."[1] The community seems to have attracted people who were interested in music, with some even transferring their allegiance from other monasteries so they could sing and study there.[2] More surviving documents of pre-Reformation polyphonic music can plausibly be linked to Canterbury than to any other single church, of any sort, anywhere in England.[3]

Tallis arrived there during a time of radical restructuring at the beginning of the 1540s. Like many other English cathedrals, Canterbury had remained a monastic church into the sixteenth century, maintained by a community of monks who sang all the principal services. This created a problem at the Reformation. Cathedrals were an important part of the ecclesiastical and administrative fabric of the country; they could

Tallis. Kerry McCarthy, Oxford University Press (2020). © Oxford University Press.
DOI: 10.1093/oso/9780190635213.001.0001.

not simply be destroyed, abandoned, given as prizes to the nobility, or sold to the highest bidder, as other monastic houses were. Henry and his advisers decided that the best solution was to keep these cathedrals in place and refound them under new auspices. The king offered paid positions to any of the brethren who wanted to go on living in their old home under the new regime—in the case of Canterbury, exactly half of them took up the offer—but the system had already begun its slow process of changing beyond recognition.[4]

One of the earliest changes was musical. Now that the complex liturgical routine of the cathedral was no longer being carried out by a monastic community, a new team of professional musicians had to be recruited to do the job. Tallis's name appears on the earliest surviving list of those musicians.[5] The list (Figure 4.1) is undated. It names a "Master of the Choristers," twelve adult singers ("Vicars"), and ten boy choristers. (The vicars were lay musicians who went by that name because they were, at least in theory, performing a vicarious task: they deputized for the clergy, who had the official duty of singing every note of the church services but could rarely fulfill that obligation in practice.) Tallis is the first singer on the roster. It is certainly not an alphabetical roster, and the musicians are not named by seniority as they were in Chapel Royal rosters, because their posts were all newly created. They may well be listed in some approximate order of prestige or rank; second place among the singers is given to Thomas Wood, who had been the most important member of the pre-Reformation lay staff at Canterbury, directing the small but musically accomplished Lady Chapel choir.[6] Tallis's prominent place at the top of the list might simply reflect his having been chosen first, at a very early stage in the process of forming the new foundation.

The Canterbury roster is different from all the other documents of Tallis's career because it is simply a list of names. There are no amounts of money, no dates, no allotments of goods, no other details—just a long list of people. Even the unusually tall and narrow format of the document seems designed for this exact purpose. It shows an institution being built up and repopulated in an idealistic, almost utopian way. The musicians take up less than a page of the full document: they are only one part of a much larger group of more than 160 people, from the senior canons and other high clergy to the bell ringers (six), horse keepers (four),

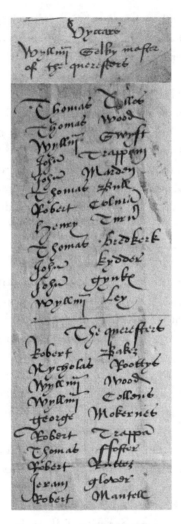

Figure 4.1 List of "Vyccars" and "The queresters" at the new foundation of Canterbury. Reproduced courtesy of the Chapter of Canterbury Cathedral.

and cooks (two).[7] The choice of a dean (a secular substitute for the old monastic prior) to oversee the reorganized cathedral remained a point of controversy for a long time, and no dean is named in the list, which suggests that it was compiled before the official refoundation took place on 8 April 1541.[8] It is easy to suspect that this list is more a master plan than a documentary record of people who were already securely in place and performing their duties. When the actual payment records start to appear in 1542–43, with the singers being paid what seems to have been the going rate of £8 per year, Tallis is nowhere to be found.[9] Ten of the original twelve singers named in the foundation document are still present, but Tallis is gone. The new replacements are conspicuously located at the bottom of the list.

Given the fact that Tallis was already an established member of the Chapel Royal by 1543–44, his time at Canterbury may have been brief. One later document suggests indirectly that he did not linger for long: a petition to the Queen in the late 1570s (see Chapter 5) claimed that he "hath served your Majesty and your royal ancestors these forty years."[10] That document was quite likely written by his younger colleague Byrd, who was prone to forceful rhetoric or even overstatement when it suited his purposes, but even a generous reading of "these forty years" would hint at an affiliation with the Chapel Royal that began very early in the 1540s. There is a remote but still real possibility that Tallis never took up his Canterbury post at all, that he was a musical prize unsuccessfully pursued. Even if that was the case, it is still striking to see him as the first lay singer named at the new foundation of England's most important cathedral.

Henry VIII liked to think of the cathedral refoundation project as one of his own bright ideas. There is no sign that he had any direct role in the choice of musicians, but he was actively interested in the whole process and seems to have approached it with great optimism. A document in the king's own handwriting shows his utopian ambitions: now that "the slothful and ungodly life" of the old monastic cathedrals was suppressed, their vast resources could be used to have "children brought up in learning, clerks nourished in the universities, old servants decayed to have livings, almshouses for poor folk to be sustained in, readers of Greek, Hebrew, and Latin to have good stipends, daily alms to be ministered, mending of highways . . . ."[11] Thomas Cranmer, who was Archbishop of Canterbury at the time, was enthusiastic about many of the items in the king's list. He saw the reform of his cathedral as an opportunity to build up a powerful educational establishment. The roster of the new foundation includes two dozen scholars to be sent to Oxford and Cambridge at the church's expense, as well as a large group of grammar school pupils and their schoolmaster. Provisions were made for Canterbury choristers to stay at the cathedral and enter the grammar school after their voices had changed, even if they had passed the official age limit for new arrivals, who normally had to be fourteen or under.[12] The foundation charter of the cathedral goes into great detail about the grammar school curriculum, including reading lists and examination practices.[13] Unfortunately there is nothing of the kind about the musical training of the choristers, just a note that they should have "sonorous voices fit for singing" and that their choirmaster should be a skilled teacher, singer, and organist.

One distinctive feature of post-Reformation Canterbury which already appears at this very early stage is the appointment of the Six Preachers, six clergymen hired to provide the cathedral and the surrounding parishes with a regular supply of sermons. Cranmer set up this group of six (in accordance with the king's personal wishes, he said) as "three of the old learning and three of the new": half traditionalists and half evangelicals, or, to put it in more blunt and perhaps more anachronistic terms, half Catholics and half Protestants.[14] This unusual scheme reflects the desire for balance and moderation found in some reforming circles, but there is also a whiff of mischief about it. It was not an arrangement that could last. It is no surprise that there was already serious conflict among the clergy by summer 1541, just a few months after the new foundation was launched.[15]

Life among the new musicians at Canterbury Cathedral, at least in these first years, seems to have been less troubled. The choir was certainly kept very busy. Liturgical practice at the cathedral was ostentatiously conservative in the early 1540s, following the Sarum rite, the time-honored national rite of England (see Chapter 7), down to the smallest detail. Special books were produced to help bring the old ceremonies into conformity with the new principles of the Church of England. One such book appeared in 1541 just as the new foundation was made: a revised Sarum breviary printed by Edward Whitchurch, "newly printed and cleansed of many defects, in which the falsely inserted name of the Roman pontiff is omitted, along with other things incompatible with the statute of our most Christian king."[16] Most of the "cleansing" was superficial, not going much beyond the omission of undesirable names and a few politically inexpedient feast days. In the case of almost all existing musical books, the only real action required would have been some token defacement of music for Becket and the careful erasure of the word "Pope." (When Reginald Pole briefly restored the cathedral to full Catholic observance in the 1550s, those were the only two things he needed to fix in the old books.)[17] The rest went on more or less exactly as it had in so many pre-Reformation cathedrals. The enclosed area where the choir sang its principal services was still decorated with rich tapestries of biblical scenes, and dozens of candles illuminated the altars and the choir stalls, using more than two hundred pounds of beeswax each year.[18] The great sevenfold *Gaude* window in honor of the Virgin (see Chapter 16) was still undisturbed. All the singing was in Latin, with many hours of chant each day and generous portions of polyphony.

The first signs of real liturgical change appeared in 1547, only months after the death of Henry VIII. Tallis had long since moved on by then, but these new rules give some useful indirect evidence about daily life in the choir earlier in the 1540s, when he was recruited to join the group.[19] The Canterbury musicians were ordered in 1547 to stop singing sequences, the long and wide-ranging chants given a place of honor at feast-day masses. "All masses by note" which had been "sung in other places of the church" were now to take place only in the main choir area: in other words, sung mass could no longer be performed at the side altars dedicated to various saints. The young choristers were no longer to have their "crown shaven," a practice that had recalled the old tradition of monastic and clerical tonsure. Psalms were to be sung with "leisure and deliberation." "Talking or jangling" was now strictly banned during services, with permanent expulsion from the choir after the third warning. These injunctions add up to an incomplete and negative portrait, but they offer a glimpse into the choir just after the new foundation in 1541: musically luxurious, somewhat archaic, and perhaps a little too casual for reforming tastes. It is no surprise that decorum was a sore point. These singers were on display. In some ways, Canterbury Cathedral took on an even more important role in the course of the Reformation as it became the headquarters of an independent national church. It no longer had its old fame as a pilgrim destination, but it had a new reputation to uphold.

With a full-time staff of élite lay musicians now singing all the services, the cathedral also needed an even broader repertory of polyphonic music than before. Tallis was a logical first choice for the new foundation, since he was active as a composer. Another member of the original group of twelve, Thomas Bull, came from Oxford, where he had enjoyed a busy career as a music copyist. One attractive theory suggests that Bull may have been the person who assembled the music in the Peterhouse partbooks (Chapter 10), intending it for the use of the new choir at Canterbury.[20] The singers would certainly have required music of just that kind: polyphonic "masses by note," substantial settings of the Magnificat in Latin to sing at vespers, and a selection of votive antiphons. This was the old-fashioned musical culture of the great cathedrals during Henry's last years. It was a situation detested by more radical reformers such as George Joye, who railed in 1541 against "matins mongers, idle evensong upheapers, and *Salve* singers."[21] Joye's words are not an inaccurate description of the Canterbury choir at that exact moment, who may well have been singing Tallis's own *Salve intemerata* (prominently featured in the Peterhouse books) to conclude their evening devotions.

Tallis's colleague William Selby was the "Master of the Choristers" named in the original roster of the new foundation. Selby stayed at Canterbury and kept his job for more than forty years, not retiring fully until 1584, the year before Tallis's death.[22] A salaried musical post at England's mother church was an appealing choice in an unstable era. Many of the other original musicians also stayed, some for a considerable length of time. Tallis, as usual, is more elusive. He appears once in a single document and then he is gone. (This recurring problem will end in the next chapter, when he enters the Chapel Royal and starts to leave a more substantial paper trail.) Whatever length of time he may actually have spent at Canterbury Cathedral, the record of his recruitment there is valuable because it shows him at a critical juncture in his career: what happens to an exceptionally talented musician when his familiar social context starts to fall apart? This document is also significant because it shows Tallis (at least in passing) as part of a living musical tradition that has continued to the present day. A visitor to Canterbury, or to any other English cathedral, can still walk into the building on virtually any day of the year and hear a professional choir sing an evening service with psalms, a choral Magnificat, and an anthem—the direct descendant of what Tallis would have sung there almost 500 years ago.

CHAPTER FIVE

The Chapel Royal (1543–85), I

COMMUNITY AND CEREMONY

TALLIS SPENT THE LAST FOUR DECADES OF HIS LIFE AS A MEMBER OF the English Chapel Royal. Unlike the churches where he had worked during the first part of his career, the Chapel was not a building or a single physical location. It was a group of musicians and clergy employed to serve the reigning monarch wherever he or she might go. Tallis was now part of the complex itinerant machinery of the royal household, called upon to make music in a wide range of places. He served four very different sovereigns in this role: Henry VIII and his three heirs Edward, Mary, and Elizabeth. The Tudor monarchs were constantly on the road, moving among a number of royal residences according to changing seasons, political vicissitudes, and personal whim. This chapter is an exploration of Tallis's place in the Chapel Royal community and an account of the musical and ideological upheavals that took place while he was there. The following chapter (Chapter 6) is a closer look at the various sites where Tallis and his Chapel colleagues would have sung.

Tallis first appears as a Gentleman of the Chapel (a courtesy rank given to all royal singers) in a list made in 1543 or 1544.[1] The list has nothing directly to do with music; it is a roster of names compiled for tax purposes. This type of document, known as a lay subsidy roll, records a special tax on land and income that was periodically imposed on the English people to help pay for large national projects.[2] The lay subsidy of 1543–44 was collected to raise money for Henry's newly

Tallis. Kerry McCarthy, Oxford University Press (2020). © Oxford University Press.
DOI: 10.1093/oso/9780190635213.001.0001.

declared wars against Scotland and France. The subsidy roll containing Tallis's name survives in two separate copies. These are fascinating if unwieldy documents, made up of many long pieces of parchment sewn together end to end and rolled up tightly for storage. Every member of the king's personal staff is named individually. The roster starts with Sir Thomas Cheney, royal treasurer and Warden of the Cinque Ports, and makes its way gradually down to the professionals and skilled servants who did most of the work of running the royal household. The names of Tallis and his colleagues occur around the middle of the list. Tallis is shown as receiving a standard Chapel Royal salary of £11 8s per year, with a few shillings appropriated for the war effort.

A variety of secular musicians are also present on the list, including half a dozen members of the Italian Bassano family (conspicuously paid several times as much as the Chapel singers), the distinguished Flemish lutenist and composer Philip van Wilder (see Chapter 11), a consort of five recorder players, and no fewer than seventeen trumpeters. Henry maintained a large musical establishment that incorporated many different sounds and styles.[3] He was one of the Renaissance monarchs who clearly loved music for its own sake. In fact he had been a keen amateur composer in his youth, before other matters took up his time and energy. Some of the thirty-five surviving works attributed to him are awkward student exercises, but others are delightful songs such as *Pastime with good company* and *Green groweth the holly*. If we believe an early-sixteenth-century informant, he even composed two masses at the age of nineteen and had his own Chapel sing them.[4] Those days were long gone by the 1540s, but Henry's court was still known for outstanding music when Tallis arrived. The impressive list of names in the roster of 1543–44 speaks for itself.

This roll is the earliest of about thirty-five documents that mention Tallis by name during his Chapel years. The documents fall into four basic groups. The first group, the most straightforward (and generally the dullest), consists of a series of lay subsidies and other financial assessments, following Tallis from the 1540s through the year of his death in 1585.[5] He eventually became one of the better-paid Chapel musicians, although there seems to have been a sharp drop in salary in the last decade of his life, most likely tied to retirement from active duty as a singer and organist. These tax documents do not offer biographical

details, just appraisals of "goods," "wages," and "fee." The one exception is an assessment dated 8 March 1568, which mentions that he is a
resident of Greenwich, a few miles downriver from central London.

The second group of documents is more personal, revealing Tallis's
connections with other musicians. Most of the items in this second
group are wills made by various Gentlemen of the Chapel. Given the
almost complete lack of surviving letters and other private writings
among professional church musicians in Tudor England, their wills
offer a valuable perspective on life in their community. Every will had
to be ratified by witnesses, and the actual executor of the will was
almost always a close family member, but there was an important third
role specified in many wills: that of overseer. Overseers were chosen to
support the executor and help look after the surviving family. In many
ways this was comparable to the role of godparent at a child's baptism—
a position of trust and elective kinship that went beyond administrative or legal responsibilities. Tudor wills often described overseers in
affectionate terms such as "trusty and well-beloved friend" or "loving
neighbor."[6] Tallis chose his wife Joan as his executor and two Chapel
colleagues as his overseers: one was Richard Granwall (see Chapter 17),
who went on to take care of Joan in her old age, and the other was,
unsurprisingly, William Byrd. An almost identical pattern occurs in
the will made in 1558 by John Sheppard, who chose his wife Elizabeth
as executor and "Mr. Danyell, Subdean of the Queen's Chapel" as
his overseer, also appointed to act as a guardian for Sheppard's two
children.[7]

Tallis is named in several Chapel Royal wills. The earliest was
made by Richard Pygott in 1549. He was an accomplished composer
and performer who had been choirmaster in Cardinal Wolsey's private chapel, a formidable musical establishment which managed under
Pygott's direction to defeat the Chapel Royal in a sight-reading contest
(a story told later in this chapter.[8]) After Wolsey fell from political grace
at the end of the 1520s and his choir was disbanded, Pygott quickly
found a place in the king's household. When he died twenty years
later, he named Tallis as one of his overseers and left him a gift of two
months' salary.[9] That was just one of many bequests made by an older
man who had grown prosperous under the pre-Reformation system of
musical patronage.[10] Pygott's will includes horses, jewels, real estate in

Greenwich and elsewhere, and some respectable sums of money. He also made a special bequest "unto my fellows of the King's Majesty's Chapel," as Tallis did a generation later when he left a donation toward the annual Chapel feast.

The next will mentioning Tallis was made a few years later by Thomas Bury, a Gentleman of the Chapel who had also served as one of Pygott's overseers.[11] Bury's father had been a member of the Stationers' Company, a specialist in the London book and paper trade. Bury sang as a boy chorister in the private chapel of Lady Margaret Beaufort, who personally sent him to study at Eton from 1504 to 1509, where he would have sung from a splendid and very new choirbook.[12] He entered the Chapel Royal early in Henry's reign and served him for several decades, accompanying him in 1520 to his eighteen-day diplomatic summit with the French king at the Field of the Cloth of Gold. During the upheavals of the 1530s, Bury was given a paid (and conveniently non-residential) honorary post as a canon of the collegiate church of Penkridge. He had to ask for special permission to keep collecting that income when he married in the 1540s. When he made his will in February 1554, he left his house in Greenwich to his wife Joan and asked her to distribute food to the poor in his memory. Tallis was just a witness to the will, not an overseer, but he had a far more important connection to the Bury family: by the end of 1555 he had married Joan (see Chapter 17) and moved into her home, where he would live until his death.

Another close associate was Richard Bower, who chose Tallis as one of his two overseers in 1561. Bower was master of the choristers in the Chapel Royal, in charge of training and supervising the boys. By the late 1550s, he and Tallis had become distinguished enough figures at court to be honored by Queen Mary with a lucrative joint lease giving them the annual rent paid for a manor on the Isle of Thanet.[13] Bower was yet another member of the Chapel who lived in Greenwich. Like Tallis, he is buried in the local parish church of St. Alfege, or at least was buried there until the destruction and total renovation of the building in the early eighteenth century. Also like Tallis, he had a gravestone with a brass memorial plate near the altar. The other overseer named in Bower's will alongside Tallis was an unusual choice: the eminent lawyer William Roper, son-in-law and biographer of Thomas

More. Roper was a pillar of the English Catholic community (where he had settled after a youthful fascination with Lutheranism) and a well-known patron of musicians. He became something of a father figure to the Company of Parish Clerks, the London church singers' guild, whose meeting hall displayed a portrait of Roper with a scroll describing him as "a worthy benefactor of this Company." The portrait hung in a place of honor in the hall until December 1940, when it was destroyed in the Blitz.[14] Generosity to musicians seems to have run in the family: William Roper's son Anthony was later thanked by Joan Tallis for "his good favors showed to my late husband and me."[15]

One unusual document in this second group is a letter sent to Byrd in April 1580. It is an extremely rare example of private correspondence among, and about, musicians in Tallis's immediate circle.[16] The writer signs himself "Richard Sugeham," a surname otherwise unknown in Tudor England. He speaks in studiedly cautious terms. He has an introduction to make to Byrd ("I send unto you a very dear friend of mine who is very desirous to be acquainted with you, who will show you many things which perhaps you will like well to know") and a request for music ("I crave of you certain songs.") He ends with a postscript, where he finally drops his vagueness and mentions some names: "I pray you remember me to Mr. Tallis, Mr. Blitheman, Mr. More, Mr. Mundy, and the rest, my good friends." All four of those "good friends" were senior members of the Chapel Royal at the time. ("Mr. More" was John More, now the least familiar of the group because he seems not to have been active as a composer.) "Sugeham" may well have been some kind of pseudonym or alias. The author was right to be wary; his letter has survived because it was intercepted by the Elizabethan secret service in an attempt to find evidence of international Catholic conspiracies. In fact the letter appears to have been sent from across the English Channel. The mysterious writer's friendship with the four older Gentlemen of the Chapel named in the text, including Tallis, is of course no indication of their religious beliefs or loyalties, but there is certainly a hint that they may have had some place in a broader circle that included recusant sympathizers in England and émigré Catholics such as the Paget brothers.

The third set of documents tracing Tallis's presence at court is the series of lists made when the Gentlemen of the Chapel received new ceremonial livery for important events in the life of the monarchy: black clothing for royal funerals, scarlet clothing for coronations. Livery lists were not infallible (Sheppard was issued a new suit three weeks after his own funeral) or even immune to silly mistakes (Tallis is called "Thomas Tailor" in that same list), but they are useful evidence of who was present, or expected to be present, on the historic occasions when one regime gave way to another. Unlike tax records, where the ordering of names could be haphazard or inconsistent, Chapel Royal livery rosters are arranged by order of seniority. The longest-serving musician is named first. Tallis can be seen gradually moving up the list as the years go by: he is sixteenth in 1547 at the coronation of Edward, eighth in 1553 at the coronation of Mary, and seventh in 1559 at the coronation of Elizabeth.[17]

Perhaps the most unusual clothing list for the Chapel is the account of apparel worn in a (now lost) morality play performed by the Gentlemen shortly after Mary's coronation.[18] There are twenty-three costumes in all, a perfect fit for the size of the group in 1553. The characters are clothed in a variety of vivid outfits, including a purple gown for the protagonist *Genus Humanum* (Everyman, the Human Race), wings for the Good Angel and the Bad Angel, "a woman's cassock of russet satin" for Scarcity, and "ash-colored" clothing for Feebleness. Unfortunately no personal names are given in the list, only names of characters, so we are unlikely ever to know what part Tallis played. This was also the last known occasion on which the adult singers of the Chapel acted on stage in a court play. By the end of Mary's short reign, those duties had been taken over by the boys.

The fourth and last group of documents from Tallis's Chapel Royal years has to do with a well-known event in his later life: Elizabeth's grant of a printing monopoly to him and Byrd on 22 January 1575. The original handwritten document conferring the monopoly—the so-called "letters patent"—is a long and dense text in highly repetitive legal jargon.[19] When Tallis and Byrd launched their publishing venture later that year with the joint volume of Latin motets they called *Cantiones sacrae* (see Chapter 14), they included a printed page with the "extract and effect" of the letters patent. This new version of the document was shorter, cleaned up for non-specialist readers, with many of the redundancies and technical terms cut out. Given Byrd's known affinity for tinkering with legal texts, he may well have done the job himself. The message was clear: the two composers now had the exclusive right for the next twenty-one years to print "songs in parts, either in English, Latin, French, Italian, or other tongues that may serve for music either in church or chamber, or otherwise to be played or sung."[20] They also had a monopoly on printed music paper with blank staves, and on importing "any song or songs made and printed in any foreign country, to sell or put to sale." The penalty for non-compliance was a fine of 40 shillings, paid to the Queen, and surrender of all the illicitly produced or imported music, directly to the composers.

This looked like a lucrative plan in theory, but Tallis and Byrd seem to have lost a lot of money within the first couple of years, whether through over-ambitious publishing of motets or through other expenses associated with managing a monopoly. The next document in this series, written in 1577, is their direct and rather abject petition to the Queen for a new source of income: "Your Majesty, of your princely goodness, intending the benefit of us your said poor servants, did give us about two years past a license for the printing of music. So it is, most gracious sovereign, that the same hath fallen out to our great loss and hindrance, to the value of two hundred marks at least."[21] A mark was two-thirds of a pound, so this was slightly over £133, not a trivial amount for two musicians in Elizabethan England. One attractive hypothesis suggests that the lost 200 marks may have been a bribe or gratuity of the type that often had to be paid to an agent at court in order to gain an important royal privilege.[22] The composers' request for more income was granted in the form of annual rents on royal lands, and they (and Tallis's heirs) retained the music monopoly for its full twenty-one-year term.[23]

The *Cantiones* of 1575 contain another valuable piece of biographical information: an introductory poem by the courtier and musician Ferdinand Heyborne, who often wrote (as he did here) under his alternate family surname Richardson. He calls Tallis "my great master," then turns to Byrd, praising him as the youthful hope of English music and referring to Tallis as "a master common to me and you."[24] This could be taken simply to mean that Tallis was revered as a magisterial figure in the world of Elizabethan court music, but a plain reading of the text suggests that Tallis was in fact Byrd's teacher at some point.

It is probably not a reference to Byrd's childhood musical training, because there is no evidence that Byrd was ever a boy chorister of the Chapel Royal. His older brothers Simon and John Byrd were choristers at St. Paul's Cathedral, but it is also not known whether he followed them there. The only hint of an actual document that might possibly concern his early life is a list of the choristers of St. George's Chapel, Windsor, drawn up in 1548 as that prosperous royal foundation was being assessed and reorganized along more Protestant lines. The ten boys are mentioned only by surname, and the seventh boy (Figure 5.1) is "Byrd": not an entirely improbable place to find a talented young musician who would have been eight or perhaps nine years old at the time, and whose later career would show some connections with the musical establishment at Windsor.[25] (There is also a record of a chorister named "Wyllyam Byrd" at Westminster Abbey in the early 1540s. This document is enticing, but it cannot be reconciled with any of the existing information about the composer's age and birthdate. Its primary value is as a reminder to biographers that his name was dangerously common in Tudor England.[26])

Figure 5.1 "Byrd" listed as the seventh of ten choristers at St. George's Chapel, Windsor, in 1548. St. George's Chapel Archives. Reproduced by permission of the Dean and Canons of Windsor.

Tallis and Byrd may well have met in the later 1550s, when the younger man seems already to have become involved in Chapel Royal circles to some extent, collaborating with Sheppard and Mundy on a setting of the long psalm *In exitu Israel* found in the Gyffard partbooks (see Chapter 11).[27] The seventeenth-century writer Anthony à Wood noted that Byrd was "bred up to music under Tho. Tallis." It is a phrase that suggests a young child rather than a working composer close to the age of twenty, although Wood may have taken his information directly from Richardson's poem without further consideration of the details.[28] Whenever this musical apprenticeship began, it had matured into a close professional and personal bond by the mid-1570s. It is surely no coincidence that Byrd chose Tallis to be the godfather of his newborn son the year after their joint collection of music was published, and that he named the boy Thomas.

The only other witness to Tallis's teaching activity is the Elizabethan translator, courtier, polymath, and wit John Harington, now better known as the inventor of the flush toilet than for any of his numerous literary exploits. Harington wrote in 1595 that his father (also a courtier, and also named John) had been "much skilled in music, which was pleasing to the King, and which he learnt in the fellowship of good Master Tallis when a young man."[29] He then quoted a satirical poem which his father had set to music. The poem is a piece of Latin doggerel on the vain and dissolute lives of monks, beginning *O tu qui dans oracula.*[30] It is given a date of 1546 and entitled "The monks' hymn to Saint Satan, chanted daily in their cells, till goodly King Henry spoiled their singing." Harington repeats his father's anecdote that "King Henry was used in pleasant mood to sing this verse"— although the king's pleasant moods were rare enough by 1546—and he describes his father's musical setting as a three-part canon: "The music of this hymn is a canon in what the musicians call *subdiapason* and *diatesseron*, a practice peculiar to the learned in that period of time when Tallis flourished, whose works abound in such labored compositions; and no wonder his scholars adopted the manner of their master, who was so truly excellent." Convoluted musical canons, like the decadent practices of monks, were a relic of the bad old days.

There is certainly no reason to doubt that John Harington senior gained his musical skills "in the fellowship of good Master Tallis" during the turbulent last years of Henry's reign, since he was already in royal service by 1538 at the age of about twenty. For Harington, as for the much younger Ferdinand Heyborne, musical training with Tallis seems to have been more an enjoyable means of social advancement than part of a professional career of the sort pursued by Byrd. Harington's anti-clerical burlesque would also seem to put him at a considerable distance from Byrd, who ended up as a devout recusant and used his compositional talents in the service of the English Catholic community—although even Byrd in his own youth appears to have made a musical setting of the words "from Turk and Pope defend us, Lord."[31]

One very important thing is missing in all these documents of Tallis's time in and around the Chapel Royal. There is no direct record of the music that he sang, played, or composed for his four sovereigns. We have no surviving music lists or eyewitness accounts of specific pieces being performed. It is possible to make an educated guess about some of the repertory by looking at the personnel of the Chapel, the style of their compositions, and a few loosely associated sources such as John Baldwin's manuscripts (see Chapter 15), but nothing survives from Tallis's time that could be called a true Chapel Royal anthology. Even the group's basic daily routine is only known in the most general terms. The full Chapel normally accompanied the sovereign from October through June. After the feast day of St. Peter and Paul on 29 June, most of the musicians left for a three-month break (this "quarter of liberty" was the most important of their traditional vacation periods) while a smaller version of the court went on its more extensive summer travels.[32] The Eltham Ordinances of 1526 say that only six adult singers and six boy choristers needed to follow the court "in riding, journeying, and progresses" during the off-season; this skeleton group had limited duties, reduced to the singing of a daily Lady Mass in the morning and a daily votive antiphon in the afternoon, as well as a Mass of the day on Sundays and holy days.[33]

The stripped-down schedule of the summer Chapel during Henry's reign was not too different from what the entire group seems to have been doing all year round in Tallis's later life, after the Reformation had drastically reduced the number and complexity of daily offices. By 1604, the next time the duties of the Gentlemen were spelled out in any detail, the requirement even on the most important days was to be present "at both services."[34] An annual rota had also been established by that point, giving the Gentlemen every other month off for much of the year. Beyond these basic outlines, we know almost nothing about the actual musical routine of the sixteenth-century Chapel. The lack of information is especially unfortunate because these were the years of Tallis's career that saw the broadest changes in musical practice. He was safely established in a lifelong post from the mid-1540s onward, but the ideological instability around him was greater than ever, and it had a direct effect on the music he wrote and performed.

Just as Tallis was entering the Chapel, the first real cracks were starting to appear in what were still basically traditional practices of church music and liturgy. The so-called King's Book of 1543, an official book "set forth for the institution and erudition of the common people," still allowed salutation of the Virgin Mary and (though with copious health warnings attached) prayer for the dead. 1543 was also the year when weekly Bible readings in English were ordered in all churches. In 1544, an official ritual text in English was sung in public by professional musicians for the first time. This was the new English litany, a long and eloquent series of prayers written by Cranmer, including a solemn invocation against "the tyranny of the bishop of Rome and all his detestable enormities." (Cranmer's litany is still in the Book of Common Prayer, with that phrase discreetly removed.) We know that the litany was performed by the Chapel Royal—one thing we can be absolutely sure was sung by them during Tallis's forty-year tenure—because it was almost immediately published in a musical setting for five voices "according to the notes used in the King's Majesty's chapel."[35] That five-part music is not preserved in its original printed form, but it is highly likely to have been the five-part litany composed by Tallis himself, a simple but effective piece which survived in other sources and soon became a musical fixture in the Church of England. The new litany in English was at the margins of normal liturgical practice (quite literally at the margins, since it was sung while walking around outside the church building), but it was the first step in what would eventually become a quick and overwhelming process of musical transformation. Outdoor processions were reliably attention-getting: consider the Tudor chronicler Henry Machyn, who had an insatiable interest in open-air ritual and ceremony, and who was more likely to comment on a good procession than on anything that happened inside a church. This was a highly effective way of introducing new teachings and new practices.

The new litany of 1544 did not just consist of the five-part music "used in the King's Majesty's chapel" and its simpler plainsong cousin. There was also an "Exhortation to Prayer," a brief instructional homily, which was required by royal mandate to be read out loud before the litany was performed.[36] There was even a little preface outlining the right way for the priest to intone the litany ("so loud and so plainly that it may well be understood of the hearers"), how the choir should respond ("soberly and devoutly"), and proper behavior for the congregation during "this common prayer of procession" ("such among the people as have books, and can read, may read them quietly and softly to themselves"). This is the first time a newly composed piece of church music in England was issued with a user's manual. The new ideals seem to have caught on. By the end of 1544, Cranmer was writing directly to the king, offering his help in making more English-texted music of the same type.[37] Some other things at court still remained quite conservative, such as the rich and largely unreformed schedule of religious holidays, including observances such as Michaelmas and All Souls' Day that had been scrubbed from the official calendar. (Cranmer did not approve: "If in the court you do keep such holy days and fasting days, when shall we persuade the people to cease from keeping them?")[38]

This sort of eclectic traditionalism, finely calibrated to suit Henry's personal tastes, could not and did not survive his death. His son Edward's coronation in 1547 was still an old-fashioned affair, with grand vestments and a "solemnly sung" mass, but things began to change almost immediately afterwards as real Reformation practices took hold. The Chapel Royal was soon noticed for being modern: during Edward's first year, compline "was sang [sic] in English in the king's chapel, before any act of Parliament enjoined it."[39] The Chapel was also invoked as a model for other choirs to follow during the confusing early days of the new reign. By September 1548 the Duke of Somerset, regent for the young Edward, was writing to the staff of various Cambridge colleges in a tone of obvious frustration, ordering them to use only the rites "presently used in the king's majesty's chapel, and none other."[40]

The Reformation changed the musical repertory of the Chapel, but the institution itself remained as robust as ever. There was no decrease in the number of adult singers, and the king's household still had the right to recruit boys (willing or unwilling) from virtually any other choral foundation in England and take them into royal service. Edward gave direct commissions to his Chapel choirmaster Richard Bower and to his secular choirmaster Philip van Wilder, one "to take up from time to time as many children to serve in the same Chapel as he shall think meet," the other "to take to the King's use such and as many singing children and choristers as he or his deputy should think good."[41] The impressment of young singers was not unlike the periodic Tudor military conscription of able-bodied young men, though it filled a much smaller and more specialized niche. There were also plenty of excellent grown-up musicians who were there voluntarily, including a number of distinguished composers. Sheppard joined the group during Edward's reign, and what survives of his English-texted music is complex enough to suggest that austerity was not always the order of the day in the Protestant Chapel, even if it was practiced or expected elsewhere.

Just six years after the Gentlemen of the Chapel were issued scarlet livery for Edward's coronation, they were provided with new clothing for the coronation of a new monarch, his Catholic half-sister Mary. This led to an even more sweeping set of musical changes. As Mary came to power in autumn 1553, her Chapel returned quickly to full pre-Reformation practice, singing in Latin and performing all the traditional ceremonies.[42] When Mary married King Philip of Spain in 1554, Tallis and his colleagues joined forces with the choir of Winchester Cathedral for the wedding there on 25 July—the feast day of St. James, the Apostle Santiago, an auspicious date for any Spanish monarch. "During high mass time," an observer wrote, "the Queen's Chapel matched with the choir, and the organs used such sweet proportion of music and harmony as the like (I suppose) was never before invented or heard."[43] Whatever musical restraint might have been exercised earlier in the 1550s, it was clearly a thing of the past now. Philip brought a group of his own musicians from home, who served alongside the English Chapel at court and sang mass together with them in December 1554. The organist Antonio de Cabezón, famous for his improvisations and his sets of variations, was part of Philip's musical establishment in England, as was the Flemish composer Philippe de Monte, who later took up a musical correspondence with Byrd. The Spanish royal entourage even carried out their own separate ceremonies, including a Corpus Christi procession in 1555 through the streets of Kingston upon Thames with Philip's *capilla real* "and all its music."[44]

If Mary had lived for more than a few years after her coronation, or if she had produced an heir, Tallis's career as a composer would have gone in a very different direction. Instead there was yet another swerve in beliefs and practices under Mary's half-sister Elizabeth at the end of the 1550s. One crucial step was to restore the use of the vernacular Book of Common Prayer which had first been established a decade earlier. While Elizabeth waited for this restoration to take effect, she made some pointed changes in her Chapel, including the immediate sacking of the dean and subdean (both known for their Catholic views) and the revival of the sung litany in English.[45] Once the Book of Common Prayer was reissued in its new edition of 1559, the Chapel was bound to follow its texts and rites. There are just a few isolated reports of what this sounded like in musical terms. When guests attended services at Elizabeth's court, they remarked on the richly decorated buildings, the furnishings, the clothing, and the ceremonies, but they only very rarely said anything about the music. One service in 1565 was begun "by the gentlemen of the Chapel and the cornets," suggesting that wind instruments and voices sounded together; another service in 1598, in the presence of the Queen on a Sunday morning, "scarce exceeded half an hour" but had "excellent music."[46]

Elizabeth took after her father Henry in several ways that had a direct effect on musicians: she had good taste in music, a liking for old-fashioned religious ceremony, and a strong will. She took steps to ensure that choral singing could continue within the restrictions imposed by the Book of Common Prayer. In a set of injunctions published in 1559, she made room before or after services for anthems to be sung "in the best sort of melody and music that may be conveniently devised," and declared that professional choirs in large churches should not have their funding taken away or their numbers reduced.[47]

There are some signs that Elizabeth's own household chapel was a breeding ground for unusually complex music in English of a type that may not have been cultivated or even tolerated elsewhere. William

Harrison described the typical post-Reformation fare in 1577 in his contribution to Raphael Holinshed's *Chronicles of England*: "in cathedral and collegiate churches . . . the choir singeth the answers, the creed, and sundry other things appointed, but in so plain (I say) and distinct manner, that each one present may understand what they sing, every word having but one note, though the whole harmony cunningly consist of many parts, and those very cunningly set by the skillful in that science."[48] The use of rich harmonies and even of polyphony is not out of the question in cathedrals and colleges, but Harrison's composers are considered cunning and skillful *because* they can set every word in such a "plain . . . and distinct manner" while also writing music that is aesthetically pleasing. Tallis went well beyond that level of complexity in some of his English-texted works. He was clearly writing for a somewhat relaxed situation at Elizabeth's court. His Te Deum "for meanes" (see Chapter 12) is far from simple or austere. Another Te Deum by Tallis that survives only in a single mid-sixteenth-century fragment from Ludlow (a remote outpost of the royal household) is clearly a notch or two above plain style, with hints of luxury scoring such as divided bass parts.[49] Judging from the even more elaborate English service music written by slightly younger colleagues such as Mundy and Parsons, the Elizabethan Chapel Royal appears to have kept some old practices such as ceremonial polyphonic singing at a large lectern in the middle of the choir area (the technical term was *in medio chori*) by a select group of soloists.[50] There is absolutely no evidence that the Chapel sang anything in Latin after 1558, but the handful of surviving hints suggest that their music in English during Tallis's later years may have been lavish enough at times to equal that of any sixteenth-century Catholic court, including the use of wind instruments and double-choir or even triple-choir singing.

Even less is known about keyboard music in the Chapel. Tallis calls himself "Organist of the Queen's Majesty's private Chapel" in 1575 on the title page of the *Cantiones*, but he is never given that title or description in any extant Chapel records. At the beginning of the sixteenth century, the duty of organist still seems to have been shared among the Gentlemen according to their skill; the royal household regulations of the 1470s had required them to be expert singers but merely "sufficient in organ playing."[51] Henry VIII went several steps further by bringing the virtuoso organist Dionysius Memo from St. Mark's in Venice to join his musical staff. In 1534, he had the chapel organ at his Greenwich palace repainted with the heraldic insignia of Anne Boleyn.[52] Organ playing very nearly did not survive the radical changes in mid-sixteenth-century England: the Bishops' Convocation of 1563 came perilously close to approving a set of sweeping Calvinist-style reforms, one of which required "that the use of organs and curious singing be removed." Fifty-seven members of the clergy voted for these reforms and fifty-eight voted against them. Elaborate keyboard music was still being played in some places—Byrd got into trouble for it at Lincoln Cathedral just a few years after this controversy—but institutional support for it had begun to collapse. Between 1510 and 1539, twelve or more new organs were being built per decade in England. Between 1540 and 1569, the number of new organs dropped to four per decade. Between 1570 and 1579, not a single one was built, at the royal court or anywhere else.[53]

Tallis joined the Chapel Royal at the exact time when the professional practice of sacred music in England was being centralized under the new auspices of a state church. The royal musical establishment never became a monopoly in the strict sense, but the Chapel took on a more isolated role as so many other choral institutions, including chantries, monasteries, and various private foundations, were dismantled one by one. There seems to have been much more competition among pre-Reformation choirs, and in fact the royal singers were outclassed at least once in the early sixteenth century. The scholar and diplomat Richard Pace wrote to Cardinal Wolsey in 1518, saying that the king had "plainly shown unto Cornysh [choirmaster of the Chapel Royal at the time] that your Grace's [Wolsey's] chapel is better than his: and proved the same by this reason, that if any manner of new song should be brought unto both of the said chapels to be sung *ex improviso* [at sight], then the said song should be better and more surely handled by your chapel than by his."[54] (Pace went on to say in the same letter that "Cornysh is completely unable to stomach this.") Henry loved public contests and tournaments, and it is no surprise to see him calling for one among élite singers, apparently with an eye to improving the status of his own choir. Pace was writing to Wolsey again the next day, this time about Henry's desire to poach an unusually talented boy singer from

Wolsey's chapel. This embarrassing royal defeat would probably not have happened fifty years later; the competition was simply not there.

Unlike Byrd, who eventually turned to a different way of life among the clandestine Catholics of rural Essex, Tallis seems never to have withdrawn from the Chapel Royal community in any deliberate fashion as he grew older. He stayed in Greenwich among his old colleagues and neighbors, and he mentioned the Chapel four times in his will: while identifying himself as a member in the very first lines, while making a bequest toward their feast, while discussing the music monopoly, and while naming his overseers. (Byrd, in his considerably longer will, never mentioned the Chapel at all.) It is hard to know whether Tallis was still involved with everyday music-making at court during his last years, although it is telling that his annual "fee" by June 1585 had returned to £11, the same basic wage he had earned four decades earlier as a junior member of the group.[55] His share of the music patent seems to have been intended in some ways to compensate for active work that was coming to an end or at least slowing down. The additional letter sent to the Queen in 1577, begging for extra income to supplement the patent, made an appeal for pity toward an elderly man, saying that Tallis was now "very aged." There is no direct evidence of how retirement from active Chapel duty was handled in Tallis's day, but appointments to the Chapel were for life, and a document from the early seventeenth century takes it for granted that there will be "such of the Gentlemen as are grown aged or taken with sickness, so that there is no expectation of their service any more."[56]

The other rhetorical strategy used in the letter to Elizabeth was an appeal to Tallis's loyalty, the pointed reminder that he had "served your Majesty and your royal ancestors these forty years."[57] We have seen that Tallis was still a parish musician in London in 1537, with at least three more unexpected twists in his career ahead of him, so "these forty years" must have been a slight exaggeration in 1577—not unlike the liberties taken by his younger colleague and friend Richard Granwall, who later made an almost identical claim of forty years' royal service when he had certainly not been with the Chapel quite that long.[58] The underlying message was still clear. By this point in his life, Tallis had earned his reputation as a faithful servant who had remained at his post under four sovereigns. Robert Dow's laudatory verses written in the

1580s take exactly the same approach, as does the epitaph composed at Tallis's death in 1585. The tumultuous early stages of his career, as outlined in the first four chapters of this book, seem largely to have vanished from popular memory as the Elizabethan era went on. His fame was now as a lifelong Gentleman of the Chapel, a model of musical prestige and stability.

CHAPTER SIX

The Chapel Royal (1543–85), II

A JOURNEY DOWN THE THAMES

HENRY VIII OWNED SIXTY PALACES, CASTLES, AND HOUSES BY THE time Tallis joined the Chapel Royal. The king and his royal successors moved freely among their many residences, and they often ventured even further afield in the complex rituals of travel and hospitality known as progresses, but most of the significant events of court life took place in a handful of select locations. These were called the "standing houses"—the well-established large venues that were always ready to host the king or queen, at short notice if necessary. The most important Tudor standing houses were located along the Thames within relatively easy reach of London. This chapter is a journey down the river as Tallis would have known it, visiting the distinguished residences where he made music for his four sovereigns. The itinerary begins at Windsor Castle and ends more than forty miles downstream in Greenwich, where Tallis lived when he was not on tour with the royal household singers.

Most things in and around London have changed beyond recognition since Tallis's day, but the course of the Thames has remained the same. The river is still the most distinctive physical feature of the city. In Tudor times, it was also the most important transport network and thoroughfare in the area. There was only one bridge in London, a very short walk upstream from Tallis's former parish of St. Mary-at-Hill (see Chapter 2); otherwise a coin was paid to the ferryman to cross over. Journeys were often made by boat whenever weather and

Tallis. Kerry McCarthy, Oxford University Press (2020). © Oxford University Press.
DOI: 10.1093/oso/9780190635213.001.0001.

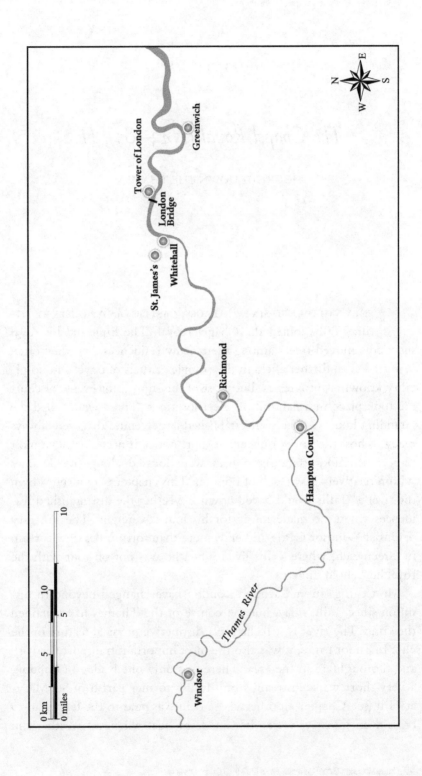

geography allowed. (This is still clear a century later in the diary of Samuel Pepys, much of whose peripatetic London life was spent on the river.) Travel by water was a relatively comfortable, prestigious, and private way to move from place to place, avoiding the mud and jostle of the public roads. Each of the Tudor sovereigns had a fleet of royal barges at his or her disposal. These barges could be dressed up for pageants, mock battles, and other spectacles, but they were most often used for the simple business of moving people from one place to another.[1] Hundreds of courtiers and staff accompanied the monarch from house to house during the annual nine-month season when the full court was in session. Tallis, as a Gentleman of the Chapel Royal, was one of them. We can follow him on these "removings" and explore the buildings where he would have sung and played. Some of the most significant royal palaces, including Greenwich, Whitehall, and Richmond, have survived only in fragments and archaeological finds. Others, such as Hampton Court, St. James's, and the Tower, still exist in various forms today and even have their Tudor chapel buildings intact to some degree. Many of the palaces were also depicted in considerable detail in mid-sixteenth-century drawings by Anton van den Wyngaerde.[2] Each of these sites has something to reveal about Tallis's experience with the Chapel Royal.

After nearly a thousand years of construction and reconstruction, Windsor Castle still stands on the hill where William the Conqueror began building it, overlooking the towns and the green countryside west of London. It was the most remote spot on the primary circuit of Tudor royal houses—a very long day's journey by boat up the Thames from the city, or two days' journey by the horse carts used by many lesser members of the traveling household. By the sixteenth century, much of the focus of court life had shifted to the newer, more fashionable, and more centrally located residences, but Windsor still had an important role to play for the Tudor monarchs. Henry spent some of his happiest days hunting in the large forested deer park that adjoined the castle. Elizabeth liked the place enough to put a substantial amount of new work into it, including updated lodgings for herself and a complete renovation of her private chapel. The court was sometimes present there for various holidays, especially during the half of the year that fell between Easter and All Saints' Day, when relatively mild weather could be hoped for.[3]

The area within the walls of Windsor Castle is dominated by two large structures: the imposing round tower at the center of the castle and the monumental Gothic chapel of St. George in the lower courtyard. This chapel is an unusually apt illustration of the kind of church that the sixteenth-century monarchs and their household musicians did *not* use. St. George's was not a Chapel Royal site at all. It was founded and maintained under royal auspices, but it was an entirely separate, self-sufficient establishment with its own full-time resident choir and its own building, constructed on a grand scale to accommodate ceremonies such as the annual festivities in honor of the Knights of the Garter. The appealingly named boy chorister "Byrd" mentioned in Chapter 5 belonged to this separate choir of St. George's; so did the reform-minded and mischievous singers Testwood and Marbeck mentioned in Chapter 10; so did John Baldwin, the music scribe of Chapter 15, before he joined the Chapel Royal.

When the Tudor sovereigns were present at Windsor, they did not worship under the lofty Gothic vaults of St. George's. They worshipped in a smaller private chapel in a completely different part of the castle, nestled within the royal apartments. That private chapel was where the members of the Chapel Royal sang. Nothing has survived of the space as Tallis would have known it; it was extensively rebuilt, reshaped, and most recently gutted in a devastating fire in 1992 that removed the last traces of its sixteenth-century structure and decoration. We still have some descriptions and images, though, and they reveal a typical architectural pattern that was common to almost all the English royal chapels.[4]

The private household chapel at Windsor was not a monumental free-standing building. It was a single cell in a complex body of structures, rooms, halls, and passageways. It was located within the Upper Ward of the castle, in the residential area used by the Tudor monarchs, and in many ways it was an extension of the private apartments where they slept, dressed, ate, and carried out their daily lives. Access to those private rooms was highly restricted, but many people could and did attempt to catch the sovereign's eye as he or she made the indoor procession from the domestic sphere toward the royal chapel. This procession was a theatrical display in itself and a rare moment of permeability between the inner and outer circles of the court. It generally happened only on Sundays and feast days. On ordinary weekdays, the sovereign did not go to the chapel at all, and the royal prayers were said in an even tinier private oratory next door to the royal bedroom. Henry seems often to have used this time to get a head start on his paperwork for the day while mass was celebrated on the other side of a small screen.[5]

Even when Tudor monarchs worshipped in the royal chapel at Windsor or at their other palaces, they were shielded from public view by the architecture of the room. The clergy, the musicians, and the attending courtiers and staff were crowded together on the ground floor. The king or queen remained one story higher up in a secluded private box or "closet," viewing the service from above. On the most important days, the sovereign might descend into the main body of the chapel to make an offering or perform other ceremonies.[6] (The imperial ambassador Eustace Chapuys famously found himself—willingly or unwillingly—acknowledging Anne Boleyn as queen when they met face to face during one such event at Greenwich Palace.) The social divisions, upstairs and downstairs, were clearly spelled out in the stone and wood of each royal chapel. This was the room in Windsor Castle that Elizabeth refitted in 1570–71 with a luxurious neoclassical interior and new choir stalls for the singers.[7] The nature of the space is captured in 1575 in the carefully crafted diplomatic Latin of the title page to the *Cantiones sacrae* (see Chapter 14), which describes Tallis as a gentleman serving in Her Majesty's *privato sacello*, "private little chapel." The key points here are smallness, prestige, and exclusivity.

We can see these characteristics first-hand in the chapel of Hampton Court Palace, twenty winding miles down the river from Windsor. Much of the Tudor core of the palace has survived relatively intact. Cardinal Wolsey began building it in 1515 in fashionable red brick as a house where he could entertain royalty and other dignitaries. Henry took it for his own use in 1528 and expanded it to suit the even larger scale of his court. By the time Tallis joined the Chapel, Hampton Court had already become one of the most important royal residences. It was especially valued for entertaining. During the last part of his reign, Henry often spent the twelve days of Christmas there. The hours of the festive season were rung out by the imposing astronomical clock in one of the inner courtyards, a technical tour de force installed in 1540 by a German clockmaker. Its original large bell is still in use. It makes the same sound that would have been heard by Tallis and his colleagues as they hurried across Clock Court on their way to the chapel. This astronomical clock is unusual because it does not just mark the hour, the day, the sign of the zodiac, and similar things: it also has a dial that shows, in real time, the tide level of the Thames eighteen miles away in central London. This information would have been vital for people traveling by boat from Hampton Court to the city, where the wrong timing could mean a delayed journey or a hazardous passage under London Bridge. The great clock, easily visible from the king's private apartments, was at the heart of the palace, and the river was the palace's lifeblood, bringing a steady flow of visitors through a large formal riverside gate (now entirely gone, alas) and watering the gardens that provided fine produce for their meals.[8]

The royal chapel at Hampton Court has picked up some baroque accretions along the way, but its basic form would still be familiar to Tallis. The spectacularly ostentatious ceiling put in by Henry in 1536 is still there, painted in his original color scheme of celestial blue and gold, covered with massive cherub-encrusted ornaments and repetitions of the king's motto *Dieu et mon droit*. The Tudor structure and floor plan of the chapel is intact. The floor plan can be described as a squat T-shape. The crossbar of the T—the west end of the chapel—is divided into upper and lower levels. On the ground floor, it is a wide and low-ceilinged ante-chapel, which functioned as a sort of vestibule, available to accommodate courtiers who wanted to attend services but had no official duties or privileges that brought them near the altar. On the upper floor, the same broad area is taken up by a suite where the sovereign could view the service from above in complete privacy. The lower branch of the T—the east end of the chapel—is modest in size but a full two stories in height, containing the choir stalls for the singers of the Chapel Royal and the sanctuary where the clergy presided over the service. On the south side there is a small organ loft originally placed there in the 1530s as part of Henry's renovations. Behind the monumental eighteenth-century wooden altarpiece, there are hints of the high lancet windows that originally caught the morning sun above the altar.

The only surviving fragments of the Tudor chapel floor can be seen in a small neglected corner of the ante-chapel: plain square clay tiles in a checkerboard pattern. Those cheap materials were not meant for show. Whenever the sovereign was present, the floor of the chapel was covered with textiles, and the walls were hung with tapestry.[9] The resulting acoustics would have been far from what we have come to expect in modern recordings and performances of Tallis's music. A big piece such as his seven-voice *Loquebantur variis linguis* (see Chapter 15)— composed for Pentecost, one of the great ceremonial "days of estate" in the royal chapels—would almost certainly have been sung in rather small, muffled, and unforgiving spaces.[10] Some of Tallis's singing at Hampton Court would also have been done outdoors, most notably in the cloister that adjoined the chapel, built as a stage set for royal prayers and processions. Even the layout of Henry's apartments at Hampton Court was designed to maximize the drama of the procession from his private residential areas into the chapel closet and beyond. Henry loved such opportunities for ceremonial display, and he went on to build another grand processional colonnade at his central London palace of Whitehall. Even as he was dissolving monastic cloisters, he was constructing new cloisters for himself.[11]

Hampton Court Palace was built on a generous scale to accommodate the whole royal entourage and any guests who might join them. This principle was tested to its limits in 1555 when Queen Mary was falsely thought to be pregnant and went into a long confinement there in preparation for childbirth, with both the English and Spanish households crowded in for a tense four months.[12] Most stays there were shorter and more convivial. If Windsor in the Tudor era was in many ways a summer palace meant for recreation, Hampton Court was a winter palace meant for hospitality.[13] We can catch the mood of the great feast days at court in a sermon preached by John Longland in the king's presence in 1538. This was actually a Good Friday sermon, asking rhetorically why the usual festive sounds, sights, and other pleasures were all missing at such an important moment in the church calendar. It is worth quoting at length because it so vividly evokes the sacred and secular soundscapes of the Tudor court.

> If it be so high a day, where are the signs and tokens of the feast?
>
> Where is the solemn ringing of bells to matins, to mass, to evensong, to divine service?
>
> Where are the solemnities of the masses said and sung, as are in the other festival days?
>
> Where are the solemn songs of descant, pricked song, faburden, square note, regals, and organs?
>
> Where are your warbling voices, reaches, and pleasant reports in your singings?
>
> Where are the rich ornaments of the altars, the rich vestments, copes, plate, and jewels, wont upon such days to be set upon the altars?
>
> Where is the great welfare, the great dinners, the double service, the delicate meats and drinks on such festival days wont to be used?
>
> Where are your musical instruments of all sorts, and your blowing to dinner with trumpets?
>
> Where are your harps, your lutes, your cymbals, your flutes, your tabrets, your drumslades and dulcimers?
>
> Where are your viols, your rebecs, your sackbuts, and your sweet soft pleasant pipes?
>
> Where are your merry communications, your merry jests, fables, and tales wont to be had at your table for merry pastime on such days?[14]

The great hall at Hampton Court still exists in its more or less original state, with its wall-to-wall tapestries and ornate hammerbeam roof. As Wyngaerde's south-facing sketch makes clear, it was the most monumental structure in the palace, with a considerably higher profile than

the chapel.[15] Tallis may well have had some memorable "great din-
ners" there during his long career at court, although it is uncertain
how often he and his colleagues actually took their everyday meals
in the great halls of the royal palaces. The daily routine of the Chapel
singers seems to have been changing significantly in the two or three
generations before the Reformation. The *Liber Niger*, the Black Book of
royal household management, gives details of the official arrangement
in the 1470s: the members of the Chapel Royal were entitled to two
meals a day, "sitting together in the hall at the Dean's board," whenever they were in residence at any palace.[16] These meals were served
at approximately 11 am (after the daily high mass had been sung) and
5 pm. The singers were also entitled to a drink and a snack after they
had finished their evening services. They were expected to be "lodging
together within the court in one chamber, or nigh thereto"—ostensibly
for the sake of delivering their evening refreshment, but probably also
to keep them within sight and close to the chapel where they would be
expected to assemble early the next morning for matins. This practice
still appears to have been on the books in 1502, when there is a reference at the palace of Westminster to the "room where the gentlemen of
the king's chapel lie."[17] By 1526, the court harbingers were being asked
to set up suitable local accommodation ("herbergage convenient") for
the members of the Chapel as they traveled from place to place, perhaps
as it became clear that it was no longer practical at the more architec-
turally refined new Tudor palaces to lodge twenty or more people in
one big room.[18]

The most important change took place just as Tallis joined the
group. An injunction issued on 28 April 1544 says that "the Gentlemen
of the Chapel . . . shall have from the last day of March forward, for
their boardwages, every of them 12d per diem."[19] "Boardwages" were
cash payments given in lieu of the room and board traditionally provided to servants. This extra daily allowance of 12d (one shilling) per
day was not a trivial amount of money at the time. It was significantly
more than the royal singers' existing wage of 7 1/2d per day (£11 8s
per year.) Even if it was only given during the nine-month season
when they were active, it more than doubled their income. It implies
what may already have been a trend of increasing professionalization,
detachment from the full-time residential machinery of the court,

and acknowledgment that many of the Gentlemen had a busy personal and commercial life outside of their court duties. A couple of
months later, in June 1544, they were given an additional bonus to
make their touring life easier: the "Gentlemen Singers" were to be
provided "at every removing, allowance of a cart for the carriage of
their stuff."[20]

Richmond Palace, the next of the great Tudor standing houses, was
located eight miles downstream from Hampton Court. It was sold off
and largely demolished during the Commonwealth; not much of it is
left now except an elegant gatehouse. If the palace were still there it
would doubtless be a major tourist attraction. Henry VII, first of the
Tudors, began the work of building Richmond in 1498 after its medieval predecessor Sheen Palace suffered a major fire.[21] By 1501, the project was largely complete, including a spectacular new chapel. A visitor
that year described its interior: "The chapel, well paved, glazed, and
hanged with cloth of Arras, the body and the choir with cloth of gold,
and the altars set with many relics, jewels, and full rich plate. In the
walls of this devout and pleasant chapel is picture [sic] of kings of this
realm . . . In the right side of the chapel is a goodly and a privy closet
for the king, richly hanged with silk and traverse carpet and cushions
for his noble grace . . . From the chapel and closets extended goodly
passages and galleries, paved, glazed, and pointed, beset with badges of
gold, as roses, portcullises, and such other."[22]

Henry VIII invited a group of Venetian ambassadors to attend a
service sung by the Chapel Royal at Richmond in 1515. A member of
their entourage wrote home about the experience in a letter that was
preserved by the diarist Marino Sanuto: "The mass was sung by His
Majesty's Chapel, which is really more divine than human; they did
not so much sing as jubilate (*non cantavano ma jubilavano*), and especially
the basses (*contrabassi*), who I think do not have their equal anywhere
in the world. I could say many things, but time does not permit me.
And when mass was over, His Majesty with the rest of the lords, and
the ambassadors with their retinue, went into the palace into a room
where a table was prepared . . . ."[23] We are fortunate that our Venetian
informant at least had time to comment on one detail of the Chapel
Royal's singing: the resonance and brilliance of the bass voices, even in
the tapestried, cushioned confines of the new Richmond chapel.

Richmond Palace was particularly significant for the religious life of the pre-Reformation court because it was part of a larger complex that included several monasteries. The palace was built and rebuilt when English royal piety was at its peak. It was designed to be surrounded by powerhouses of prayer and learning. Henry V had founded the neighboring Charterhouse of Sheen in 1414 and the Brigittine abbey of Sion just across the river in 1415. Henry VII added a third foundation around 1500, an Observant Franciscan friary, which was closest of all to the royal household; in fact it was fully integrated into the architecture of the new Tudor palace, with a covered gallery leading to the friary church so courtiers could visit without being exposed to the weather.[24] A similar friary had been set up within the precincts of Greenwich Palace in 1485. The Observant Franciscans were a particularly austere subset of the Franciscan order who took very seriously the ideal of poverty espoused by their founder.[25] People did not go to the friaries to be awed by gold, jewels, silk, and impressive murals of the king's royal ancestors. They also did not go there to hear elaborate music; the Observants had strict rules against such things. The friaries were places for confession, for meditation, for spiritual advice, and for hearing challenging sermons that were free of courtly flattery.

This arrangement came to a quick and violent end in the 1530s. When the friary and the two other adjoining royal monasteries were dissolved, Richmond Palace was left standing amid swathes of attractive newly-acquired parkland. The palace with its grounds was given as a consolation prize to Anne of Cleves, Henry VIII's fourth wife, after their brief marriage in 1540. (Anne seems to have considered this a lucky escape and lived peacefully for seventeen more years.) The chapel at Richmond was one of the first places where renewed ceremonial and musical grandeur was noticed at the beginning of Queen Mary's reign. Bess of Hardwick, Countess of Shrewsbury, spoke with her there in September 1553 as she "came from evensong, which was sung in the chapel by all the singing men of the same, with playing of the organs of the solemnest manner."[26] Richmond was not the most modern or fashionable of sixteenth-century palaces—it had been built on what was essentially a late-medieval footprint, and its significance declined further with the fall of the monasteries—but it was still enjoyed by the later Tudors, not least because it was more conveniently situated than

Hampton Court or Windsor but still remote enough to be a country retreat. It was one of Elizabeth's three most frequently used residences.[27] She died there in 1603.

Downstream from Richmond, the river continues to widen as it runs past Chelsea and turns north. Shortly after passing Lambeth Palace, the residence of the Archbishop of Canterbury, the royal barges would have reached the district of Westminster (in Tallis's day a separate entity from London proper) and the palace of Whitehall. Those two names, Westminster and Whitehall, are still shorthand for the legislative and administrative machinery of the British government. Westminster had been the traditional meeting place of Parliament since the thirteenth century and a significant residence for the kings of England since Anglo-Saxon times. The medieval palace of Westminster was severely damaged by fire in 1512. Henry VIII took the opportunity to reclaim this traditional site of power in 1530 by appropriating a nearby mansion, another luxury home owned by Wolsey, and rebuilding it on a massive scale to suit the needs of his court. Wolsey's residence had gone by the name of York Place; Henry's new palace soon picked up the nickname of Whitehall.

By the end of the 1530s, Whitehall Palace had taken on the role of official seat of government and administrative center of the realm. It was designated by an act of Parliament in 1536 as "the king's palace at Westminster forever"; in fact it was the only Tudor royal house given the official title of "palace," with all that implied in terms of absolute imperial power.[28] The word *palatium* in Tallis's *Gaude gloriosa* (see Chapter 16), the "palace" where the Virgin was enthroned, had unmistakable political overtones. In a rapidly shifting society, Tudor Whitehall seems to have offered some degree of institutional stability. The Chapel Royal was very often in residence there, and many sixteenth-century court musicians chose to live in or near Westminster. Some of them owned significant property in the area and were involved with local commerce and social life. The parish church of St. Margaret's, Westminster was itself the center of a thriving musical community.[29]

Tudor Whitehall was the largest royal residence in Europe at the time, covering a sprawling twenty-three acres of land between Westminster Abbey and the river.[30] Almost no visible traces of the palace are left above ground, but twentieth-century excavations revealed the nature and extent of the buildings. The palace incorporated a large private orchard as well as a sports complex with tennis courts, bowling alleys, and a tiltyard. Long covered galleries led to monumental royal apartments. A lavishly appointed space was created for the Chapel Royal to sing in. Two "foundations" were dug in 1536 directly under the two facing sets of choir stalls in the chapel; these seem to have been hollow acoustic chambers of a type found in many English churches, designed to enhance the resonance of the singers' voices.[31] The new stalls themselves were made by John Ripley, the king's master joiner, and carved in grand heraldic style "with beasts standing upon them."[32] Some of the Whitehall buildings were constructed on land newly reclaimed from the Thames by a vast retaining wall, itself topped by a formal covered walkway that ran more than 400 feet along the waterfront.[33] Henry's new cloister within the palace was even more ambitious because it was built on two levels with a sheltered upper gallery for spectators, who could crowd in to watch processions and other ceremonies from above. Tallis's polyphonic litany of 1544 (see Chapter 5) may well have been sung there for the first time. The Whitehall cloister was also an important venue for preaching from the late 1540s onward.[34] A large pulpit was set up in the middle of the courtyard, where sermons could be "heard of more than four times so many people as could have stood in the king's chapel."[35]

The Reformation changed the music and the rituals at the palace, but it seems to have had rather little long-term impact on the level of magnificent display. A guest who was present in 1565 (for the christening of one of Elizabeth's godchildren) described the furnishings in the chapel. After the usual enumeration of gold and jewels, he noted that "rich tapestry" covered both the front and back of the choir stalls, wall hangings of luxury cloth covered "the upper part of the chapel from the table of administration to the stalls," and a large part of the chapel "under foot was laid with carpets."[36] Once again, there were almost no exposed hard surfaces anywhere in the room. Even the large baptismal font was lined with linen cloth and hung with tapestry. Elaborate sets of gilded candlesticks were fastened onto the choir stalls, "so that the whole lights set there were eighty-three": there would have been no problem reading complex polyphony on a dark winter evening.

About a fifteen-minute walk northwest from the site of Whitehall, across St. James's Park (which has been miraculously preserved into the twenty-first century as a green space), is the much smaller St. James's Palace. It was built in the 1530s as an auxiliary Westminster residence and a private home for younger members of the royal family. Henry had the ceiling of the original chapel refitted at the very end of the decade, using a striking Renaissance design published just a few years earlier by the Venetian architect Sebastiano Serlio.[37] The king optimistically decorated it with the date 1540 and the initials, mottoes, and heraldic symbols of Anne of Cleves, who he hoped would provide him with further heirs to the throne.[38] The Tudor chapel at St. James's is a tiny jewel box. It was even tinier in its original form, before the royal closet on the upper level was made much smaller and the screen separating the traditional low ante-chapel from the main chapel was knocked out. (The resulting extra section of "Tudor" ceiling is a later imitation.) It takes just fourteen steps to walk from the back of the original church to the altar. Singers in the choir stalls face one another at close range. It would have been a very tight fit indeed when the full or nearly full complement of the Chapel Royal was present there. Hot weather (and Tudor ceremonial garb) would have made these close quarters even more stifling; it must have been a relief that the court did not continue its usual round of chapel observances during July and August.

Past Westminster, the Thames turns eastward again and flows toward the City of London. In Tallis's day this stretch of the river was lined with the townhouses of bishops and gentry, including the grand Renaissance edifice of Old Somerset House. The next Chapel Royal site, the Tower of London, is at the far edge of the City, just east of the old wall and still visible from the river in a largely unobstructed view. The Tower was no longer a significant court residence by the sixteenth century. It was notorious as a place of violence, used more often as a prison and military arsenal than a palace. Tudor sovereigns generally did not stay there unless they had a good reason to, as each of them did on the night before the traditional coronation procession from the Tower to Westminster. The site nonetheless has something to tell us about Tallis's world because its royal chapel of St. Peter ad Vincula, built in 1519–20, has been preserved in a remarkably intact state. The austere Spanish chestnut roof, uncovered by Victorian restorers, is original. So are the unadorned windows with their low Tudor arches. When the rows of modern chairs are removed, the interior of the chapel appears more or less as an early-sixteenth-century observer would have seen it. The effect is quite different from the gilded luxury of the other surviving royal chapels. The status of St. Peter ad Vincula as (at best) a secondary place of worship seems to have kept it safe from ambitious redecoration.

After passing by the Tower, the river loops into one more deep bend as it approaches Greenwich, the last stop on this royal household itinerary. Even now there is a sense of turning a corner away from the frenetic center of the city. Greenwich was actually still something of a secluded rural retreat in the Tudor era, despite being only five miles by water from the Tower. The royal palace there, much like Richmond Palace, was built by Henry VII at the turn of the sixteenth century on the site of an older residence, then was neglected and demolished in the seventeenth century. The only known remnants of its chapel came to light unexpectedly in 2005 during routine construction work in a Greenwich car park. What emerged about four feet below modern ground level was a clay tile floor almost identical to the traces left in the chapel at Hampton Court—plain red, black, and white in a simple alternating pattern—along with Tudor brickwork that marked the east end where the altar stood. Greenwich Palace also had a closely attached Observant Franciscan friary that played an important role in the ceremonial life of the court. Catherine of Aragon was a member of the Franciscan third order, a lay associate of the friars, and when the royal household stayed at Greenwich (as they so often did in her day), she would get up at midnight and pray matins with them in their church.[39] Like the friary at Richmond, it was valued as a place to receive the sacraments. Henry VIII was baptized there, as were his children Mary and Elizabeth. (Edward, the youngest, was baptized at Hampton Court; by that point the Franciscan brethren were no longer in royal favor.)

Greenwich Palace was especially well-loved in the early years of the sixteenth century. In fact Henry VIII celebrated more than half of the major holidays there in the course of his reign.[40] It is no surprise that many Chapel singers came to live nearby, even as changing fashions and political circumstances began leading the court to spend more time elsewhere. As we have seen in Chapter 5, Tallis was part of a close-knit local community of musicians in Greenwich. His own family home was acquired in 1555 via an older member of the Chapel, his wife Joan's first husband Thomas Bury, who had served during the years when the court was very often resident there. The house was centrally located within easy sight of St. Alfege's parish church, on the east side of Stockwell Street where it meets Church Street. It eventually became an inn, the Old Greyhound, and then another private home whose location can be seen on an early-nineteenth-century map.[41] The exact spot where Tallis lived, where he slept in his featherbed with the Flemish tapestry coverlet (see Chapter 17), is now the bustling entrance to a university library.

DOCUMENTS OF TALLIS'S MUSIC

CHAPTER SEVEN

Setting the Stage

THE *ANTIPHONALE* OF 1519–20

T HE FIRST (AND OLDEST) MUSICAL DOCUMENT IN THIS BOOK IS A vast treasury of chant for use in church. It does not contain any of Tallis's own compositions. What it offers the modern reader is a view of the musical world in which Tallis was educated and in which he began his career. It includes two dozen plainsong melodies he used in his own works; even more importantly, it contains a thousand melodies he would have sung and improvised on. We do not know where he served his apprenticeship as a young musician, but we can look over his shoulder at the pages of a collection he would have known well.

The *Antiphonale ad usum ecclesiae Sarum* was the most monumental single publication of music in sixteenth-century England.[1] Its title can be roughly translated as "book of antiphons for the use of the church of Salisbury." It was printed in two large volumes, one in 1519 and one in 1520. The preface to the *Antiphonale* describes it as "an incomparable treasury . . . in which the divine praises and heavenly songs are portrayed as with a paintbrush and colors." This music was not new in 1519: it was the traditional chant that had been sung for centuries in the rite of Salisbury (or Sarum), the liturgy used by almost all pre-Reformation churches in the British Isles, including all of Tallis's known places of employment before he joined the Chapel Royal. The *Antiphonale* of 1519–20 was a new reimagining of an old repertory. Its 1,093 pages were produced in the finest Renaissance style, printed in Paris (no English press could manage the task) with black type on red

Tallis. Kerry McCarthy, Oxford University Press (2020). © Oxford University Press.
DOI: 10.1093/oso/9780190635213.001.0001.

staves for ease of reading. Some luxury copies were even printed on vellum instead of paper. The book's subtitle boasts that it is "adorned with elegant pictures": these elaborate woodcut images, featured on the most important pages, preserve something of the tradition of hand-illuminated manuscripts. The editors, a team of experts from King's College, Cambridge, described their work as a "collation of the oldest and best sources." This was an optimistic project, even a utopian one in many ways. The people who worked on it could hardly have imagined that their book would be controversial in twenty years and outlawed in thirty. It seems to have been intended as a musical reference work for the ages.

Unlike most liturgical books, the *Antiphonale* is not a book for clergy; it is a book for musicians. It contains nearly everything chanted by the choir during the complex daily and nightly round of services. (The only music not included is the music for the mass, which is found in a separate collection called the *Graduale*.) Every church that hoped to maintain any sort of sung liturgy beyond daily mass would have needed at least one *Antiphonale*. By the beginning of the sixteenth century, something like twenty thousand such books were in use in England.[2] At that point, they were all copied by hand. Some of these manuscripts were beautiful objects—one late-fifteenth-century singer in London described his copy as "his principal jewel"—while others were "old," "feeble," "sore broken," or so worn as to be unusable.[3] The new printed *Antiphonale* was offered as a uniform and easy-to-use substitute for the existing patchwork of manuscript copies. The cost of the two-volume work, in its standard paper edition, was approximately thirty shillings. This was not a trivial expenditure (it was three-fourths of Tallis's annual wage as organist at Dover Priory) but it would have been a wise purchase for any church that wished to cultivate singing. The preface even boasts that the price is "so cheap" as to leave prospective buyers with "no excuse" for failing to acquire it.[4] The large print and generous dimensions of the book, with pages nearly sixteen inches high, made it suitable to be placed on a desk, stand, or lectern and shared among several singers.

The *Antiphonale* is organized in the form of a giant calendar. The *Pars Hyemalis* (the winter volume) covers the six months from the first week of Advent, around the beginning of December, through Trinity Sunday in late May or early June. The *Pars Estivalis* (the summer volume) covers the other half of the year. The elaborate seasonal ceremonies surrounding Christmas and Easter make the winter half of the book heftier than its summer counterpart. The music in both volumes is interspersed with closely-spaced rubrics, sometimes pages of them at once, instructing people what to sing when. The introduction to the 1549 Book of Common Prayer a generation later complained about "the number and hardness of the rules" in pre-Reformation worship: "many times there was more business to find out what should be read than to read it when it was found out." Those words were written by the English reformer Thomas Cranmer, who spoke from experience. (In fact he was paraphrasing a slightly less extravagant statement by a Spanish Catholic priest, Francisco de Quinoñez, who had proposed a thorough revision and simplification of the Latin liturgy in the 1530s.)[5] The singers who used the *Antiphonale* day after day would certainly have needed a good command of Latin and a sharp eye for detail.

To help musicians find their way around these massive books, each of the two volumes also includes a compact printed calendar, with each month outlined on a single page. Readers seeking the start of the liturgical year in Advent would find themselves directed to the beginning of the winter volume. The December calendar page in the *Antiphonale* includes a rich assortment of saints' days and feast days. Winter solstice falls on 12 December: the old Julian calendar had gradually drifted from the annual solar cycle since the days of ancient Rome. The sun passes through its astrological houses from Sagittarius into Capricorn. The reader is informed (perhaps a bit pessimistically, even for English latitudes) that "the night has 18 hours and the day has 6." The music for December would have been sung with generous use of candles, despite the quixotic efforts of some English churches to do away with artificial light and train their singers to perform this vast repertory from memory.[6] December, like every month in the calendar, also includes some homespun Latin maxims about staying healthy during the season:

> Warm clothing is sensible for the body during the month of
>   December.
> Let bathing not be trusted, but let drinking of the cup be valued.
> Let your drink be warm, in total opposition to the chill.[7]

The first event of the church year, and the first page of music in the *Antiphonale*, is the singing of vespers on Saturday evening at the very beginning of Advent. The editors follow the time-honored principle found in so many liturgical books: give a full explanation the first time around and let the reader apply this knowledge to future events. The rubrics set the scene. "When the bells have been rung in the customary manner, and the candles have been lit . . . the presiding priest sings, with a clear voice, *Deus in adiutorium meum intende*": "O God, come to my assistance." After this comes a set of basic instructions on singing the psalms at vespers and combining them with the correct seasonal music.

Near the end of the psalmody, "three boys, having received permission from the leader of the choir, go out to vest themselves, two for carrying the candles and one for the censer." The young Tallis would doubtless have performed this duty in the course of his training as a chorister. What follows soon after (Figure 7.1) is the first substantial piece of music in the book: *Ecce dies veniunt*, the responsory for the first day of Advent.

> Behold, the days are coming, says the Lord,
> and I will raise up a righteous seed for David:
> and he shall reign as king, and he shall be wise,
> and he shall bring forth judgment and justice on earth,
> and this is the name they shall call him: our Lord, the Just One.
> In those days Judah shall be saved, and Israel shall dwell in confidence.

The *Antiphonale* specifies that this piece is to be sung by "clerks of the second form." The "forms" were the rows of seating in which the staff of larger churches in Tudor England took their places during services. This threefold arrangement can still be seen today in the choir stalls of most English cathedrals. Clerks of the first form, the uppermost row of seats, were the senior clerics who presided over the liturgy; clerks of the third form, the lowest row of seats, were the boy choristers. The second form belonged to the lay vicars or lay clerks, the professional musicians whose job it was to perform the most difficult and complicated parts of the choral services. The musical setting of *Ecce dies veniunt* was entrusted to the paid singers, and it is suitably elaborate, with a lively melody spanning more than an octave and a complex set of internal repetitions and refrains. The service of vespers in the *Antiphonale*

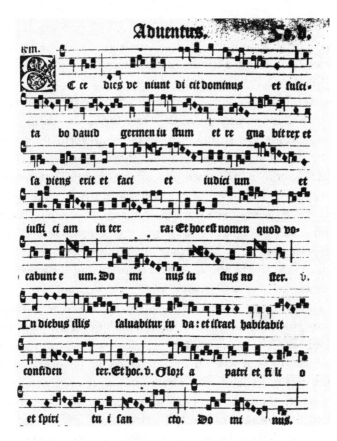

Figure 7.1   *Ecce dies veniunt*, for the first Sunday of Advent, from the Sarum *Antiphonale* (1519–20). Christ Church, Oxford. Reproduced by permission.

includes one of these responsories on every prominent feast day of the year. Tallis himself set a number of them to polyphonic music, always preserving the chant melody or at least a rough paraphrase of it.

The seasonal preparations of Advent reach their high point a few weeks later at the midnight service on Christmas Eve. On this night, there are nine responsories of even greater splendor, including the memorable *O magnum mysterium*. The Gospel reading for the occasion is the long genealogy of Christ according to Matthew, set in the *Antiphonale* to a special melody used only for this purpose. The Te Deum, the hymn of rejoicing at matins, is intoned by a priest "in a silk cope." Even the poorest churches in pre-Reformation England generally had at least one silk vestment, however old and patched, to lend some grandeur to feast days. The antiphons of Christmas are begun by the clergy in order of seniority, "beginning with the most distinguished person, according to the rank of each."

A few days later, on 28 December, that tidy arrangement is turned upside down. This is the feast of the Holy Innocents, patron saints of choirboys, and the young musicians of the third form are given their day in the sun. The boys make a solemn procession into the upper reaches of the choir and take their places there. For the next twenty-four hours, the church belongs to them. They lead the services and direct the music while the senior clergy perform menial tasks such as carrying books and holding candles. The rites in the *Antiphonale* even provide for the appointment of a "boy bishop" who presides over the day's festivities. He is elected by the choristers from among their number and dressed in a miniature set of vestments for the occasion. An inventory of the London parish church of St. Mary-at-Hill, where Tallis sang in the 1530s, includes a miter for the boy bishop, "garnished with silver . . . and pearl and counterfeit stone." The silver garnish was melted down and sold in 1549 when the full force of the Reformation hit the parish; just five years later, as Catholic rites were briefly restored, the church's records show another small miter being crafted, this time with a more frugal adornment of lace.[8] The boy bishop was allowed to exercise some of the liturgical duties of a real bishop, preaching a sermon for the day and giving the episcopal blessing to his fellow-musicians. (The very simple melody, barely more than a monotone, is helpfully written out in full in the *Antiphonale* for boys who are not used to imparting episcopal blessings.)[9] The small bishop and his retinue went from house to house during the day, visiting their "subjects" and accepting gifts. All of the choristers could expect special treats, new clothing, generous meals, and the excitement of seeing their strictly regimented world in disarray for a day.

In some English churches, this topsy-turvy reversal of roles took place on 6 December, the feast of St. Nicholas, another traditional patron of choristers and scholars (including the Company of Parish Clerks, which would have been Tallis's own guild during his time as a professional singer in the City.) This was the case in the Chapel Royal, where these "superstitious and childish observances" finally disappeared for good in the mid-1540s after at least one unsuccessful attempt to ban them.[10] The whole thing, on whatever date it was celebrated, was a somewhat milder version of the Feast of Fools or "Lord of Misrule" festivities that took place around Christmas in many churches and households across Europe.[11] The emphasis in England seems more often to have been on harmless fun than on real subversion and chaos, although Queen Mary's authorities in 1554 (who were otherwise whole-heartedly in favor of reviving old Catholic customs) made a last-minute effort to ban the St. Nicholas celebrations in London, perhaps for fear that they would make a bad impression on the foreign dignitaries who were present for the country's formal reconciliation with Rome earlier that week. This was noted by the diarist Henry Machyn, who also observed two years later in December 1556 that the festivities were back in full swing: "Saint Nicholas went abroad in most parts of London singing after the old fashion, and was received with many good people into their houses, and had as much good cheer as ever they had in many places."[12]

The ceremonies in honor of St. Nicholas or the Holy Innocents would have been a welcome change in the daily routine of sixteenth-century choristers. That routine was not always a happy one. The familiar litany of "choristers' laments" included long hours, harsh classroom discipline, and cruel or incompetent elders. The Tudor choirmaster John Redford wrote a (presumably tongue-in-cheek) complaint, a dozen verses long, for his own boys to sing: "He plucketh us by the nose, he plucketh us by the hawse [neck], / He plucketh us by the ears with his most unhappy paws, / And all for this peevish prick-song, not worth two straws / We poor silly boys abide much woe."[13] A chorister in another poem is berated during an elementary singing lesson: "What hast thou done, Walter, since Saturday at noon? / Thou holdest not a note, by God, in right tune."[14] "O painful time," wrote Thomas Tusser, looking back on his childhood years as a chorister, sent away from home against his will in the 1530s and pressed into service in a series of church foundations that offered little more than stale bread and frequent beatings.[15] Even allowing for the satirical and formulaic nature of these texts, it is clear that the life of a very young musician in Renaissance England could be somewhat grim at times. Not all Tudor teachers were the gentle and reasonable "Master" of Morley's *Plain and Easy Introduction to Practical Music.*

One fascinating glimpse into the choristers' classroom is offered by the English-Latin phrasebooks which became popular in the early sixteenth century. Bilingual collections of *vulgaria*—"colloquial things"—were published for young beginners, allowing them to build their Latin skills with everyday phrases before venturing into the more treacherous waters of the classics.[16] These phrases reflect the usual preoccupations of children: food ("The fried eggs and bacon I ate at breakfast"), games ("Would God we might go play"), family ("My father is a great man"), school life ("We have played a comedy of Latin"), and insults of various sorts ("Thou stinkest").[17] There is also plenty of music.

> What part singest thou? *Qua voce cantas?*
> He playeth well at organs. *Bene pulsat organa.*
> The chanter or setter of the choir was absent. *Phonostus aberat.*
> The choir singeth side for side. *Chorus alternis canit.*
> This is good descant. *Haec est mera symphonia.*[18]

Some Tudor phrasebooks for children included more elaborate sentiments about music. One such sentence declares that "Melody made with man's natural voice, well tuned and proportioned, is sweeter than any melody by instrument."[19] That thought was shared (and perhaps even learned at school) by Byrd, who said exactly the same thing in 1588 in the preface to his first English songbook: "There is not any music of instruments whatsoever comparable to that which is made of the voices of men, where the voices are good, and the same well sorted and ordered."[20]

It is clear from these textbooks that young pupils were often actors as well as musicians. ("I am principal player," one fictional child boasts. "I have played my part without any fail.")[21] Most children's plays were private exercises in the classroom, but some boys, including the choristers of the Chapel Royal and St. Paul's Cathedral, also acted in public for eager audiences. A German visitor to Elizabethan England noted in his diary that he was delighted by the *"Kinder-comoedia"* ("children's comedy") performed at Blackfriars by the Queen's choristers, who also offered lavish musical entertainment before the play.[22] In many ways, the annual December festival of the Boy Bishop was just another theatrical production: a chance for young performers to play senior clergy, complete with pomp, regalia, and lines befitting the role.

The celebration of the Holy Innocents lasted only one day, but the splendid music continued throughout the Christmas season. The very next day, 29 December, was dedicated to St. Thomas Becket, the twelfth-century Archbishop of Canterbury who was murdered in his own cathedral by the agents of Henry II. The *Antiphonale* gives instructions to offer incense to "the image of blessed Thomas the martyr" while a special piece of music is sung in his honor: it is tacitly assumed that every church would have an image of him displayed for public veneration. He stood as a potent symbol for the fraught church-state relations of medieval England, and he was, for obvious reasons, the first saint to be expunged from the liturgical calendar in the English Reformation. His shrines and images were destroyed by direct command of Henry VIII. Henry's proclamation, issued in November 1538, also said that liturgical texts referring to Becket must be "erased and put out of all the books."[23] In a copy of the *Antiphonale* now at Christ Church, Oxford, all the music for 29 December—covering a generous twelve folio pages—is crossed out with angry scratches and blots in thick, dark ink. One post-Reformation primer, published in 1552, kept Becket's place in the calendar, presumably for the sake of calculating dates and reading old documents. In that calendar he is designated not as bishop or martyr but as "traitor."[24] There is almost no surviving English polyphonic music in his honor, and nothing at all from the sixteenth century except a single stray fragment of one piece, *Gaude pastor* by Tallis's slightly older colleague Richard Pygott. Given Becket's great popularity in England up to the very moment of the Reformation, this absence is doubtless the result of deliberate suppression. If Tallis (quite possibly a namesake of the saint) ever wrote anything for him or for his feast day, it has been lost without a trace.

The Christmas festivities went on into the New Year, through Twelfth Night and Epiphany on 6 January, after which the season of leisure and feasting ended and normal work was resumed. (The calendar in the *Antiphonale* reassures us that bathing is now safe during January.) The very end of the Christmas cycle comes with the celebration of Candlemas, also known as the feast of the Purification, on 2 February. This day commemorates the ritual presentation of the infant Jesus to the temple forty days after his birth, as was the law at the time for all firstborn Jewish male children. Figure 7.2 shows the first page

In die purificationis.

¶ In Purificatione beate
marie virginis ad primas vesperas an.
O admirabile comerciū. ps. Dixit dūs.
an. Quando natus. ps. Confitebor tibi.
an. Rubum quem. ps. Beatus vir. an.
Germinauit radix. ps. De profundis.
an. Magnum hereditatis. ps. Memen-
to dūe. Quere omnes aſie in circunciſio-
ne domini. fo. xciiij.　　　Capitulum.

Ecce ego mitto angelū meum qui
preparabit viam ante faciem me-
am. et statim veniet ad templum sanctū
ſuum dominator quem vos queritis: et
angelus testamenti quem vos vultis.
r. Deo gratias.

Responsorium.

Vide te · mira culum ma tris do mi ni

concepit vir go viri lis igna ra con ſor

ci j. Stans one ra ta no bi li onere ma

ti a. Et ma trem ſe le tam co gno ſcit. Que ſe

nes cit vx o rem. v. Hec ſpe

Figure 7.2　The celebration of Candlemas, from the Sarum *Antiphonale* (1519–20). Christ Church, Oxford. Reproduced by permission.

of music for Candlemas in the *Antiphonale.* The New Testament scene has been transported to early-sixteenth-century Europe: the temple has a geometric tile floor, a carved altarpiece, and a luxuriously draped altar cloth with five embroidered crosses. Mary and Joseph bring their offerings to the altar. A tonsured cleric holds the service book open for the elderly Simeon as he carries the infant in his arms. What Simeon is presumably singing is the Nunc Dimittis—"Lord, now lettest thou thy servant depart in peace"—sung every day at evening services in England both before and after the Reformation.

Candlemas was, quite fittingly, a day for grand processions. In the ritual of the Chapel Royal, the "most ancient earl and greatest of blood" had the privilege of carrying a specially blessed candle alongside the monarch.[25] In February 1506, this procession included Philip of Castile, future brother-in-law of Henry VIII, who was received at court as a guest of honor after his entire fleet was shipwrecked in the English Channel on its way to Spain. Philip was traveling with an impressive retinue of musicians, including the composers Pierre de la Rue and Alexander Agricola, who found themselves taking an unplanned three-month holiday in England while their ships were repaired and restocked.[26] Candlemas at court that year was even more festive than usual, and included a sermon in French, presumably the closest they all had to a common language. The ceremonies outlined in the *Antiphonale* are somewhat more humble, but there is no lack of music, including a trio of important pieces sung at vespers: the responsory *Videte miraculum* (seen in Figure 7.2), the hymn *Quod chorus vatum*, and the antiphon *Homo erat in Jerusalem.* Tallis wrote polyphonic settings of the first two, perhaps as a deliberately matched pair for the day. Like his other works of this kind, they are built around the plainsong, shaped in every way by its form and contour. In fact Tallis uses the full chant melody as one of his polyphonic parts in both pieces. In the case of *Videte miraculum*— which we will revisit in more detail in Chapter 15—the person assigned to the tenor line could simply sing his part in plain equal notes from the *Antiphonale* without much difficulty. What Tallis is doing in a large ceremonial setting of this sort is what a late-medieval author would have called a "gloss": a creative elaboration and exposition on the primary text, which remains intact as the centerpiece of the work.

This chapter has offered a brief musical tour through the seasons of Advent and Christmas as Tallis would have known them as a young musician. Those seasons take up only a small part of the *Antiphonale*. The remaining pages of the collection, nearly eight hundred of them, are full of equally elaborate melodies, texts, and rubrics. Francisco de Quiñoñez wrote in the preface to his revised breviary that it took almost as much time to figure out the order of the traditional Divine Office as it did to celebrate the actual services. He said something else in the same essay, something less well-known because Cranmer did not borrow it for the introduction to his English prayer book: that the span of a human life is scarcely enough to learn all the details of the traditional Office thoroughly.[27] Quiñoñez was not exaggerating when he said that, and his statement captures a note of fascination as well as tedium. This intricate edifice of music and ritual is enough to keep an intelligent person occupied for half a century or more. An English chorister in the early sixteenth century would have sung thousands of hours of plainsong in the course of his youthful training, and many more as an adult professional. It left a distinctive stamp on all the polyphonic works of Tallis's generation, even the works which were not based on chant in any direct way.

Studying a book such as the *Antiphonale* can give us a good deal of insight into the world of Tallis's early career. It is easy to forget that splendid pieces of composed polyphony such as his own *Videte miraculum* were the exception rather than the rule. Almost all the day-to-day music heard in church before the Reformation was unison chant or direct unwritten improvisation on it. Plainsong was the very substance of early-sixteenth-century English choral music. Its role is summed up in a poem published in the 1530s with the delightful title *A comparison between four birds, the Lark, the Nightingale, the Thrush, and the Cuckoo, for their singing, who should be chanter of the choir.* The humble cuckoo, with his plain melody, listens to the boasts of his three flamboyant singing colleagues and sums up his own case with a simple question: "What is descant without plainsong?"[28] He wins the contest.

CHAPTER EIGHT

Earliest Traces

HE OLDEST SURVIVING SOURCE OF TALLIS'S MUSIC IS A SLIM HAND-written volume of works for five voices. It contains two dozen pieces, but only one of them is by Tallis: his elaborate musical invocation to the Virgin Mary that begins with the words *Salve intemerata Virgo*, "Hail, undefiled Virgin." This manuscript shows Tallis in the company of an older generation of English composers, some of whom had already begun their careers in the late fifteenth century.[1] The volume is now held in the British Library under the unassuming title of Harley 1709. It is named after a former owner, the antiquarian collector Robert Harley, and the book's original location on the shelf as item number 1709 in his hoard of more than seven thousand old manuscripts. Harley 1708, its neighbor on one side, is a beautifully illuminated thirteenth-century monastic manuscript that records the numerous legal privileges of Reading Abbey. Harley 1710, its neighbor on the other side, is a large lectionary in English compiled just before the turn of the fifteenth century, a collection of vernacular readings from the Bible in the pioneering (and extremely controversial) Lollard translation made under the supervision of John Wycliffe. The ordering of these books is arbitrary, of course, but it is hard not to see in them a reflection of the conflicting cultural forces that would tear England apart during Tallis's lifetime.

Harley 1709 is a more humble document. It is made of paper rather than vellum. It is written in dark brown ink with no colorful decoration, although the scribe entices the reader's eye to the beginning of each piece

Tallis. Kerry McCarthy, Oxford University Press (2020). © Oxford University Press.
DOI: 10.1093/oso/9780190635213.001.0001.

of music with an ornate initial. It is a well-designed and easily handled object: about 7.5 by 10.5 inches, 19 by 26.5 cm, a little smaller than a standard piece of modern printer paper (A4 or US Letter), and not at all unlike the music that a modern singer might hold during a performance. The most crucial detail about Harley 1709 is what is missing from it. It is a single book from what was originally a set of five, and it contains only one of five voice parts. *Salve intemerata* eventually became one of Tallis's most popular and widely disseminated works, but it cannot be sung from this book alone; it needs to be reconstructed with the help of other sources. A set of musical partbooks, like the infant in the famous judgment of Solomon, was of little use to anyone once it was divided. Some sixteenth-century owners of partbooks took precautions to make sure their set stayed together. One set of six was inscribed in 1530 with a note declaring that "William Forrest is the rightful owner of this book with five others belonging to it."[2] That set, the Forrest-Heyther partbooks, has survived to our own day in complete form; the four companions of Harley 1709, produced around the same time, have vanished without a trace.

The first page of this manuscript (Figure 8.1) offers some basic information about its contents: "Medius / xxiii antemns [anthems] in these bokes." The word "Medius," in large ornamental lettering on a thick and sturdy piece of parchment, has been cut out from what seems to have been the otherwise lost original cover of the book and pasted onto the page. This is a note to the performer, showing which voice part is contained in this particular book. The voice name "Medius" does not fit into the familiar four-part arrangement (soprano, alto, tenor, and bass, with doubled parts as needed) of most Renaissance music. The young Tallis, like other English church composers in the early sixteenth century, used five different vocal parts in five overlapping but distinct ranges. Those parts were called treble (or *triplex* in Latin), mean (or *medius* in Latin), contratenor, tenor, and bass. The English practice of writing in five rather than four basic layers created a richer, more complex sound. Many of these pieces, including Tallis's own *Salve intemerata*, made generous use of a total span of more than three octaves. Harley 1709 was used by the person—or shared by the small group of people—who sang the second part from the top. Much of the music in the book is in what would nowadays be considered the higher sort of alto register, but these two dozen pieces are variable in range and

Figure 8.1 First page of Harley 1709, showing voice part ("Medius") and summary of contents ("xxiii antemns in these bokes"). © The British Library Board. Reproduced by permission.

structure, and the *medius* book, the "mean" book, contains everything from a couple of bracingly high second soprano lines to some mellower parts which spend much of their time below middle C. It was a distinctively English and sometimes quite challenging part to sing. Tallis's colleague John Heywood wrote a whole poem about it:

> Long have I been a singing man,
> And sundry parts oft have I sung,
> But one part, since I first began,
> I could nor can sing, old nor young:
> The mean I mean, which part showeth well
> Above all parts most to excel.
>
> The bass and treble are extremes;
> The tenor standeth sturdily;
> The counter rangeth then, meseems;

> The mean must make our melody:
> Whereby the mean declareth well
> Above all parts most to excel.
>
> The mean in compass is so large
> That every part must join thereto;
> It hath an oar in every barge,
> To sing, to say, to think, to do . . .[3]

After a few more stanzas, Heywood's poem reveals itself as a rather conventional moral allegory in praise of the "golden mean" and moderation in all things. The musical image is what remains in the memory, though: the *medius* part, at the heart of the typical pre-Reformation choral sound, wide in compass and melodious in nature, putting its oar in at every opportunity. That is the single voice which has survived from this set of partbooks, the oldest known fragment of Tallis's music.

According to the title page, there are "23 anthems in these books." The word "anthem" is simply an English version of "antiphon." By the sixteenth century, it had become the usual term for what musicians in other countries called the motet. Sir Thomas Hoby's 1561 English translation of Castiglione's *Book of the Courtier*, telling an anecdote about a motet by Josquin, renders *un mottetto* as "a certain anthem."[4] The Peterhouse partbooks (see Chapter 10), slightly younger and much better-preserved cousins of Harley 1709, refer to one of Taverner's motets as "the anthem *Mater Christi*."[5] In an inventory made in 1529 of all the Latin polyphonic music held at King's College, Cambridge, the very first item is a set of five leather-bound books "containing the most solemn anthems of five parts."[6] "Solemn" in this context did not mean somber or gloomy; it meant majestic, formal, dignified. The particular set of books used at King's can no longer be traced, but the solemn anthems of five parts that make up Harley 1709, including Tallis's *Salve intemerata*, are clearly what has survived of a similar collection.

The word "anthem" persisted after the Reformation, and musicians ever since then have used it to refer to freely composed devotional works in English, often sung as a special treat ("for the comforting of such as delight in music") after evensong.[7] Anthems in pre-Reformation England were sung in Latin, but their basic musical function was not too different. They were most often sung at the close of evening services as a festive conclusion to the day's worship. They had a wide variety of forms and texts which were not dictated by liturgical requirements. Pieces of this sort are often called "votive antiphons" in modern parlance. "Votive antiphon" is not a Tudor term—it was coined in the twentieth century—but it is an apt description of this type of music: a prayer freely offered by the singers, most often to the Virgin Mary, as a votive candle might be lit in front of a shrine.[8] In many cases, these evening devotions were the most elaborate works in a choir's whole repertory. This was music by and for musicians.

Salve intemerata, like many other votive antiphons of its generation, is a substantial piece of music. It takes a good fifteen or twenty minutes to sing; one recent recording takes twenty-three. It has little in common with the pithy, compact, easily accessible motets by Tallis (such as *O nata lux*) which have become familiar to many singers and listeners. It is quite likely the earliest of his works explored in detail in this book; it may also be the most remote to modern ears. On a casual first listening, there are long stretches where not much seems to be happening, interspersed with abrupt changes of texture and some moments of great intensity. Nearly half of the music consists of duets and trios sung by various combinations of voices while the others sit silent. Given the rich scoring Tallis has at his disposal, there is a sense of something being deliberately held back for much of the piece. It is a long journey to the splendid Amen on the final page.

The words set by Tallis offer a clue to the underlying principles of the music.[9] *Salve intemerata* is a long, rhetorically complex prose text which has recently been identified as a prayer written by Cuthbert Tunstall, a bishop and scholar who (like Tallis) weathered the storms of the Reformation era in a career that spanned more than half a century.[10] Tunstall was, among other things, a noted preacher and an advocate of preaching. Listening to a sixteenth-century sermon could require a considerable attention span and a strong memory. Some Tudor sermons (such as the simple vernacular feast-day sermons of John Mirk's *Festial*, ubiquitous in English parishes right up to the point of reform) were short and sweet, easily accessible to almost any listener. More formal sermons, especially the Latin sermons delivered to learned audiences, often posed a challenge. One of the most memorable sermons of this type preached in early Tudor England, John Colet's famous Convocation sermon (1512) on the corruption of the clergy and its remedies, is a typical example.[11] It is a solid half-hour of complex rhetoric. (In fact half an hour was a relatively modest duration for this sort of sermon. Some were much longer.) Colet's sermon is organized as two halves, each divided in turn into various sub-sections with their own themes and arguments, finally building to a fiery sequence of repetitions in the last minutes. His impassioned pleas at the end make rather little sense without what has come before. This sort of performance can ask a lot of its listeners, even listeners fluent in Latin. The basic idea and structure of *Salve intemerata* is similar to that of Colet's sermon, even though the votive antiphon is (at least in principle) addressed to a heavenly audience rather than an earthly one.

Composing a twenty-minute piece offered Tallis some musical opportunities that were not as readily available in smaller forms. A key principle of Tudor aesthetics, in music as well as in the visual and verbal arts, was the principle of *varietas*, of variety. The scholar and prolific author Thomas Starkey wrote in 1536 about "this wonderful variety and nature of things . . . this variety, wherein standeth all natural beauty."[12] A collection of proverbs published in London a few years later declared that "Nothing is sweet unless it be interlaced with variety and sundryness."[13] Preachers, poets, painters, and composers all made use of what was various and sundry to hold the attention of their audiences. One of the guiding principles in *Salve intemerata* is the constant use of new mixtures of voices. All votive antiphons of this generation make heavy use of the contrast between reduced-voice sections—what contemporary singers called "counterverses"—and the sound of the full ensemble. These verses appear to have been sung by soloists, and in fact they seem to have been welcome opportunities to show off: in one sixteenth-century anecdote (revisited in Chapter 10), a long piece with a rich selection of "counterverses" is brought out after vespers in honor of a visiting singer known for his vocal prowess, and another solo singer deliberately mangles the text in his own "counterverse" as a gesture of religious protest.[14] That was obviously an unusual evening for the choir, but the personalities of individual singers would have been on display whenever solo verses were sung. In the case of *Salve intemerata*, it is worth noting that no two solo passages ever use the same exact grouping of voices. Given the length of the piece and the large number of contrasting sections, it is almost impossible for that detail to have been coincidental. The distinctive sound of the full choir is also held back for effect throughout much of the piece, although we hear more of it as time goes on.

One important aspect of *varietas* was the reluctance to repeat oneself literally. Another Tudor arbiter of eloquence, Thomas Wilson, wrote about this in his *Art of Rhetoric*: "For if the repetition should be naked, and only set forth in plain words, without any change of speech or shift of rhetoric, neither should the hearers take pleasure, nor yet the matter take effect . . . Thus, in repeating, art may be used."[15] There is necessarily a great deal of redundancy in a piece of polyphonic music where multiple voices share similar phrases, but Tallis made a point of using art in repeating. *Salve intemerata* is made up of intertwining melodies which imitate each other, but very rarely in a mechanical or slavish fashion. Each phrase of the text is expressed in a slightly different form by each voice, adjusted to fit the ebb and flow of the musical texture.

In many early Tudor votive antiphons, including a number of the pieces in Harley 1709, there is also an extra ingredient in the sections where the full choir is singing: the interplay of short phrases is set against a pre-existing chant melody sung in long notes by the tenor. "The tenor standeth sturdily"—as Heywood describes it—while the other voices create an elaborate musical filigree around it. There seems to be no cantus firmus of this kind in Tallis's *Salve intemerata*. If there is, it is so well hidden that it has resisted all attempts to dig it out of the score. The tenor part still reverts to an old-fashioned sturdiness now and then, especially at the very end of the piece, the setting of the single word *Amen*, where it slows down to a glacial pace while the bass voice accompanies it with a long, elegant, free-flowing melodic sequence. English music of the early sixteenth century has gained a reputation for soaring treble voices, but the bass part is definitely the star of the show here: as Henry VIII's Venetian guest remarked (see Chapter 6) after hearing the Chapel Royal perform in 1515, "they did not so much sing as jubilate, and especially the basses, who I think do not have their equal anywhere in the world."[16]

When Tallis composed *Salve intemerata*, he was drawing on a well-established tradition of styles and techniques. What we see in the rest of this manuscript, the other pages of Harley 1709, is the exact sort of music he would have taken as a model for his own early works. More than one-third of the works still cannot be matched to any known author, but the collection is a roll call of prominent names, including Taverner, Ludford, Cornysh, Fayrfax, Davy, and of course Tallis himself, who was quite likely the youngest composer included. Some of these were already venerable figures in English music by the time Tallis started his own career.

The first piece in the manuscript is Taverner's *Gaude plurimum*, one of the most popular English votive antiphons of its generation. Taverner's date of birth is unknown, but he appears to have been somewhat older than Tallis; he was appointed master of the choristers at Wolsey's ambitious new Cardinal College in 1526 and died in October 1545. His music was given the place of honor at the beginning of the manuscript, and this copy of *Gaude plurimum* shows some visible signs of use. There is a grimy thumbprint worn into the margin, at the place where the book would have been held open by singers. A small grammatical error in the Latin text (one of many such errors throughout the manuscript) has been corrected in black ink by someone other than the original scribe. Given the wide circulation of Taverner's piece in the first half of the sixteenth century, it is hard to imagine that Tallis did not know it. In fact it shares some characteristics with *Salve intemerata*, including its general structural plan and a number of distinctive scoring decisions along the way.

Some of the works in Harley 1709 come from an even earlier generation of musicians. Robert Fayrfax has the distinction of being the first English composer whose exact birthday we know: he was born on 23 April 1464, "around ten o'clock at night," as noted in a family book of hours by the sort of educated gentry who considered such things worth remembering for the purpose of tracing pedigrees and casting horoscopes.[17] Fayrfax was awarded doctorates in music from both Cambridge and Oxford, and served for more than two decades in the Chapel Royal. He repeatedly gave ceremonial New Year's Day gifts to the king, including a "book of anthems" (now lost) for which he was rewarded £20, almost twice Tallis's entire annual income when he joined the Chapel a generation later.[18] Fayrfax's colleague William

Cornysh, whose music is also preserved in Harley 1709, was a musician, poet, actor, and, as he called himself, "chapelman with the most famous king Henry the seventh." Cornysh left a handful of votive antiphons and other elaborate Latin works, but the bulk of his surviving compositions (which may in fact have been written by a son of the same name) are English songs of various sorts, including the memorable Passion carol *Woefully arrayed*.

A particularly fascinating set of four pieces in this manuscript comes from the composer Richard Davy. These four works have a well-documented history: they had already been copied together, as a group, into the monumental Eton Choirbook at the turn of the century. One of them, *O Domine caeli terraeque creator*, has the most exact date of composition known for any of the pieces in Harley 1709. It was written between 1490 and 1492, while Davy was choirmaster at Magdalen College, Oxford. The Eton scribe, who is not otherwise given to gossipy marginalia, says that "Richard Davy composed this anthem in one day." If the story is true, it was an impressive achievement: the piece is as substantial as *Salve intemerata* and if anything even more ornate. (Davy chose—or, one rather suspects, was given—the Holy Week antiphon *Symon dormis* as the cantus firmus: "Simon, are you sleeping? Could you not stay awake one hour?")[19]

The Eton Choirbook is perhaps the most impressive single document of early English music. It is a beautifully produced and illuminated book on fine vellum, two feet tall, designed to be put on display as a ceremonial object at the center of evening devotions.[20] Singers in other countries, especially in southern Europe and its colonies, continued to use similar books throughout the whole sixteenth century and even beyond, but large folio choirbooks were already going out of fashion in England by the time Tallis composed *Salve intemerata*.[21] The simpler format of Harley 1709 is closer to what most musicians of Tallis's generation would have used from day to day. These smaller items were more practical, but they were also more vulnerable: the orphan status of this partbook, missing all the rest of its set, is proof enough of that. A large amount of English music circulated in even more portable and ephemeral form, as "scrolls," "rolls," and individual leaves.[22] Such humble items are mentioned often in contemporary records, but only a handful of them survive.

We know very little about the specific origins of Harley 1709. It includes a piece by Fayrfax with a prominent prayer "for our illustrious king Henry the eighth," but that in itself does not narrow things down very much: it applies to a span of nearly forty years, from 1509 to 1547, what must have been more or less the first half of Tallis's life. If the manuscript was created by and for a particular community, as the Eton Choirbook was, there are no traces left of that connection. There are also no clues to the identity of the skilled but unostentatious scribe who copied these twenty-six pieces. (The note that there are "xxiii anthems in this book" is not accurate. There are twenty-six, not twenty-three. Either the scribe was somehow confused and wrote "xxiii" instead of the similar-looking "xxvi," or he continued to add music after writing the inscription.) There is some evidence that Tallis's *Salve intemerata* was actually meant to be the final item in the anthology. Unlike any other piece in the book, it finishes with the note *corrigitur*, "it is corrected," an indication that the music has been proofread. Figure 8.2 shows the last notes of Tallis's music with the last syllable of the Amen, followed by the word *finis* (confirming that this is indeed the end of the piece) and the word *corrigitur.* This sort of annotation in a Tudor manuscript is not always a guarantee that the music is flawless—there is at least one clear wrong note left in *Salve intemerata*, fairly early on—but it is a sign that it has been checked and prepared for use. If the note *corrigitur* does not apply to the whole manuscript up to that point, it is a sign that *Salve intemerata* was singled out for special care and attention. If it applies to

Figure 8.2   Harley 1709, end of Tallis's *Salve intemerata* with notes "finis" and "corrigitur," f. 49r. © The British Library Board. Reproduced by permission.

the whole manuscript up to that point, the scribe was choosing to draw a line under this particular work. Either way, Tallis's piece (which was likely quite new when it was copied) seems to have had a notable place in the collection.

We know equally little about the specific origins of *Salve inteme-rata* itself. It is not a particularly unusual item among Tallis's surviving works; in fact he composed three other big votive antiphons of a similar sort. *Ave Dei patris filia* and *Ave rosa sine spinis* are both five-part pieces with broadly comparable structures. *Gaude gloriosa* (discussed in detail in Chapter 16) is scored for a six-part ensemble with complex divisi, unusual extremes of range, and fuller textures in general; it may or may not be a significantly later work than the others, although it is certainly more flamboyant. The verbal text of *Salve intemerata* first appears in a printed book in 1527, a book of hours produced by Nicolas Prévost in Paris for English use, although there is no reason why a prayer by such a distinguished churchman as Cuthbert Tunstall could not have circulated even earlier in some other form.[23] However Tallis encoun-tered this text, it was clearly not a trivial undertaking for him to set it to music. Unlike the simple rhymed poetry of a common devotional text such as *Ave rosa sine spinis*, it does not break easily into bite-sized pieces. Working with almost two hundred words of dense, rhetorically complex prose requires the composer to make some structural decisions before starting the actual business of composing.

Tallis sometimes responds to this sort of prose in unexpected ways. He is not averse to starting a new section of music in the middle of a sentence, even in the middle of a phrase. Perhaps the most striking deci-sion he makes is near the beginning of the prayer, as the speaker first addresses the Virgin: "from the womb of your mother Anne, that most holy woman, you were sanctified and illuminated." When the name of Anne is mentioned, Tallis abruptly ends his opening duet and brings in a new group of voices, including a prominent high treble part. The resulting section of the piece, beginning with the words *Annae mulieris*, certainly makes no grammatical sense by itself. Could there have been a special devotion to St. Anne, cultivated by some patron or at some particular church, which prompted Tallis to write her name in lights at this point in the motet? (The mind inevitably wanders to the festivities at the coronation of the pregnant Anne Boleyn in 1533, which included poetry in praise of the "most holy fertility" of her saintly namesake, as well as a pageant depicting St. Anne surrounded by children and grandchildren.[24] Any direct connection here is highly unlikely, but this is one clear example of an old popular devotion that was still thriving in England as the first stage of the Reformation started to take hold.)

Whatever may have prompted the composition of *Salve intemerata*, it outlived its original context and went on to become one of Tallis's most popular works. It survives in twenty-one different manuscript sources, surpassing even Taverner's evergreen *Gaude plurimum*, which is preserved in only twenty.[25] It is found in the company of an incredibly diverse range of other music, from Fayrfax to Morley to Lassus. It was still being sung and appreciated at the end of the sixteenth century. Many English musicians also collected and recopied its various trio sections as free-standing gems of three-part polyphony—including the radiant *Annae mulieris*, whether or not its original Latin words made any sense on their own. Even in a world of drastically changing musical styles, there still seems to have been a place for a select few "classics" such as this challenging and beautiful piece.

CHAPTER NINE

The Mulliner Book

WHEN TALLIS FIRST TURNS UP IN THE HISTORICAL RECORD IN 1530 at Dover Priory, he is called "player of the organs." When he makes his last important public appearance as the senior partner in the *Cantiones* of 1575, he is described as "Organist." Much of his professional life seems to have been spent at the keyboard. An organist's life, then as now, involved a lot of improvisation, and what has survived of Tallis's organ music is almost certainly the barest residue of fifty years of music-making, much of it extemporaneous or at least unwritten. We can no longer hear him play, but we can capture something of his style by listening to and playing the few keyboard works that are left. Almost all of those works are preserved in a mid-sixteenth-century manuscript called the Mulliner Book.

Thomas Mulliner's collection of keyboard music (now British Library Add. MS 30513) is an eclectic anthology of more than 130 pieces.[1] It begins with a couple of popular tunes and an ornate galliard before starting to explore the Tudor tradition of liturgical organ music, including a dozen chant settings by Tallis. Along the way, it takes in a wide variety of sacred and secular vocal works adapted for keyboard. There are also a number of freely composed pieces called "point," "fancy," or "voluntary"; in fact those last two terms are seen here for the first time in an English musical source. The book contains another unexpected treasure: the small handful of Tallis's surviving secular songs, which

Tallis. Kerry McCarthy, Oxford University Press (2020). © Oxford University Press.
DOI: 10.1093/oso/9780190635213.001.0001.

will be discussed in the latter part of this chapter along with his few known works for viols.

Not much is known about Mulliner outside the covers of his book. He seems to have sung at Corpus Christi College, Oxford, in the late 1550s, and he was appointed organist at Magdalen College in March 1563.[2] He was clearly an associate of the London musician and poet John Heywood, because the title page of his manuscript bears a Latin inscription stating that "I am Thomas Mulliner's book, with John Heywood as witness." He had access to an unusually rich selection of music, perhaps with the help of Heywood, who was connected with both St. Paul's Cathedral and the royal court. He may even have been an apprentice of Heywood, as the composer and musical memoirist Thomas Whythorne had been a few years earlier.[3] More than half of the music he collected is firmly in the pre-Reformation tradition, including almost thirty chant-based pieces by John Redford, who died in 1547. Composing on chant melodies would remain a fashionable exercise in some circles through the end of the century, but the plainsong settings in the Mulliner book are a rare opportunity to see what this sort of music looked like when it was still part of everyday life. (There are only two other documents, also in the British Library, that bring us equally close to the living tradition: Royal Appendix 56, an organ book begun around 1530, and Add. MS 29996, whose core is an important collection of pre-Reformation keyboard works which made its way several generations later into the hands of the antiquarian-minded organist Thomas Tomkins. Unfortunately neither book contains anything by Tallis.)[4]

Like a modern book of organ music, the Mulliner Book is in oblong form, landscape rather than portrait. It is not a presentation copy like the famous Lady Nevell's Book produced a generation later, but it is carefully and legibly written. The first item by Tallis, the brief *Natus est nobis* (no. 9 in the collection), gives an idea of Mulliner's style as a scribe. Figure 9.1 shows the whole piece, which is split across two separate pages in the original. The music is written on one twelve-line stave, with a single F clef in the bass for orientation. Mulliner abandoned this large stave later in the book and switched to two separate staves, one for each hand, but the basic layout remained consistent. Notes are not grouped together by beams, but the left-hand part is

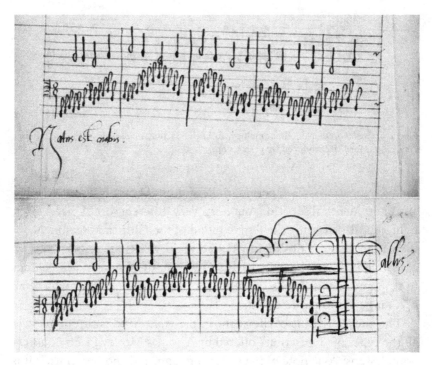

Figure 9.1   *Natus est nobis* in the Mulliner Book, British Library Add. MS 30513,
ff. 12v–13r. © The British Library Board. Reproduced by permission.

divided into convenient groups of six by a series of small dots. The only
decoration is the rather wild flourish on the last chord of the piece, a
common addition in manuscripts of this sort.

    Natus est nobis is a good place to start because it is the simplest of
Tallis's surviving keyboard works. Like all the older liturgical items
collected by Mulliner, it is based on a piece of plainsong, designed to
substitute for it or alternate with it in performance. The original melody in this case is a very brief chant (Figure 9.2) for Christmas: "Today
is born to us in the city of David a Saviour, who is Christ the Lord."
It is sung at the end of the day, as a refrain to the psalms at compline,
on Christmas Day and during the whole week following. Compline in
pre-Reformation England was a relatively stable and unchanging service, but it picked up a distinct seasonal coloring at special times of the
year, often through the use of special antiphons. The imposing *Media
vita* set to music by John Sheppard is another antiphon for compline,

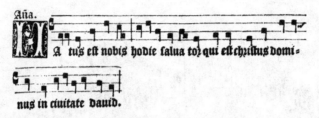

Figure 9.2 *Natus est nobis*, chant melody, from the Sarum *Antiphonale* (1519–20). Christ Church, Oxford. Reproduced by permission.

sung during a two-week period in the depths of Lent. *Natus est nobis* has an almost identical function, but it is a very different sort of piece: brief, light, joyful, reflecting the festive mood of the Christmas season. More than a quarter of Tallis's Latin-texted vocal works are associated with compline in some way. His keyboard setting of *Natus est nobis* belongs to the same robust English tradition of evening services, for which the best music was often reserved.

The alternating lilt of the chant in the right hand is the simplest of all the types of "figuration" offered by Thomas Morley in his counter-point lessons: "one note of the plainsong long, and another short."[5] It is a technique that Tallis occasionally uses in his Latin hymn settings for voices (see Chapter 15), where the melody is likewise featured in the top part. What he places underneath the melody here is an unbroken series of running quavers (eighth notes) in the left hand, four to each long note and two to each short note, moving stepwise whenever possible. This is one of the most common ways in which students were taught to adorn a piece of plainsong at the keyboard, and its place near the beginning of Mulliner's notebook suggests that he found it useful as an example and a model.[6]

Most of Tallis's other organ works carry the tune discreetly in an inner part, with one note of the chant assigned to each semibreve. This steady flow of notes is shifted or ornamented at times, but it is never interrupted or tampered with in any serious way. There are ten such pieces in the Mulliner Book. Once again, the primary focus is on the adornment of evening services, with almost all of this music intended for vespers during either the Christmas season or the Lenten season. (Lent certainly had its severity in the Sarum rite, but there appears to have been no ban on organ playing.) All ten of these organ pieces are hymn verses which were played in alternation with singing. The organist took the odd-numbered verses and the singers took the even-numbered verses. The organist's side of the exchange was rooted in a flourishing tradition of keyboard improvisation; in fact many Tudor organ verses seem to have originated to some extent in everyday improvisational practices before being revisited, polished up, and set down in stable written form for future use.[7]

One of the more memorable hymn verses in the Mulliner book is Tallis's irrepressibly playful *Iste confessor* (no. 106). Like all of Tallis's organ verses, it has a single recurring theme that weaves its way through the music. The four-note theme, perhaps inspired by the hops and skips in the chant melody, is a wide-leaping figure that migrates constantly between the top voice and the bass before dissolving into an exuberant final flourish. Another verse with a very different theme—and thus a very different sound—is Tallis's first setting of *Ecce tempus idoneum* (no. 100), an evening hymn for the same two weeks in mid-Lent when *Media vita* was sung. The plainsong melody of *Ecce tempus* runs half-concealed through the middle of the texture while the simple four-note figure sounds over and over against it. This figure is heard more than twenty times, usually creating a brief dissonance on its second note, quite often a plangent major or minor seventh. These four notes, and the mood they create, are practically identical to Tallis's setting of the word *miraculum* at the beginning of his choral responsory *Videte miraculum* (see Chapter 15). There is almost no external adornment; it is the regular rhythm of dissonance and resolution that gives the music its energy.

Some of the organists in the Mulliner anthology take greater liberties with their raw materials than Tallis seems to have been willing to take. There is often a freer use of extreme ranges (Redford in particular is never hesitant to explore the low end of the keyboard) and of virtuosic figuration. Sixteenth-century musicians were fascinated by the possibilities of "breaking" chant melodies, of paraphrasing and ornamenting them, sometimes beyond the point of recognition. "In the works of Mr. Redford, Mr. Tallis . . . and divers others," Morley writes in his *Plain and Easy Introduction*, "you shall find such variety of breaking of plainsongs, as one not very well skilled in music should scant discern any plainsong at all."[8]

Morley, who wrote those words in the 1590s, may well have had access to a more diverse and adventurous selection of Tallis's organ music than we have today. There are only a few extant keyboard works where Tallis is really showing off. That very small group of pieces (none of them collected by Mulliner) includes his *Lesson two parts in one*. One of the manuscript sources of the *Lesson* attributes it to the early-seventeenth-century keyboard virtuoso John Bull, an inaccurate guess but no great surprise given the character of the piece.[9] The *Lesson two parts in one*, as its name suggests, contains a vigorous and strict two-part canon: one part shadows the other precisely, a fifth lower, at the distance of only one beat. Both of these canonic parts are played by the right hand. The left hand accompanies almost the entire piece with fast non-stop runs of notes in the bass, while the two right-hand voices pass through a dizzying array of different ideas and combinations, showing the almost endless variety of ways in which two parts can be made to mesh and interplay in very close imitation. Tallis loved composing canons—they can be found in just about every genre and type of his music—but this one is uniquely relentless. In some ways it seems to be not so much a bravura piece for performance as a highly concentrated collection of techniques for two-part canonic writing. It is not at all unlike the popular Renaissance guides to verbal eloquence that overwhelm the reader with useful figures of speech, one after another. The quintessential book of this sort in Tallis's day was the *Copia* of Erasmus—the title means "abundance"—which famously offers more than a hundred elegant ways to say "Thank you for your letter." (The *Copia* itself had strong English connections: it was dedicated to John Colet and offered for use in his school in London.) No one was expected to use all those verbal variations at once. They were a set of rhetorical building blocks, and the hope was that the person who practiced with them would gradually learn to communicate with confidence and fluency in whatever situations arose.[10] Any Tudor organist who made a careful study of the *Lesson two parts in one* would have been able to generate music of his own in a similar style.

A comparable (though far from identical) atmosphere is present in Tallis's two most substantial keyboard pieces, the two extremely long and highly ornamented settings of the melody *Felix namque*. They are both preserved amid a collection of more or less exclusively secular music in the Fitzwilliam Virginal Book, where they are dated 1562 and 1564. These settings have come a long way from their original roots in the *Felix namque* offertory sung or played at the pre-Reformation Lady Mass. Once again, Tallis is creating an encyclopedic exercise in figuration of all sorts. There are various arpeggios, fanfares, canons, syncopations, rhythmic proportions, and other devices, each technique applied in turn to accompany a snippet of chant in long notes. This method has not always fared well with modern critics. Willi Apel had this to say about Tallis's two *Felix namque* settings: "I do not hesitate to call them the most horrible specimens of a genre that is always quite problematic."[11] They can be exhausting to sit through, but they also reveal the sheer richness of Tallis's musical invention. Anyone who wanted or needed to extemporize in an ornate style would have found them a useful storehouse of ideas.[12] Like the *Lesson two parts in one*, they ultimately seem designed to make life easier for Tallis's fellow-musicians, not to make it more difficult.

The actual sound of this music can be difficult to recover because no complete English organs have been preserved from Tallis's day. The smaller organ at the church of St. Alfege in Greenwich, his home parish during the second half of his life, still has a substantial section of keyboard (now on the middle manual) that seems to have belonged to the original "pair [set] of organs" inventoried there in 1552. Those keys have clearly seen heavy service, and the D just above middle C has a deep indentation worn into it from repeated use. Valuable evidence can often be found in the soundboard of an organ, a large slab of wood carved with holes and wind channels to direct pressurized air into the pipes. A couple of sixteenth-century English soundboards have been preserved, most notably an impressive specimen which was discovered in the 1970s doing duty as a farmhouse door at Wetheringsett in Suffolk.[13] An examination of growth rings shows that it was still part of a healthy oak tree around 1525 and was incorporated into a musical instrument not long after. The complex grid of precision holes and grooves in the Wetheringsett soundboard is a technical diagram that gives us information about the specifics of this organ. It had seven separate stops and forty-six keys, fully chromatic from bottom C up to a″, able to accommodate everything in the Mulliner Book and every known organ work by Tallis.[14] It was an elaborate piece of machinery that would have taken considerable skill to build, maintain, and play. (The author of the anonymous early-sixteenth-century Leconfield Proverbs knew about this sort of thing: "The sweet organ pipes comforteth a steadfast mind. Wrong handling of the stops may cause them cipher from their kind.")[15] There is no trace left of the "great large pair of organs" present at Waltham Abbey when Tallis was sent away at the dissolution in 1540, but that may well have been an even more monumental instrument, given the abbey's wealth and prestige.

Organ music was only one of Thomas Mulliner's interests. His anthology also includes more than thirty keyboard arrangements of songs, anthems, and various other vocal works. There is even an excerpt (no. 119) from Tallis's ubiquitous *Salve intemerata*. (Mulliner chose one of the ornate trios which Tallis quite pointedly did not use in his own parody mass: see Chapter 10.) A few of the songs are of foreign provenance, including a pair of pieces called *La doune cella* and *La shy myze*. The phrases "doune cella" and "shy myze" appear to be corruptions of the well-known French chanson texts "Dont vient cela" and "J'ai mis mon coeur," set to music variously by Dufay, Crecquillon, Sermisy, Gombert, and Lassus, among others. They were two pieces that seem often to have traveled as a pair. In one of Giles Farnaby's *Canzonets* published in 1598, we hear that "Pearse did dance with Petronella / Lasiamiza and Laduncella," and the two titles also occur together in a sixteenth-century English manual of choreography.[16]

Most of the songs in Mulliner's collection are clearly of English origin. There are songs from courtly circles (including *Defiled is my name*, associated with Anne Boleyn), songs based on myth and legend (*The wretched wandering prince of Troy*), and at least one song (*Where griping grief the heart would wound*) in praise of music itself. Four of the Mulliner songs are works by Tallis with secular titles in English. Being keyboard arrangements, they do not have any words beyond their initial headings, and two of them have proved difficult if not impossible to reunite with their original texts. One of this pair, *O ye tender babes* (no. 83), appears to have been a setting by Tallis of some sort of metrical poem which is now lost.[17] There is a prose text by the Tudor grammarian

William Lily that begins "You tender babes of England," but that text cannot be shoehorned into Tallis's music without making some uncharacteristic repetitions and turning a number of awkward corners.[18] The piece by Tallis that Mulliner calls *Fond youth is a bubble* (no. 25) is not unique to his anthology; it is also found with a sacred text in another sixteenth-century source. Those sacred words, *Purge me O Lord from all my sin*, fit the music remarkably well from start to finish, and the style is entirely typical of Tallis's English anthems.[19] The eighteenth-century musician Thomas Warren, indefatigable secretary of the London Catch Club, made a copy of this piece from the Mulliner Book and optimistically underlaid it with what seemed to be a likely text (beginning "For youth is a bubble blown up with breath") from the February section of the *Shepherd's Calendar* by Edmund Spenser.[20] Unfortunately Spenser's poem came along too late to have had any possible effect on Tallis's song or Mulliner's arrangement of it. It seems almost certain that the anthem *Purge me O Lord* was the original, and that we are not dealing here with a secular song at all.

With those two cases out of the way, we can turn to the two songs by Tallis which are much less problematic. Both of these songs, *Like as the doleful dove* (no. 115) and *When shall my sorrowful sighing slack* (no. 85), owe a great deal to international trends in secular music. Chansons of the northern European sort became very popular in England during the second quarter of the sixteenth century. Musicians of Tallis's generation were eager consumers and imitators of contemporary Flemish and French songs, which at the time were just as fashionable as Italian madrigals would be fifty years later. This sort of song could take various stylistic forms, from the simpler, more declamatory kind of chanson associated with Sermisy—what might be called the "Parisian" type—to the more leisurely and contrapuntal "Flemish" chansons of Crecquillon and Clemens. Those are simplistic designations, of course, but they reflect two general tendencies among song composers of the era, two different ways of setting a secular poem to music. We are fortunate to have an example of Tallis working in both traditions.

Like as the doleful dove is the more straightforward of these two songs. The Mulliner Book is its only source. Its text is a poem by the Chapel Royal musician and prolific author William Hunnis. The words were not printed until 1576, in a popular anthology called *The Paradise of*

Dainty Devices, but Hunnis was already producing poems by 1550 and many of his literary works seem to have been written quite early in his life.[21] This poem certainly has an old-fashioned flavor, with its heavy alliteration and its echoes of mid-sixteenth-century theatre, especially of the lugubrious songs commonly heard in choirboy plays.

> Like as the doleful dove delights alone to be,
> And doth refuse the bloomed branch, choosing the leafless tree,
> Whereon wailing his chance, with bitter tears besprent [sprinkled],
> Doth with his bill his tender breast oft pierce and all to-rent [tear
>   apart];
> Whose grievous groanings though, whose grips of pining pain,
> Whose ghastly looks, whose bloody streams outflowing from
>   each vein,
> Whose falling from the tree, whose panting on the ground,
> Examples be of mine estate, though there appear no wound.

Tallis's setting of this poem is one of the most austere things he ever wrote. The melody moves within a restricted range: it does not even budge from its initial pitch of B flat until the end of the first line. (Might this reflect the monotonous song of the dove?) The text is declaimed simply and elegantly, one phrase at a time, in all voices together, with no polyphony of any kind except for some vestigial ornamentation at a couple of the cadences. The ends of lines are marked by simultaneous one-beat rests in all the parts. In its form and style, *Like as the doleful dove* is more reminiscent of Tallis's "tunes" for Archbishop Parker's psalter (see Chapter 13) than anything else he is known to have composed.

This song, like many other simple sixteenth-century tunes in English, might originally have been designed for solo singing with instrumental accompaniment. The transcription in Mulliner's book descends to low D and even low C in the bass part. Tudor singers were certainly willing and able to produce these notes—Morley approves of them when used "upon an extremity for the ditty's sake or in notes taken for diapasons [octaves] in the bass," and they occur from time to time in such situations—but in this context they may point to some sort of instrumental involvement.[22] The preface to the *Paradise of Dainty Devices* includes a note that all the poetry in the collection is "aptly made to be set to any song in five parts, or sung to instrument."[23] Like many of Tallis's other English-texted works, this particular song is set in only four parts. The four-voice texture is another link to the clear and uncluttered musical language of the Parisian chanson, which he may well have had in mind while composing *Like as the doleful dove*. He even begins with the characteristic long-short-short rhythm used again and again as an opening gambit by Sermisy and his associates.

When shall my sorrowful sighing slack is a different sort of piece. It was the most popular of Tallis's secular works, making its way into no fewer than twelve manuscripts, eight of them Scottish.[24] The words are by Henry Howard, earl of Surrey, a courtly poet who was executed at the age of thirty in 1547 as perhaps the last victim of Henry VIII's rampant paranoia.[25] It is another mournful text, this time set as a series of urgent questions.

When shall my sorrowful sighing slack?
When shall my woeful wailing cease?
When shall my tears and mourning make
Mercy and pity me to release?
When shall the pensive heart find peace?
When shall the heart find quiet rest
That hath been long with thought oppressed?

How long shall I in woe lament?
How long shall I in care complain?
How long shall danger me torment,
Augmenting still my deadly pain?
Till hope and dread between them twain
Agree that hope have her request,
Till then live I with thought oppressed.

What Tallis creates out of these verses is a real polyphonic song, with four fully independent parts imitating one another and weaving a continuous web of sound. He repeats the last line of the stanza to create a well-rounded eight-line form with a recognizable refrain. His setting recalls the musical style of many chansons by Clemens and other northern composers, and indeed it circulated alongside a number of those pieces. The soprano part appears to be the primary melody, with clearly defined phrases and careful support from the other parts, but (unlike the top voice of *Like as the doleful dove*) it is not a tune accompanied by chords: it is just one distinct strand in a complex network.

This kind of song takes some musical skill to handle, and the many different versions that survive are hints that it had a complicated history. It was ornamented in various ways, copied out from memory, arranged for keyboard and disentangled again into four parts, apparently revised at some point by Tallis himself, and imitated by the Scottish composer John Black, who created a four-voice "Report upone quhan sall my sorifull siching slaik"—the only named tribute to a work by Tallis until the *Fantasia* of Vaughan Williams several centuries later.[26] Given the popularity of urbane French (and French-style) songs in sixteenth-century Scotland, it is no surprise that Tallis's piece became one of the greatest hits of its generation there.

There is one more small but important group of pieces to be mentioned here: Tallis's few surviving works for viol consort. These works are not in the Mulliner book, but they belong to the same broad tradition of mid-sixteenth-century instrumental and secular music. By the time Tallis joined the royal household in the 1540s, a group of Italian viol players were in residence at court, and he may well have been working with them in some capacity. There were also other options for performing textless music; one significant manuscript source of Tallis's instrumental works, a large Elizabethan book designed for convivial use around a table, has a handwritten title page that describes it as "A book of In Nomines and other solfaing songs of 5, 6, 7, and 8 parts for voices or instruments."[27] A "solfaing song" was a wordless piece sung to the traditional syllables (sol, fa, mi, re . . .) that were used for sight-reading. Morley complained at the end of the century about the tedium of "singing only the bare note" in this way, but it seems to have been a very popular practice, and one instrumental piece attributed to Tallis is actually called *A solfing song* by one of its scribes.[28] The same piece also appears anonymously in the midst of a collection of works by the king's lutenist and secular music master Philip van Wilder, this time given the garbled French title *Je nilli croyss*. The music itself, whether it is by Tallis or by his expatriate colleague, could certainly pass muster as a French chanson of its generation. Another instrumental work, an elegant five-part fantasia, took a more easily discernible journey. It began life as a textless piece by Tallis, probably for viol consort, and was eventually reworked by the composer himself into the Latin motet *O sacrum convivium* (see Chapter 14).[29]

Tallis wrote two In Nomines which were almost certainly composed for viols. They stand near the beginning of a 150-year tradition.[30] This genre had its origins in instrumental transcriptions of a famous passage from one of Taverner's masses and soon took on a life of its own as a distinctively English type of chamber music. Unlike some composers who used the In Nomine as a vehicle to experiment with arcane rhythms and exotic musical devices, Tallis produced two pieces that often feel like creative glosses on Taverner's original. They share Taverner's modest four-part texture and his placement of the plainsong tune in the alto voice. Tallis's contemporary Thomas Wode, who copied both of them, called them "very well set" and "done very well."[31] The second and somewhat more extroverted In Nomine is particularly striking because of its opening gesture, the classic fanfare of the Renaissance instrumental canzona: this was the sound of the secular court.

However Mulliner managed to assemble his whole collection of music, he was a lucky man to have it at his fingertips. He seems to have been well aware of its value. A note on the last page makes a plea for return if lost: "If anyone finds it wandering and lacking its master, return the book to me: you have my name in the margin. Thomas Mulliner." Another inscription, at the beginning of the book, shows how broadly Mulliner's musical explorations seem to have ranged. It is a short Latin poem he borrowed from a continental music theorist, Nicolaus Wollick, who wrote these lines in his *Enchiridion musices* (Handbook of Music) in 1512.

> Ah, omnipotent Father, if you are swayed by any prayers,
> grant, I beg you, auspicious sailing to me as I begin.
> So that I may be able to seek out what is most pleasing to the Muses,
> offer your right hand to me, serene Virgin, in my misery.[32]

"To seek out what is most pleasing to the Muses": it is hard to imagine any better wish for the musical anthologist, then or now.

CHAPTER TEN

The Peterhouse Partbooks

T HE NEXT DOCUMENT OF TALLIS'S VOCAL MUSIC SHOWS HIM IN
the company of a somewhat younger group of composers. Many
members of the familiar old guard from Harley 1709 (see Chapter 8) are
still present, but they are now joined by some of Tallis's real contemporaries, musicians such as Christopher Tye and John Marbeck who, like
him, would have to negotiate the upheavals of the early Reformation as
they established their own careers. This manuscript seems at first glance
to be a rather sedate and conservative anthology of Latin church music,
but a closer look reveals some surprisingly broad horizons. The collection includes works by Jacquet of Mantua and a mysterious "Lupus
Italus."[1] The whole thing is copied on French paper, although that in
itself was not too unusual in élite Tudor circles.[2] The handwriting veers
back and forth between a fashionable Renaissance italic and the essentially late-medieval script still used in almost all English church music
of the era. A few pieces even appear to have been edited or given new
words to comply with the needs of changing times.

This collection of music is now known as the Peterhouse partbooks.[3]
These books had a less harsh fate than Harley 1709: they were originally a
set of five, and four of them have been preserved.[4] They take their name
from the library of Peterhouse College, Cambridge, where they found
a safe home (perhaps donated by the sympathetic seventeenth-century
high churchman John Cosin) after their contents had become obsolete. The Peterhouse books are the most substantial single collection of

Tallis. Kerry McCarthy, Oxford University Press (2020). © Oxford University Press.
DOI: 10.1093/oso/9780190635213.001.0001.

sacred music to survive from their generation. They contain nineteen complete masses, seven Magnificats, and forty-six assorted antiphons and motets. If the lost tenor book and some leaves torn from the treble book were still present, they would add up to more than a thousand pages of music in all. Only a few of Tallis's works are included: the large votive antiphon *Ave rosa sine spinis*, the even larger *Salve intemerata* (which the scribe managed to copy twice, for reasons we will explore later), and the mass which Tallis based on *Salve intemerata*.

These books are especially valuable in studying Tallis because they are the only more or less complete source of his *Salve intemerata* mass, one of just three masses he is known to have composed. The number will already be familiar to admirers of Byrd's music—three masses within a long career—but the older composer's situation was different. Tallis's three masses are not a matched set. They have almost nothing in common with one another in terms of musical style. His unnamed four-voice mass (see Chapter 11) is a relatively simple piece with close ties to the first generation of reformed church music in English. His seven-voice *Puer natus* mass (see Chapter 16) is a beautifully crafted work of what might be called speculative music, with an esoteric mathematical code governing the lengths of notes. His five-voice *Salve intemerata* mass, the one we see here in the Peterhouse books, is a derived mass—what is often called a parody mass—in which a pre-existing piece of music (Tallis's own motet in this case) is reworked into a new and closely related mass setting. This was a remarkably European thing for Tallis to have done. It is no great surprise that the one foreign mass included in this manuscript is a similar treatment of Andrea de Silva's motet *Surrexit pastor bonus*. That mass is the piece attributed to "Lupus Italus," who can be identified only as one of the large and confusing pack of sixteenth-century musicians named Lupus, Lupo, or Lupi.[5] Tallis and his Italian colleague were not alone in this practice: at least half a dozen of the Peterhouse masses make various uses of polyphonic parody and recomposition.

What we see in this manuscript, among other things, is a cross-section through the repertory of Latin mass settings that would have been performed by a skilled, well-connected group of English musicians just before the Reformation put an abrupt end to the genre. These masses show a wide variety of styles. At one end of the continuum are pieces such as the Mean Mass by Taverner and a similar unnamed mass by Tye, both rather modest in range and dimensions, with clear and uncluttered textures. (Taverner's Mean Mass earned its title because of its restricted scoring: the customary high treble part is absent, and the topmost voice is in the lower, more moderate *medius* range.) At the other extreme are the masses *O quam glorifica* and *Tecum principium* by Fayrfax, the two most substantial pieces in the Peterhouse set. They are constructed on the grandest scale. Fayrfax submitted *O quam glorifica* as the test piece for his Oxford doctorate, and he displayed his skill in a series of obscure and dizzying rhythmic irregularities. What survives in these partbooks is actually a sixteenth-century arrangement into simpler notation of an hour-long piece that would otherwise have been almost unperformable.[6]

Not all contemporary listeners were impressed with this sort of thing. "Good God," the Augustinian canon Robert Richardson wrote in 1530, "how much good time they waste vainly nowadays in England and Scotland in the singing of one mass."[7] Even more good time would have been wasted if the Tudor mass had not effectively been made up of three-and-a-half movements rather than the standard five. English musicians almost never set the Kyrie in polyphony by the beginning of the sixteenth century—its simple text had filled up with complex, highly variable interpolations (known as tropes) which made life difficult for composers—and large cuts were almost always made in the second half of the Credo. Tudor settings of the creed routinely skipped from the middle of the text directly to *Et exspecto resurrectionem mortuorum* ("And I look for the resurrection of the dead") or to the final Amen. Even with these limits in place, the general effect of some early-sixteenth-century English masses was to overwhelm with sheer bulk and virtuosity.

Tallis's *Missa Salve intemerata* is not one of those masses. It is not a shock-and-awe production like Fayrfax's *O quam glorifica*. In fact it has more in common, in many ways, with the short masses by Taverner and Tye also preserved in the Peterhouse books. The original motet *Salve intemerata* is a large, ornate piece by any reckoning, but Tallis's adaptation brings it down to a more modest scale. The making of this mass is a gentle but unmistakable exercise in compression and modernization. It is worth looking at in some detail because it gives us an unusually direct view of Tallis at work: revisiting his own music, analyzing it, making decisions about it, and adapting it to meet a new set of requirements.

Every movement of the *Salve intemerata* mass starts with a shared theme taken directly from the beginning of the motet. This theme is a severely cropped version of the original opening duet. It is always followed by another brief two-voice passage, borrowed from slightly later in the piece. Once this unifying device is out of the way, Tallis takes each movement in a somewhat different direction. Unlike (for example) Fayrfax in his mass on *O bone Jesu*, he does not work his way through the original piece from beginning to end and borrow excerpts from it more or less in order. Unlike Taverner in his mass "upon the anthem *Mater Christi*" (as the Peterhouse scribe aptly calls it), he does not adapt and reuse every single bar of the original. There is a distinct sense that he is choosing the raw material that best fits each situation. He saves two of the most exuberant cadential passages for important moments in the Sanctus. He uses the resonant last section of the motet to give shape and weight to the Gloria, although he brings it to an abrupt stop just as the final Amen begins. That whole splendid conclusion is held back until it finally appears in full at the end of the mass, unedited and unexpected, as his setting of *Dona nobis pacem*. (Figure 10.1 shows the bass part at this point as copied by the Peterhouse scribe.)

Figure 10.1   Conclusion of *Salve intemerata* mass in the Peterhouse partbooks, with attribution to "Talys" (Peterhouse, Perne Library, MS 32, f. 91v). Reproduced by kind permission of the Master and Fellows of Peterhouse, Cambridge.

Aside from the consistent opening theme, hardly any section of the original piece is used more than once. Some sections are never used at all. The materials *not* used are almost always the elaborate passages of three-voice polyphony, sometimes with very long runs of notes on a single syllable, which give the original work so much of its distinctive flavor and texture. The difficult, obscure adornment—what a medieval rhetorician would have called the *ornatus difficilis*—has been carefully trimmed by Tallis and excluded from his mass. What he adds instead at times is a quite different sort of adornment: the stark block chords at the name *Jesu*, or the cheeky little "English cadence" at *sedet ad dexteram Patris*, both gestures of a type found nowhere in the motet.

About four-fifths of the mass is adapted in some way from the original, although it can be hard at times to tell when Tallis is reusing his own work and when he is just choosing to write in a very similar style. The mass gains independence from its source material as it goes on. By the time Tallis reaches the last two movements, the Sanctus and the Agnus, there are some substantial stretches of more or less freely composed music. The freely composed sections are fascinating in their own right. Some of this new music has a close kinship with the masses by Taverner that are present in the Peterhouse books. There are many echoes of Taverner's own parody masses, *Mater Christi* and the so-called *Small Devotion*; there are also many echoes of Taverner's Mean Mass, and it is surely no coincidence that the only other source of the *Salve intemerata* mass (Tenbury 1464, an eclectic and captivating bass partbook) presents the two side by side. Tallis seems to have looked to Taverner for guidance in writing an effective mass on a less-than-grand scale, just as Byrd did half a century later when he composed his mass for four voices.[8]

During these years of Tallis's career, there was clearly an active interest in simplifying musical styles. It is hard to untangle the various reasons for this. Some of it can be traced to the growing influence of Continental composers and their music. Early-sixteenth-century musicians from other nations could certainly be long-winded and arcane themselves, but they also offered some new ways of organizing sound that made a strong impression on their English contemporaries. French, Flemish, and Italian music had already been widely available in England for more than a full generation when the Peterhouse books came into being. Half of the significant music manuscripts that survive from the early Tudor era contain foreign works of some sort.[9] Much of that music was brought in via the diplomatic activities of the royal court and the hiring of foreign musicians. There was clearly more going on than the occasional importing of attractive books by connoisseurs: these were close connections between musical cultures. The mass by "Lupo the Italian" found in the Peterhouse collection is a case in point. It was first printed by Girolamo Scotto in Venice in 1543, and again by Antonio Gardano in 1547. That seems rather late for the journey to England and full incorporation into the local repertory of Latin masses before such music was banned. In fact the copy in the Peterhouse books turns out to be independent of those printed versions: it includes a setting of the Benedictus which is omitted by both publishers, and it goes its own way in a number of important details.[10] This mass had already been circulating in Europe in various private manuscripts, and that is exactly how it came to England—as part of a living repertory copied and shared by a network of professional musicians, not just as a fashionable printed item brought home from Venice. It is a tightly constructed imitative mass, clear and direct, and it appears here in a matter-of-fact way alongside a whole range of English masses, including masses by Taverner, Tye, and Tallis that show signs of experimentation with the same principles.

Tallis's generation of composers in England had also inherited a strong native tradition of what could be called everyday music, with plainer lines and sparser textures, linked to the familiar practices of improvisation in churches and schools. Some of the trend toward simpler music in the 1530s and 1540s was a creative continuation of such practices. Some of it had to do with humanist appeals to clarity and intelligibility. Some of it, of course, had to do with the beginnings of the Reformation. All of these influences were present at this point in Tallis's career. They would have cataclysmic effects before long, but those cataclysmic effects are not yet visible in the Peterhouse anthology. It is easy to view it with hindsight as the last gasp of a dying tradition—John Jebb, the nineteenth-century vicar who first catalogued it, described its contents with visible disdain as "striking evidence of the need of a Reformation at that time"—but it does not look or feel like a document with a short life expectancy.[11] This is a large, fluent, confident, varied supply of music, obviously put together by and for people who expected to make use of it for quite a while.

A few of the younger composers in the Peterhouse books certainly appear to have felt the need of a Reformation. John Marbeck (also spelled Merbecke), a more or less exact contemporary of Tallis, is the most spectacular example.[12] He is represented in the Peterhouse manuscript by a large votive antiphon on the traditional Marian text *Ave Dei patris filia*, also set elsewhere by Tallis. By 1537 Marbeck was already copying out excerpts from the works of Calvin and other reformers into his private notebook. He was well-connected with evangelical circles and involved with the trade in subversive books and letters. In 1543 he was arrested for heresy along with three of his colleagues at Windsor, and all four were sentenced to burning at the stake.[13] Marbeck was pardoned just hours before the sentence was to be carried out, after a sleepless night spent preparing for execution. The other three were less fortunate. One of the men executed was his fellow-musician Robert Testwood, the subject of a string of colorful anecdotes in John Foxe's *Book of Martyrs*, most of them taking place in the chapel at Windsor where he and Marbeck were employed as members of the choir. The last of these anecdotes has to do with an impromptu musical duel between Testwood and a visiting singer named Robert Philips. They sang together in a piece of music containing an unusually effusive prayer to the Virgin Mary, and things did not go as planned. Foxe tells the story in his own words:

> Robert Philips was so notable a singing man (wherein he gloried) that wheresoever he came, the best and longest song, with most counterverses in it, should be set up at his coming. And so his chance being now to be at Windsor, against his coming to the Anthem, a long song was set up, called *Lauda vivi*. In the which song there was one counterverse toward the end that began on this wise: *O redemptrix et salvatrix*. Which verse of all other, Robert Philips would sing, because he knew that Testwood could not abide that ditty. Now Testwood, knowing his mind well enough, joined with him at the other part: and when he heard Robert Philips begin to fetch his flourish with *O redemptrix et salvatrix*, repeating the same one in another's neck, Testwood was as quick on the other side to answer him again with *Non redemptrix, nec salvatrix*, and so striving together with *O* and

Non, who should have the mastery, they made an end of the verse. Whereat was good laughing in sleeves of some . . .[14]

Lauda vivi Alpha et O is a work by Fayrfax that survives in a number of sixteenth-century manuscripts, including the Peterhouse partbooks themselves. There is indeed a "counterverse" toward the end of this long piece that addresses the Virgin Mary with the words *O redemptrix et salvatrix*, "O redeemer and savior." Those are rather strong words, even to Catholic ears, and it is no surprise that the vehemently evangelical Testwood "could not abide that ditty." His response was to make a joke of it. He sang the text in his own part as *Non redemptrix nec salvatrix*, "Neither redeemer nor savior."

Testwood was not the only person who found those words troublesome. Whoever copied out the Peterhouse books (or whoever provided the exemplar) changed them as well. Unlike all the other sources of *Lauda vivi*, this manuscript does not call Mary "redeemer" or "savior." The text is discreetly changed to the much less extravagant *O precatrix et adjutrix*, "O intercessor and helper." We catch a glimpse here of two different reactions to the same problematic text: the Peterhouse scribe nudging it back toward orthodox moderation, and a radical performer in the choir at Windsor subverting it completely. Those were two general tendencies seen in religious reform during these years, and it was far from clear at the time which side would prevail. It is no great surprise that a few other pieces in the Peterhouse collection also have their words tampered with in various ways. Motets for St. Alban and for St. Anne are adapted to honor Mary; a piece for St. William of York is given a new text addressing Christ.[15] There seems to be a tendency here to move away from the extravagant local veneration of saints toward a more general and somewhat blander devotional practice.

No such changes were made to Tallis's music in the Peterhouse books. His works appear here in plain and straightforward form. The only unusual fact is that the motet *Salve intemerata* is copied twice, in two separate and substantially different versions. The two copies are not very far apart in the manuscript, with only thirteen items (of a total of seventy-two) separating them. It is easy enough to imagine a scribe not recognizing the same music in a different-looking exemplar, although it is hard to believe that such a huge piece with such an unusual prose text would not trigger at least a faint recollection at some point in the long process of copying. If it was all done in error, it was not the only mistake of this sort made by the Peterhouse scribe. He was also well into an unintentional second copy of a mass by Hugh Aston before he realized what he was doing. His reaction in that case was to stop in his tracks, glue the offending pages together, and carry on with the next piece. He did nothing of the sort with the second copy of *Salve inte-merata*: he finished the whole thing and left it intact, although he did not list it again in the index.

Why did such a skilled and fluent scribe end up recopying almost 250 bars of complex polyphony? It may well have been a simple lapse of memory, but is also possible that he may suddenly have had access to a better or newer version of the piece. Given the tangled history of many of Tallis's works, with multiple revisions and reworkings, the second version of *Salve intemerata* might even have had a more direct link to the composer himself. That possibility would fit well with the hypothesis (see Chapter 4) that this collection of music was made for Canterbury Cathedral at the beginning of the 1540s, when the entire establish-ment was refounded under the auspices of the new national church with a new group of professional musicians.[16] Those singers would have needed new music, of a quite different sort from what the monks of the old cathedral and their handful of lay helpers had been singing. A link with Canterbury would certainly explain the presence of an unusual antiphon (*Exultet in hac die*) in honor of St. Augustine of Canterbury, the only piece in the Peterhouse books having to do with a saint who is not a New Testament figure such as Mary, John the Baptist, or the Holy Innocents. It would also explain the presence in these books of a sub-stantial hoard of music, some of it quite obscure, that appears to be asso-ciated in various ways with Magdalen College, Oxford: one of the new singers at Canterbury, Thomas Bull, arrived directly from Magdalen and was already well-known as a music copyist. Tallis himself was of course another musician hired for the new foundation, and it is tempt-ing (if perhaps slightly far-fetched) to imagine him offering a new and improved *Salve intemerata* for his colleagues to sing.

Whether or not this music was assembled for Canterbury, or for another one of the new cathedral foundations, it reflects what would have been sung in a first-rate choir of exactly that sort. All but four of the 71 pieces include substantial parts for boys' voices—the four exceptions are carefully labeled "men" in the index—so there must have been an expert group of young choristers as well as adult singers, all working together to provide music for mass, for vespers, and for the evening votive antiphon. In fact the Peterhouse partbooks are unusual because they include a variety of music for all three of those observances, rather than restricting themselves to only one or two genres as so many other manuscripts did. In some ways this seems to be a ready-made kit for the five-part polyphonic adornment of the whole Latin liturgy. It comes across as a project undertaken carefully but with a certain urgency. Mistakes are made, are (usually) corrected, and the scribe moves on without much fuss or regret. This is not the leisurely and rather perfectionist work of an antiquarian such as John Baldwin (see Chapter 15) in the later sixteenth century, who took the better part of two decades to finish his own anthology of music. Whoever did this job, he was well-connected enough to have access to two different versions of Tallis's *Salve intemerata*, along with the most diverse repertory found in any English church manuscript of its generation—everything from Robert Fayrfax's esoteric works to the beautiful and rather lugubrious motet *Aspice Domine* by Jacquet of Mantua. This was a range of styles present during Tallis's most formative years as a composer. He himself would produce at least one erudite cantus firmus mass and some of the most striking penitental motets of the sixteenth century. What we see in the Peterhouse collection is a remarkable snapshot of the rich musical world that surrounded his larger Latin works.

CHAPTER ELEVEN

The Gyffard Partbooks

T HE PREVIOUS FEW CHAPTERS OF THIS BOOK HAVE SHOWN TALLIS'S
music developing against the relatively stable backdrop of the
traditional Latin liturgy and the culture of pre-Reformation England.
Musical styles shifted and composers went in and out of fashion, but
it all took place within a familiar context. Almost none of that context would survive the upheavals of the mid-sixteenth century. Things
will look very different just a few pages from now: the singers will be
singing in English, for radically simplified church services, drawing on
a sometimes bewildering range of new influences. The Gyffard partbooks are worth a close look because they mark the end of an era. This
set of four sturdy little manuscripts—each about the size of a literary
paperback, 14 x 20 cm, 5.5 x 8 inches—is the last document of Tallis's
music that has to do exclusively with the old Latin rite.[1] After this,
everything changes.

With each case study so far, we have seen Tallis in the company
of various musicians: the learned Renaissance restorers of traditional plainchant (Chapter 7), the old masters of the Eton Choirbook
(Chapter 8), the virtuoso organists who made music in and around
London (Chapter 9), and the magnificent church composers who were
active during the reign of Henry VIII (Chapter 10.) Something new is
happening in the Gyffard books. A number of the composers here are
younger than Tallis. He appears alongside junior colleagues such as
John Sheppard, William Mundy, and even (in one case) the very young

Tallis. Kerry McCarthy, Oxford University Press (2020). © Oxford University Press.
DOI: 10.1093/oso/9780190635213.001.0001.

William Byrd.[2] The Gyffard scribe has a useful habit of ordering sets of pieces by the seniority of their composers. Tallis, by this point in his life, is usually somewhere in the middle.

Every manuscript of sixteenth-century music can be considered a miraculous survival in some way, but the Gyffard books are in a class of their own because approximately 95 percent of their content is unique.[3] There are a hundred pieces in these books, and all but a few of them would have been irretrievably lost if they had not been preserved here. This rather alarming statistic can be traced to the nature of the music itself. These are works for four voices, with a handful for just three voices. Smaller-scale Latin polyphony of this kind seems not to have been in great demand among later connoisseurs—it did not offer them the kaleidoscopic scorings and lush textures that already meant "old English church music" by the time of Tallis's death in 1585—so most of it simply fell by the wayside. In fact the four-part and three-part music that makes up the Gyffard collection turns out to be anything but dull or trivial. This is a treasury of fascinating and often beautiful repertory, including the *Western Wind* masses by Sheppard, Tye, and Taverner, the only surviving English masses of their generation to be based on a secular tune.

These partbooks offer a glimpse into a side of the older tradition that we rarely see, one that is in some ways closer to the daily experience of the thousands of professional singers who were making music in England just before the final ascendancy of the Reformation. These are not grand pieces of the *Salve intemerata* type. (It is no coincidence that we get a break from *Salve intemerata* in this chapter.) This is a different soundscape: richly detailed everyday music, written for small groups of skilled musicians. The Gyffard books show what Tallis did when he was asked to create Catholic music on a slightly more subdued scale. Unfortunately he seems not to have joined his three colleagues in composing a *Western Wind* mass, but his works in the Gyffard collection include an untitled four-voice mass (which turns out to offer a perplexing series of riddles), a four-voice Magnificat, and a small assortment of other ritual music. There is also his striking four-voice votive antiphon *Sancte Deus*, copied alongside a very similar setting of the same text by the Flemish musician Philip van Wilder, who served with Tallis at the royal court.

Votive antiphons have been a familiar presence in the last few chapters, so *Sancte Deus* is a good place to start exploring the Gyffard books.
This is an antiphon of a rather different sort. First of all, the text (as
the opening words suggest) is a direct prayer to God rather than an
invocation of the Virgin or another saint. Prayer-motets of this kind
had a long history in English choirs—there are plenty of them in older
manuscripts—but they seem to have enjoyed a new surge of popularity as the sixteenth century went on and lavish veneration of the saints
started to become politically suspect in some circles. *Sancte Deus* is an
unusual composite text whose first line is drawn from one of the oldest Christian liturgical prayers: "Holy God, holy and mighty, holy and
immortal, have mercy on us." It seems to have been a popular musical devotion in Tallis's day, with numerous people leaving bequests
of money for settings of those words to be sung year-round in their
memory. One choral endowment "pro sancte deus" in the London parish of St. Pancras Soper Lane was made "for ever" in 1516.[4] (The optimistic donor could hardly have foreseen what would happen in the
next generation or two.) At Cardinal College, Oxford, where Taverner
was choirmaster, the regulations of 1527 specified that *Sancte Deus* was
to be sung daily in polyphony by the choristers, with their instructor
on some days and without him on other days.[5] The task at St. Paul's
Cathedral also fell to the choristers, who received regular payment from
the estate of a late-fifteenth-century bishop for singing *Sancte Deus* in
front of the crucifix by the great north door.[6] Similar arrangements
were made in Salisbury, Bristol, Leicester, and elsewhere. The paired
settings of *Sancte Deus* in the Gyffard books, one by Tallis and one by
van Wilder, cannot be traced to any specific commission of this sort,
but their composers both had very close ties to the Tudor court, and it
is quite likely that the two pieces originated at court or at least became
part of the repertory there.

It is worth reflecting in more detail on the parallel careers of Tallis
and van Wilder because they represent two different types of courtly
music-making. In fact the writing of a non-liturgical pious work such
as *Sancte Deus* is one of the relatively few places where their worlds
would have overlapped. Henry VIII and his successors had a number of
separate musical establishments, including the Chapel Royal for ritual
performance in church and a different group of musicians—eventually

known as the King's (or Queen's) Music—who performed in the domestic sphere. Van Wilder was a Gentleman of the Privy Chamber, Henry's inner circle of personal servants and entertainers. He came to hold approximately the same place in the secular household as Tallis did in the Chapel Royal, rising through the ranks over several decades to become the group's senior and most distinguished musician.[7] Van Wilder had left Flanders and settled in London by 1522. He first appears in court records in 1525/26 as a "minstrel" and, a few years later, as a "luter." By the end of the 1520s he had a post in the Privy Chamber.[8] One of his numerous duties was the maintenance and repair of the royal instrument collection. An inventory made at Henry's death in 1547 contains a very long list of "Instruments at Westminster in the charge of Philip van Wilder."[9] There are luxuriously ornate chamber organs (including several "embroidered all over with gold and damask pearls"), multiple matched sets of viols, flutes, recorders, cornets, shawms, and crumhorns, more than a dozen harpsichords and clavichords, twenty-three lutes (with twenty-three matching cases), a set of bagpipes, and "an instrument that goeth with a wheel without playing upon."

When van Wilder was not taking care of this elaborate menagerie of instruments, he served as master to the "young Minstrels" at court and as private lute tutor to Princess Mary and Prince Edward. Teaching music to the royal family could be a dangerous business—the notorious downfall of Anne Boleyn's lute tutor Mark Smeaton is only one of several such cases—but van Wilder escaped scandal and died in 1554 in what seem to have been very comfortable circumstances.[10] He had spent a quarter of a century as a high-ranking musical servant with intimate access to the monarch, access of a sort that the organist and church singer Tallis quite likely did not enjoy. Most of van Wilder's surviving vocal works are fashionable chansons with French texts, but he also produced a few motets and devotional pieces, including two in the Gyffard books: *Pater noster* (the Lord's Prayer in Latin) and *Sancte Deus*.

It is hard to tell which of the two *Sancte Deus* settings was composed first. They are clearly a matched pair, with great similarities in structure, musical gesture, voicing, and general approach. Tallis's version is somewhat tighter and more concise. Given what we know of Tallis's musical habits, it would not have been uncharacteristic of him to have taken a piece by a slightly older composer (van Wilder was given pride of place by the Gyffard scribe) and reworked its ideas in typically self-assured fashion. On the other hand, van Wilder himself was in the habit of drawing on existing works, including a motet by Josquin (*Homo quidam*) and several popular French chansons, and emulating them in his own manner. In any case, this music is unlike the other votive antiphons we have encountered so far because it relies on a different set of rhetorical devices. The style is less extravagant. The general scale is smaller. There are no changes of time signature. There are no leisurely duets or trios for reduced voices: all four parts are singing all the time. Each separate section of text is clearly marked off by pauses and barlines, with none of the artful dovetailing found in larger antiphons. Even the range of pitch is more restrained. A typical Tudor votive antiphon covers three full octaves, requiring considerable diversity of voice types; Tallis's *Sancte Deus* covers only two octaves, with the lowest part in alto clef rather than bass clef. This was the *voci pari* ("equal-voice") arrangement found in sixteenth-century music used by groups of young choristers, nuns, and other populations that required a narrower vocal compass.[11] It is enticing to link this particular scoring with a group such as the "young Minstrels" of the royal Privy Chamber, the small and rather top-heavy ensemble directed by van Wilder, which in the 1540s included six boys' voices and only three adult voices.[12]

Figure 11.1 shows the lowest part of Tallis's *Sancte Deus* in the Gyffard collection. The composer's name ("mr talles") can be seen clearly in the upper left corner. The piece takes up barely more than three pages; this is the first page. Each phrase of the short prayer is set apart as a distinct musical gesture, ending with a fermata. (The symbol used repeatedly by the Gyffard scribe—including the rather inconspicuous one at the end of the first line—looks exactly the same as the modern fermata, and has the same function.) There is certainly room for ornamentation and melodic beauty here, but it is contained within a narrower framework than the music in Tallis's large votive antiphons. A piece of this sort would have been a perfect fit for private devotion in a small space. It is no coincidence that *Sancte Deus* is found near the end of the partbooks, separate from the strict liturgical scheme that governs most of the collection. It seems to have originated as part of a somewhat different musical sphere, one that was shared on some level by Tallis and his Flemish colleague. The devotional tastes of Henry VIII remained

Figure 11.1   The first page of Tallis's *Sancte Deus* in the Gyffard partbooks (BL Add. MS 17805, f. 203r). © The British Library Board. Reproduced by permission.

surprisingly traditional until the end of his life, at least when tradition did not interfere with his political aims, and it is not at all difficult to imagine a Latin motet of this kind being performed privately at court.

However the Gyffard scribe managed to get that piece, it is something of an exception. All the other works by Tallis he included are real liturgical music, composed for use at precise moments in specific church services. A couple of them share the same unusual arrangement of parts as *Sancte Deus*: two pairs of equal voices, just a fifth apart. These are two responsories (ornate pieces sung at matins), *Hodie nobis caelorum rex* and *Audivi vocem de caelo*, which were performed in English churches by unaccompanied boys' voices. This special decorative effect was heard on only a few important days of the year.[13] In the responsory *Hodie nobis caelorum rex*, for Christmas, a small group of high voices represented the angels who sang the refrain "Glory to God in the highest." In *Audivi vocem de caelo*, for All Saints' Day, the high voices singing "Behold, the bridegroom comes" represented the wise virgins of the parable. In both cases, the boys stood with lighted candles in their hands, apart from the main group of singers. At Christmas matins, they were directed to climb up (if possible) to "a high place above the altar" to mimic the heavenly chorus. Tallis may well have written these two pieces for St. Mary-at-Hill, with its small but well-maintained choir school and its generous observance of feast days. He could also have written them for the Chapel Royal: in fact the children of the Chapel were given special payments in 1538 and 1539 for singing unspecified settings of those two exact texts on those days, so there was already a tradition in place when Tallis arrived.[14] Whichever group he had in mind, it seems to have included a number of skilled young singers.

The longest work by Tallis in the whole Gyffard collection is an untitled mass for four voices. It is the simplest of the three surviving masses attributed to him, with a subdued close-harmony sound and a relatively limited range of note values. Rhetoricians in Tallis's day often divided literary style—and, by extension, the style of other arts—into three basic categories: high, middle, and low. Tallis composed one mass, broadly speaking, in each of those three registers. This is the low one. The designation "low" was not at all considered a negative judgment on the aesthetic or moral value of a work. In fact the humble style, the simple rhetorical register, was highly esteemed in sixteenth-century England—not least among reformers who considered it the most appropriate manner of expression for church music, as we will see in the next chapter.

This four-voice mass begins to make more sense when we look at the other music copied alongside it in the Gyffard books. It is one of a series of half a dozen masses in a distinctively low style. Two of them, even simpler than Tallis's, are given the title "Plainsong Mass." They do not contain actual plainsong; the title seems to be a reference to the plainness of their musical language. In fact one of that pair, the Plainsong Mass by Sheppard, is notated (like many other Tudor works of plain polyphony) with the same set of symbols that were used to write down chant melodies.[15] Sheppard's rhythmic scope here is so limited that it is rarely necessary to use anything beyond two basic signs meaning "long note" and "short note." Taverner's Plainsong Mass, like its immediate neighbor by Tallis, is somewhat less austere: this music is written in normal polyphonic notation and enjoys more rhythmic flexibility. There is additional room to relax in the later movements, where there are fewer words to navigate. Tallis gives a sense of variety to his own mass with a range of techniques and textures, from the simple chords at the beginning of the Gloria to the tidy patterns of imitation among all four voices in the second setting of the Osanna. Once again, as in *Sancte Deus*, he is exploring a classic genre on a smaller canvas.

Some things about Tallis's four-part mass are reminiscent of the plainer music that came with the arrival of the Book of Common Prayer and the new English liturgy. This piece is clearly not a product of the full-fledged liturgical Reformation—it is in Latin, after all—but it seems to be sharing in a number of the same musical ideals. Some of those ideals were already present, and increasingly popular, in the English church of the 1530s and 1540s. In fact some of them were already present before Tallis was born. Even in a thoroughly traditional milieu, there was a time and a place for church music of a more subdued sort. Evidence of a humbler style can be found in an early Tudor collection such as the Ritson manuscript, which preserves a large amount of simple polyphony (including some masses) from around the turn of the sixteenth century, more than a full generation before evangelical reformers began calling for "plain and distinct" music. It bears repeating once again: not all of the polyphony sung in pre-Reformation churches was florid music on a grand scale. Tallis's four-part mass was heir to a different tradition.

A recent musical discovery has added a new twist to the story. The Credo of this four-voice mass turns out to have an unlikely twin: the whole movement is more or less identical with the Creed of an English service by Sheppard.[16] The only differences are in the words and the musical edits made to accommodate them. Sheppard's version seems to date from the first experimental years of English services in the late 1540s: it uses the Apostles' Creed rather than the longer and much more typical Nicene Creed used by Tallis. Tallis bridges the gap with quicker declamation and some extra material (shared with, or borrowed from, the Gloria of his own mass) that does not appear in Sheppard's service. In any case these two works, one in Latin and one in English, are essentially the same piece of music.

Which version came first? Was Tallis the borrower or the lender? Some clues can be gathered by looking at the two pieces side by side. In the English version by Sheppard, various musical phrases fit perfectly with words that mention descent, resurrection, and ascension, most notably the falling scale that spans more than an octave on the text "and descended into hell." These same musical gestures occur at what seem to be random locations in Tallis's Latin version. English composers of this generation were not given to madrigalesque illustration of sacred words, but nearly all their surviving settings of the creed (in whatever language) show the same common sense expressed by Morley, who wrote half a century later that it would be "counted great incongruity if a musician, upon the words 'he ascended into heaven,' should cause his music [to] descend."[17] Tallis's entire mass is put together in a less conventional way than Sheppard's service, with extensive note-for-note copying of music between the first two movements and what seems to be an unwillingness to commit to a unified opening theme. (In the latter aspect, it is not unlike Byrd's three masses, where opening motives recur, change, and disappear at will. Byrd certainly felt no obligation to start every single movement of a mass in the same way.)

Given the anomalies of text-setting in the Latin version, and the evidence of what seems to be some rough-and-ready editing, it is difficult not to conclude that the English version came first. That would fit well with Tallis's lifelong practice of musical borrowing and reworking—something that Sheppard, for all his vast productivity, seems never to have done in the same way. It is also within the realm of possibility that Tallis himself did not do all of the borrowing. Some of this music could easily have been adapted or arranged by someone else and copied under Tallis's name. There are a few awkward moments in the mass that seem quite untypical of Tallis's style, including one spot in the middle of "Dominus Deus Sabaoth" where the music fades out into near-oblivion and hauls itself to its feet again. If it was somehow manipulated by a third party, it would not be the only thing in the Gyffard books to have received such a treatment: there is also a (makeshift but not at all inelegant) four-voice arrangement of Taverner's popular five-voice Easter responsory *Dum transisset sabbatum*, designed so that a smaller group of singers could perform a classic work on the most important day of the church year. These musicians seem to have had no scruples about altering existing works to fit their needs. This may well have happened during the mid-1550s, when English churches were scrambling to restore traditional worship in Latin after several years of suppression. If the adaptation of the mass was done in whole or in part by someone else, Tallis's name would have been an obvious choice to invoke—much as sixteenth-century musicians and editors in other countries invoked the name of Josquin in moments of musical need, leaving a tangle of dubious attributions in their wake which have still not been fully sorted out today.[18]

However Tallis's four-part mass came into being, the complex link with Sheppard's English service is worth exploring in detail because it tells us something important about the music of this era. Musical styles did not change abruptly and completely at the Reformation. It was a period of radical transformation, not an unbridgeable gap. This chapter has to do with four-voice music in Latin; the next chapter, on the Lumley and Wanley partbooks, will have to do with four-voice music in English. There were massive upheavals as one repertory gave way to another, but there was also a certain amount of continuity. That continuity can be hard to see unless one is looking for it. It is telling that two effectively identical pieces, a Latin creed under Tallis's name and an English creed under Sheppard's name, could hide in plain sight for so long without being recognized as twins.

The four Gyffard books are an unusually clear witness of what everyday church music looked like in England just before the Latin rite came to an end. This is a meticulously well-organized collection, leading its users step by step through the mass and through the liturgical year. It might have been part of a larger repertory used in a particular church, along with matching (and now lost) anthologies for five voices and perhaps even six voices, although it is telling that the Easter section of the manuscript features a reduced-voice rearrangement of Taverner's *Dum transisset*. If the group of singers who used the Gyffard collection were not at full strength on Easter morning, it is hard to imagine when they would have been. What we appear to have here is a self-contained resource used by a small handful of musicians in the 1550s who adorned the last few years of the Sarum rite with generous amounts of four-part polyphony by Tallis and other composers.

Once again, things are not entirely as they seem. A closer look at the manuscript reveals some complications. The Gyffard books contain several different kinds of paper, and some of that paper was almost certainly produced in the 1570s, well after this sort of music had been banished from churches.[19] Along with all the carefully ordered pieces by Tallis, Tye, and Sheppard, there are a couple of accomplished (and suspiciously modern-sounding) works attributed to even younger composers such as Robert White. Some sections of the manuscript have texts written out in beautiful formal handwriting by someone who seems to have been copying the words mechanically with no idea what they meant. The grotesque spelling errors speak for themselves: *teeplum, egogo, nrstri, mumquid, vokis, euemoique,* and more than a hundred others like them. That job was not done by a working Catholic musician familiar with basic liturgical texts in Latin. The musical notation is also garbled in places. No large-scale handmade copy of music is flawless—even printed copies very rarely are—but many of the items in Gyffard, including Tallis's four-voice Magnificat and *Sancte Deus*, are so infested with small scribal errors that singing them directly from the books is a formidable challenge. Other pieces have bigger problems, such as botched divisi passages or serious confusion about rests, which render them unperformable without help from a modern editor. Even a number of the plainsong melodies are unhelpfully given at the wrong pitch. This does not seem like the sort of document that would have been assembled and used by the professionals for whom Tallis wrote his Latin church music. It is hard to avoid the conclusion that some or perhaps even all of it was put together in retrospect. The people who worked on it certainly had access to one or more older church manuscripts, which they appear to have tackled with more enthusiasm than understanding.

Much of the Gyffard anthology seems to be an imperfect carbon copy of something which did not survive—which would have had no reason for surviving. We are lucky that the thing being copied here was a real working repertory of four-part Latin-texted music, because otherwise we would have almost no idea of how Tallis and his contemporaries composed in that style. In the Gyffard books we can see one particular slice through Tallis's earlier career, preserved in almost abstract purity. The "Doctor Gyffard" whose name is scrawled in one of the books is difficult to trace, but the most likely candidate seems to be the impressive figure of Dr. Roger Gifford (d. 1597), president of the Royal College of Physicians, scholar and collector of books, a man with (somewhat guarded) Catholic sympathies and enough of an interest in music to have been appointed honorary precentor of St. David's Cathedral.[20] He did not do the hard work of copying—the partbooks are clearly not in the doctor's own handwriting—but he was just the sort of antiquarian-minded person who would have had an interest in owning such an anthology, or even an interest in overseeing its compilation.

Roger Gifford may never have had any direct contact with Tallis or the other musicians of the Chapel Royal whose names appear in these partbooks, although it is notable that he was eventually appointed one of Queen Elizabeth's personal physicians. (He also took part in ceremonial public disputes in her presence about the art of medicine. Topics for debate included the two propositions that "Slowly cooked foods are to be preferred to those that are more easily cooked" and "Life can be prolonged by medical science."[21]) What we do know is that the ambitious Dr. Gifford, or some other connoisseur like him, helped preserve this music during the difficult years when it was no longer tolerated in public. Some of Tallis's much more monumental works, pieces such as *Gaude gloriosa* or the *Puer natus* mass (see Chapter 16), also survived in exactly this sort of circumstance: music rescued from oblivion, almost by chance, for whatever combination of social or personal reasons. Documents of this type offer a bridge across the precarious decades of the Reformation. If it had not been for the diligence of the Gyffard scribes, we would have lost more or less the complete four-part Latin works of Tallis, along with those of Sheppard, Taverner, Tye, Mundy, and a number of other composers. The Gyffard partbooks do not just mark the end of an era; they are also the first musical document of their kind in England, with a primary focus on remembrance (and, it seems, idealistic preservation) of things past.[22] In the remaining chapters of this book, we will be seeing Latin church music only through the lens of retrospect and memory.

CHAPTER TWELVE

The Wanley and Lumley Partbooks

THE LITURGICAL REFORMATION IN ENGLAND DID NOT HAPPEN overnight. The style and language of public worship changed fitfully, with a good deal of local variability. Many churches went on with their familiar old music until the new Book of Common Prayer arrived at their door in 1549 with a royal imprimatur and a threat of six months' imprisonment for anyone who refused to use it.[1] In some other places, especially in and around London, there appears to have been a gradual process of creative experimentation. Tallis was near the epicenter of those early changes.

Some of the more fervent reformers had already started trying out sung services in English in the late 1530s, but the first sign of official approval did not come until 1544, when a new vernacular litany was sung by the Chapel Royal and published in various musical forms for use throughout the realm (quite likely with the help of Tallis, as we have seen in Chapter 5).[2] Henry VIII still clung tenaciously to most of the old rites, and the floodgates of real change did not open until his death in January 1547. The musicians of the Chapel Royal were singing a form of English compline three months later.[3] By November, the whole Mass Ordinary was being sung in English at Westminster Abbey.[4] Not long after Easter 1548, the choirs of St. Paul's Cathedral and "divers other parishes in London" were doing the same.[5] These new English services seem to have been a patchwork of words and music drawn from a variety of official and unofficial sources. Uniformity

Tallis. Kerry McCarthy, Oxford University Press (2020). © Oxford University Press.
DOI: 10.1093/oso/9780190635213.001.0001.

was finally imposed the following year with the first edition of the Book of Common Prayer, but even those texts did not survive for long before they were suppressed and revised in a more Protestant direction.[6] Church musicians at the time could hardly have known what would be required of them from one day to the next.

The Wanley and Lumley partbooks, the oldest surviving sources of Tallis's vernacular music, are documents of those first experimental years.[7] The vast majority of the pieces in these manuscripts are transmitted anonymously, which is no great surprise given the complex and often chaotic situation in which they originated. Many of the items cannot be traced in any other way to an individual composer, and only four of them can be identified as works by Tallis: the anthems *If ye love me* and *Hear the voice and prayer*, the penitential antiphon *Remember not*, and a setting of one of the canticles (the Benedictus, *Blessed be the Lord God of Israel*) sung at matins in the new English rite. These are four-voice works in an elegant, pared-down, sometimes severe style. Tallis composed various other pieces of that sort, but the handful found here are crucial landmarks because they can be securely dated to the first years of reform.

The Wanley collection is by far the larger of the two.[8] It contains ninety pieces of music, some of them quite extensive. Church musicians during the reign of Edward VI needed a whole new repertory in English for a rapidly changing routine of services, and they were prepared to do whatever was necessary to get it. All sorts of strategies can be found here: recycling of the Latin classics (including a couple of communion services which turn out to be adaptations of shorter masses by Taverner), very simple note-against-note counterpoint written down in minimalist "plainsong" notation, variations on old improvisational techniques, and a range of creative new compositions. Whoever assembled the Wanley set of partbooks was obviously well-connected, with access to recent works by Tallis, Tye, Sheppard, and other mid-century luminaries. The music was copied with what seems to have been unusual efficiency by a team of two scribes. The leather covers are embossed with a decorative pattern that matches the known work of a London artisan in the 1540s, and it is easy to imagine the books being used in a busy urban church, since music is provided for almost every conceivable ceremony, including weddings and funerals.[9] There are also two dozen freely composed pieces on non-liturgical texts, most of them carefully labeled "Antem." Two of the anthems are by Tallis.

When Tallis wrote his first anthems in English, he was responding to the growing demand for a humbler, more intelligible style of sacred music. The rhetorician Thomas Wilson was writing about literature in his 1553 *Art of Rhetoric*, not about singing, but he summed up the situation well:

> There are three manner of styles or inditings:
>
> The great or mighty kind, when we use great words, or vehement figures.
>
> The small kind, when we moderate our heat by meaner words, and use not the most stirring sentences.
>
> The low kind, when we use no metaphors nor translated words, nor yet use any amplifications, but go plainly to work, and speak altogether in common words.[10]

The new Protestant musical language being forged in mid-sixteenth-century England was firmly grounded in what Wilson called "the low kind": no arcane expressions, no grand flourishes, just plain speaking in intelligible terms. The choice to "go plainly to work" in this way had been one of several options available to composers before the Reformation, as we saw in the previous chapter. It was now quickly becoming an ideal for church music in almost all situations. This ideal can be seen in Cranmer's well-known desire to have "for every syllable a note" (although that particular remark, made in 1544, was aimed at chant rather than polyphony) and in many sermons and exhortations of the Reformation years. Sacred music now had a duty to edify, to inform, indeed to teach, in a style accessible to a wide range of churchgoers. Any "anthem" composed according to those evangelical principles would have little in common with the "anthems" in the manuscript Harley 1709, a book which is barely twenty years older than the Wanley books but already seems to inhabit a different world.

Tallis's anthem *If ye love me* is a four-voice setting of a New Testament text: "If ye love me, keep my commandments, and I will pray the Father, and he shall give you another comforter, that he may bide with you forever, even the Spirit of truth." Those words had an important place in the new Book of Common Prayer. They were the beginning of the Gospel reading on Pentecost, Whit Sunday, the exact day in June 1549 on which the new rites of the Church of England were officially put into effect.[11] Coincidence or not, this text had great symbolic weight. The first words are hard to miss in any case because Tallis sets them to a crystal-clear series of block chords. As in his four-voice mass, the block chords are only an opening gambit. They eventually give way to imitation between voices, first by pairs, then passing through all the parts in turn. Cranmer would have been pleased at the syllable-to-note ratio, which hovers reassuringly close to 1, but this does not prevent Tallis from writing a couple of beautifully expressive dissonances as the voices begin to descend on the words "he may bide." In fact we get to hear them twice, because the second half of the anthem is given a repeat sign. The result is a perfectly calculated miniature, barely two minutes long. Figure 12.1 shows the entire bass part as copied by the Wanley scribe.

If ye love me may well be Tallis's most frequently performed work today. Much of its fame has to do with the fact that it is short, in English, easy to sing, and suitable (with some discreet transposition) for a modern four-part church choir, but it is also an excellent piece of music in its own right. The religious upheavals of the 1540s may have been deeply unsettling for a person in Tallis's position, but this anthem shows no external signs of turmoil. It is as serene and confident as his best Latin motets.

Figure 12.1   Bass part of *If ye love me* in the Wanley partbooks (Oxford, Bodleian Library, Mus. Sch. e. 422, f. 55r). Bodleian Library. Reproduced by permission.

Where did this musical style come from? By far the closest parallel is with a type of plain, accessible music that Tallis and his colleagues already had at their disposal: the secular songs that had become so popular in England during the reign of Henry VIII. Songs of this kind were imported from abroad, written by émigré musicians such as Philip van Wilder, and cultivated (often anonymously) by Tudor composers in their own language. We have already seen two such songs by Tallis himself in the Mulliner Book. French and Flemish chansons, and their local English cousins, had a lot to offer the church musician who needed a fresh start. These pieces had clearly discernible words. Their dimensions were modest. They could be written down without arcane notation and performed without decades of specialist training. They already had a sterling pedigree in English courtly circles, where anything in an international style was in high demand. It is no surprise that many of the earliest English anthems bear a very close resemblance to chansons of just this type. In fact Thomas Caustun, one of Tallis's colleagues in the Chapel Royal, furnished a number of foreign secular songs with pious words and published them as sacred music under his own name—a ruse that went undiscovered until recent years.[12] Tallis did not do that (as far as we know), but a piece such as *Hear the voice and prayer* or *If ye love me* uses exactly the same musical devices found in Northern European chansons: plain declamation of the text, tightly organized little passages of polyphony alternating with four-part block chords, and the practice of repeating whole sections of music note-for-note. The style of the earliest English anthems would not have felt the least bit unfamiliar to singers in the late 1540s. It was a style they already knew from court and chamber. Now it was being brought into church.

Tallis went on composing this kind of small English anthem, at least occasionally, for the next two decades. The humble four-voice style was a highly useful resource in his rhetorical armory, and he did not abandon it when the turbulent years of the early Reformation were over. One anthem of this exact sort, *O Lord give thy Holy Spirit*, was not composed before the 1560s, probably not before the mid-1560s.[13] Its verbal text went through a long process of evolution and did not even exist in the form set to music by Tallis until Elizabeth's reign was already underway. Here, as elsewhere, we can see the willingness to compose in a wide range of registers as circumstances required. Tallis was still able to "go plainly to work" as he entered what seems to have been his last active decade as a composer.

The Lumley set of partbooks, the other manuscript source of Tallis's very early English-texted church music, is a smaller collection than the Wanley set and draws on a slightly different range of materials.[14] Instead of reworkings of Latin polyphony, there are psalms set to old secular tunes, such as the songs *Blow thy horn hunter* and *My love she mourneth* by the early Tudor courtly composer William Cornysh.[15] The final pages are filled up with dances and other instrumental works: these books seem to have been taken out of church by the early 1550s and used as a convenient source of blank paper. There are only two pieces by Tallis, not counting a scrawled copy of his popular song *When shall my sorrowful sighing slack*, copied near the end alongside the pavans and galliards. Those two works—*Remember not, O Lord God, our old iniquities* and an English canticle for matins—show that Tallis was capable of considerable variety, even within the "low kind" of composition. It was a more restricted palette, but it still contained a range of colors.

Remember not is by far the more subdued of the two pieces. The text is found in the King's Primer of 1545, one of the very few English devotional books that were not banned or suppressed at some point during the turbulent last years of the 1540s. The words are given there as a final refrain after the recitation of the seven penitential psalms. Tallis's setting is suitably ascetic. Each phrase is declaimed in a plain, natural rhythm, with either a rest or a fermata at the end. There is no polyphony and no imitation between voices; the music is little more than a series of chords. Almost all of it is built around a simple technique: parallel sixths between the tenor and soprano, with the alto filling in as needed, and the bass moving somewhat more freely to create a harmonic foundation. This sort of four-part harmony could have been created on the spot by a few well-practiced singers. Music theorists taught variations on the same technique to students who wanted to improvise, and many pieces of church music from this generation, including a number of the anonymous works in the Lumley and Wanley books, are constructed in exactly the same way.[16] Tallis's music is more polished than one would expect from extempore singing in church, but he still appears to be very close indeed to the improvisational practices he would have known in his everyday work—as close as he was while setting a Latin cantus firmus or creating organ verses for a hymn.

Despite its brutally simple style, *Remember not* ended up enjoying some real popularity. It survives in four distinct versions.[17] The Lumley version is the plainest. Other sources (including some of the mid-sixteenth-century printed books that will appear in the next chapter) offer different readings that are longer, more repetitious, more orna-mented, and in some cases implying two separate groups of singers in the double-choir formation characteristic of cathedrals and other large choral foundations. The piece even appears as a keyboard work in the Mulliner Book, where it coexists peacefully with music in a radically different style. *Remember not* is one of the numerous works by Tallis that show traces of significant recomposition and adaptation. It can be difficult to tell who was doing the recomposition here. Some pieces of this type, such as the five-part instrumental fantasia (see Chapter 9) that eventually took new forms as the anthem *I call and cry* and the motet *O sacrum convivium*, appear to have been reworked by Tallis himself at some length and in several stages.[18] He may well have done the same with *Remember not*, although it may also have become the common property of mid-century church musicians who altered it to meet their own needs. If these different versions in fact originated from Tallis's hand, he took nearly as much care in revising this quasi-improvised work as he did in revising an intricately wrought piece of five-voice polyphony.

Tallis's other contribution to the Lumley books, his Benedictus, is a different sort of piece. This is not the familiar Benedictus of the Mass Ordinary; it is a longer text, the canticle of Zechariah sung daily at morning prayer in the reformed liturgy. (It is in English, but it gets a prominent Latin title in Lumley, as does every other item in those partbooks. Musicians had no scruples about referring to pieces by their familiar old Latin names. Even in our own day, the canticles at even-song are still called the Magnificat and Nunc Dimittis.) Tallis's setting is an experiment in variety within the limitations of a mostly syllabic style. The four voices spend most of their time moving independently, with unexpected touches of harmonic color. Tallis even indulges in a brief victory lap of more ornate music in the final Amen: there can be no mistaking the text at this point, and the lower parts are at liberty to roam for a couple of bars underneath a long-held note in the soprano. This piece seems to have been written extremely early in the process of reform, because Tallis's version of the text is an old reading that predates the first Book of Common Prayer published in 1549.[19] Even before English services were officially approved, he was already exploring their musical possibilities and boundaries.

Tallis could produce even more elaborate service music in English when the occasion called for it. One prominent example is his five-voice Te Deum "for meanes"—in other words, including boys' voices, unlike most of the new English music of the Lumley and Wanley type, which kept to a narrower and lower vocal range. This Te Deum uses the Prayer Book text of 1549. It is a festive work, with generous musical proportions and creative use of different voice types. The verse referring to "the Virgin's womb" is set for high voices only, divided briefly into additional parts for the occasion. A passage such as this recalls the older mimetic world of *Audivi vocem* and *Hodie nobis* (see Chapter 11), the responsories for All Saints' Day and Christmas, where the high voices of boys are likewise used to evoke virgins and angels. Some sections of the Te Deum "for meanes" have suffered the loss of individual parts, but the whole thing can be reconstructed with some confidence, and it is clear that six or perhaps even seven separate voices were sometimes in play at once. Here Tallis is treading perilously close to what might be called a moderate style rather than a low style. He avoids the grand gestures and "most stirring sentences" found in many of his Latin works, but at this point he is well out of Cranmerian territory and into self-conscious rhetorical elaboration. This music has its closest kinship with other richly scored mid-century pieces such as Sheppard's Second Service and evening canticles "for trebles."[20] It is not all too far from here to the ten-part Great Service of Byrd.[21]

Tallis's Te Deum "for meanes" seems to have attracted rather little attention from musicians, in its own day or in subsequent generations. That sort of complex service music had become a niche interest, suitable only for important churches staffed with sympathetic clergy and able to support a skilled group of boy choristers. The English service by Tallis that became famous was of the solidly Cranmerian type. This was his four-part Short Service, also known to later generations as the "Dorian Service." It has the extremely rare distinction of being a sixteenth-century work that has been performed as part of a living repertory, more or less without interruption, ever since it was composed. As its name suggests, the Short Service is brief, austere, and basically unornamented. It was taken up by other composers as a model of creative plainness. Within a generation or two, it had inspired a group of other short services, some by musicians who were not necessarily given to plainness by temperament (Byrd comes to mind again, as does Morley). Tallis's Short Service persisted in everyday church use through the era of Gibbons and Tomkins, of Purcell and Blow, of Handel and Arne, and it played an important role in establishing Tallis's somewhat romanticized nineteenth-century reputation as the "Father of English Church Music."[22] An anonymous journalist who heard this "grand old gothic service" sung in 1841 praised it for its "vastness, gloomy grandeur, and ponderous solemnity." The church music reformer John Jebb, writing two years later, said that "its harmonies are perfect models for sublimity, fullness, and exquisite judgement."[23]

Those may seem like overheated reactions to one of the plainest of all Tudor compositions, but there is something surprisingly effective about its style. This was a musical language that had both staying power and political clout. Superficially unglamorous music such as the Short Service or *If ye love me* deserves as much attention as Tallis's more extravagant works, not least because it gives us a glimpse of Tallis at a crucial point of influence. He found himself in an unexpected place during the Reformation as the old certainties began to collapse one by one. He had inherited a set of traditional techniques and worked with them for many years. Now he was acting as one of the chief architects of a new musical ideal, personally serving a monarch who was supreme ruler and lawgiver of the national church. There is only one composer's name actually written down anywhere in the Wanley and Lumley books; that is Tallis's name, carefully noted at the end of his Benedictus. This may be a simple coincidence, but it reflects his situation around 1550. He was now in a position of real musical authority for the first time, even as he was deprived of many of the options and resources he had known as a younger man. At this stage of his life, less was indeed more. He did not restrict himself permanently to composing in four parts—he would be composing in forty parts before long—but these astringent first years of reform left a mark on the rest of his career.

CHAPTER THIRTEEN

Archbishop Parker's Psalter

A S THE NEW NORMS AND COMPROMISES OF THE ELIZABETHAN church slowly took shape in the 1560s, there was a growing demand for sacred music in affordable printed form. It is no surprise that several such publications included pieces by Tallis, whose name would have added prestige to any book. At that point he found himself involved, willingly or unwillingly, in the business of commercial music production. By the mid-1570s he was at the heart of the London music trade, with a royal music patent and a beautifully produced collection of his own works. It is easy to admire the *Cantiones* of 1575 as Tallis's first real venture into print, but his earlier printed music tells a different and equally fascinating story.

The first decade of Elizabeth's reign saw a surge of music publishing in England. Most of it took place under the supervision of the ambitious printer John Day, who is perhaps best remembered for his production of John Foxe's *Acts and Monuments* (also known as *Foxe's Book of Martyrs*), a massive illustrated work of Protestant history and hagiography. Music was only part of Day's publishing empire, but it was a lucrative part. It became even more lucrative as he began to produce vast quantities of popular psalm books, using rhymed metrical poetry in the Calvinist style. By far the most successful of these metrical psalters—in fact one of the best-sellers of the entire sixteenth century—was the *Whole Book of Psalms*.[1] The first edition of that book in 1562, like many of the numerous editions that would follow it, includes the top voice of Tallis's devotional

Tallis. Kerry McCarthy, Oxford University Press (2020). © Oxford University Press.
DOI: 10.1093/oso/9780190635213.001.0001.

song *O Lord in thee is all my trust*. Day's *Whole Psalms in Four Parts*, published in 1563, contains a four-voice version of that song, along with Tallis's always popular *Remember not*. In 1565, after a complex editorial process that had dragged on for five years, Day brought out a more ambitious anthology of church music including the same pair of works, as well as Tallis's anthems *If ye love me* and *Hear the voice and prayer*.[2] Finally, in 1567, Day printed a group of short psalm settings by Tallis. These psalms are a striking mixture of old and new. They are arranged according to the traditional medieval system of the eight musical modes and matched with poetic texts by Matthew Parker, an old friend of Queen Elizabeth whom she chose to serve as her first Archbishop of Canterbury.

Matthew Parker was not one of Foxe's martyrs. He had survived the anti-Protestant persecutions of the mid-1550s by staying in England and keeping very quiet. While many of his colleagues escaped temporarily to the Continent, Parker sequestered himself in a kind of domestic exile. Deprived of all his ecclesiastical duties, he found himself unexpectedly "joyful," relishing what he called "the sweetest literary leisure."[3] (He wrote those words while in hiding at a friend's house in October 1554; he was not speaking through a retrospective haze of nostalgia.) In August 1557 he made a note that he had "completed a psalter in metrical verse in the vernacular."[4] This work was published by Day a decade later as *The Whole Psalter Translated into English Metre*. Parker, who was the most senior churchman in England by that point, seems to have chosen (as did many other authors of high social standing) to keep his work relatively anonymous. The only hint of his authorship in the actual printed text of the *Whole Psalter* is the acrostic *Mattheus Parkerus* in his prefatory poem to Psalm 118. Tallis's music takes up only a tiny section of Parker's weighty tome, which also includes many pages of learned introductory material, extra poems and prayers to accompany each of the 150 psalms, networks of black and red lines to show interlocking rhyme schemes, and other supplementary features.[5] The music is the last bonus item in the book, just before the final index. There are eight psalm settings in four-part harmony, one in each of the eight musical modes, followed by the very brief final invocation *Come, Holy Ghost*. There is no reticence about naming the author here—each piece of music is clearly labeled *Talys*—but Tallis's name appears nowhere else in the volume.

The eight modes Tallis uses in these psalms are the basic set of modes he would have learned during his childhood training. They are musical scales, arrangements of pitches, within which a melody develops and resolves in characteristic ways. Modes 1 and 2 are both built on the note D, and both finally come to rest on that note, mode 1 having explored a higher vocal range than the more subdued mode 2. The same is true for the other pairs of modes: 3 and 4 on E, 5 and 6 on F, 7 and 8 on G. This eightfold system, which had its origins almost a millennium before Tallis, evolved alongside (and helped to shape) the course of European music history. The system originally applied to plainchant melodies, but it grew to encompass polyphony as well. In his four-part Parker settings, Tallis takes the traditional approach to determining the mode in a polyphonic piece: it is dictated by the tonal center, range, and behavior of the tenor voice. In fact the tenor is the true melody here, and a note to the reader specifies that "The Tenor of these parts be for the people when they will sing alone"—in other words, for unaccompanied unison singing.

Many sixteenth-century authors had more esoteric ideas about mode, going well beyond the use of musical scales and melodic gestures. Following ancient Greek and medieval precedents, they ascribed a distinct mood, ethos, and even moral character to each of the modes. Parker shared this view and applied it to Tallis's music. His psalter includes a brief rhymed guide (Figure 13.1) to the eight modes—which he calls the "eight tunes," that is "tones"—and their characteristics.

> The first is meek: devout to see,
> The second sad: in majesty.
> The third doth rage: and roughly brayeth.
> The fourth doth fawn: and flattery playeth,
> The fifth delighteth: and laugheth the more,
> The sixth bewaileth: it weepeth full sore,
> The seventh treadeth stout: in froward race,
> The eighth goeth mild: in modest pace.

Parker also includes a Latin version, which says more or less the same thing.

> Primus, modeste & religiose graditur.
> Secundus, severe cum maiestate tonat.

The nature of the eyght tunes.

~ 1 The first is méeke: deuout to sée,
\ 2 The second sad: in maiesty.
\ 3 The third doth rage: and roughly brayth.
/ 4 The fourth doth fawne: and flattry playth,
/ 5 The fyfth deligth: and laugheth the moze,
\ 6 The sirt bewayleth: it wéepeth full soze,
\ 7 The seuenth tredeth stoute: in froward race,
~ 8 The eyghte goeth milde: in modest pace.

☞ The Tenoz of these partes be foz the people when they will syng alone, the other parts, put foz greater queers, oz to suche as will syng oz play them priuatelye.

Figure 13.1   Archbishop Parker's rhymed guide to the eight modes, with "accents" in the left-hand margin to help match them with appropriate texts. Princeton Theological Seminary. Reproduced by permission.

Tertius, Indignatur & acerbe insultat.

Quartus, quasi adulatur & allicit.

Quintus, Iucunde delectat & ridet.

Sextus, Lachrimatur & plorat.

Septimus, Incitate progreditur & imperiose.

Octavus, decenter & moderate incedit.

The first walks modestly and devoutly.

The second thunders gravely with majesty.

The third is indignant and insults harshly.

The fourth, as it were, flatters and entices.

The fifth delights and laughs pleasantly.

The sixth weeps and cries.

The seventh marches on passionately and imperiously.

The eighth advances tastefully and moderately.

Some of these descriptions are quite conventional; others are more original. Most surviving lists of this sort agreed with Parker, and with the accounts of "Phrygian" music from classical antiquity, that the third mode was vehement, warlike, and irritable. Opinions about (for instance) the fifth mode are much more varied, from gloomy (Gaffurio, writing in 1518) to bacchanalian (Glarean, writing in 1547) to joyous (Finck, writing in 1556) to humble (Case, writing in 1588).[6] The Waltham Abbey manuscript owned by Tallis includes a statement by the English musician John Wylde that the fifth mode is "more cheerful and pleasant than the others."[7] Parker seems to agree with Wylde in principle as he makes his lists, but he also matches Tallis's fifth-mode setting with a poignant text of longing: "Even like the hunted hind the waterbrooks desire, / even thus my soul, that fainting is, to thee would fain aspire." Unlike many of his contemporaries, Parker is inclined to regard adjacent pairs of modes as polar opposites. In general he sticks more closely to received medieval traditions of modal ethos than to Renaissance attempts at recapturing a more ancient practice. He recalls at one point in an autobiographical note that he was trained in singing by two musicians during his youth in pre-Reformation Norwich, one a priest and one a parish clerk, both remembered by him as "stern teachers."[8] The traditional view of the eight plainsong modes, perhaps

inculcated by those two stern men of an older generation, seems to have
been the one that stuck in his mind.

The "nature of the eight tunes" was not just a matter of academic
speculation for Parker. He wanted people to sing his rhymed translations of the psalms, and he wanted them to use the right sort of music.
In fact he developed a special system to help his readers match each
psalm with a suitable mode and musical ethos. A closer examination
of the poem in Figure 13.1 shows some peculiar marks in the left-
hand margin, one next to each of the "tunes." There are three different
marks. Parker refers to them as the "sharp accent," the "grave accent,"
and the "circumflex accent" (although the last one resembles the modern tilde more than it does the modern circumflex). Every psalm text
in the final section of the psalter, from Psalm 101 onward, is furnished
with one of these marks. Each of the musical settings at the end of the
book also has a symbol of its own. Parker explains the use of these symbols in a note to the reader:

> For a difference of tunes and songs in this triple nature and diversity be
> used the three characters of the three common accents, as the sharp accent
> to joyful songs and tunes, the grave accent to sad, the circumflex accent
> to indifferent. Not yet by this meaning to prescribe a rule to prejudice
> any man's peculiar spirit or ear, for as there be diversities of tastes in men's
> palates: so be there in men's spirits, and so also in their ears. For what
> psalm or song one man's spirit shall judge grave and sad, some other shall
> think it pleasant. And what one man's ear shall think pleasant, another shall
> judge it sour and severe. I leave it to every man's spirit as God shall move
> him: and to every man's ear, as nature shall frame him. I set these only in
> example, for that it agreed to my understanding inwardly, and to mine ear
> outwardly.

In other words, Parker's three "accents" are suggestions rather than
prescriptions. If he had Tallis's specific settings in mind, this is also
the earliest surviving account of a personal response ("to mine ear")
to Tallis's music—which was followed very shortly, near the end of
the 1560s, by a patron's delighted reaction (see Chapter 16) to the new
"song of 40 parts." It is no surprise that (say) Tallis's sixth-mode psalm
setting, with its sonorous F major chords and suave modulation to
the flattened seventh, might have evoked delight or contentment to

some Elizabethan ears rather than weeping or wailing. The psalms, like any great collection of poetry, also have an emotional spectrum much broader than "joyful," "sad," and "indifferent." Parker is inviting musicians to take a flexible approach to them. This is necessary in any case because his psalm texts are in a variety of poetic meters and some of them do not match with the modally "correct" tunes given in the book.

Anyone who tries to sing from the book will quickly encounter an even more serious problem: twenty-five of Parker's psalm texts, one-sixth of the total, do not fit with any of the music at all.[9] They simply cannot be sung using the existing materials in the book. Parker was eager to experiment with unusual metrical forms, and a number of them have no parallel in Tallis's music, which sticks to a handful of relatively conventional meters. Tallis's settings of the "eight tunes" appear to be a set of samples or exemplars, not an exhaustive repertory for singing Parker's whole psalter. There is almost a sense that they were added as an afterthought; they are far from a perfect match with this "psalter in metrical verse." The archbishop had a penchant for systematic classification and taxonomy—in musical modes and in many other matters—but it is hard to know from this document whether Tallis felt the same way, or to what extent the two men were even working together directly.[10] It is entirely possible that Parker took the psalm settings from some pre-existing source without asking Tallis's permission, or even that the music was put there by the enterprising John Day to boost the commercial value of the book.

Whether or not Tallis shared Parker's ideas about the "nature of the eight tunes," his individual psalms show a range of expressive musical techniques. Perhaps the most famous is the psalm in the third mode. It was chosen in 1906 for inclusion in the *English Hymnal* by Ralph Vaughan Williams, who also used it in 1910 as the basis of his *Fantasia on a Theme by Thomas Tallis*. This is the mode, according to Parker, that "doth rage: and roughly brayeth." In his Latin account of the modes, it "is indignant and insults harshly." His own designation of "sad" was a word whose sixteenth-century meaning extended to "serious" and "severe," not just "melancholy." Parker chose to match Tallis's music with an indignant text, the beginning of Psalm 2: *Why do the nations so furiously rage together, and why do the people imagine a vain thing?*

Why fumeth in sight the Gentiles' spite,
in fury raging stout?
Why taketh in hand the people fond,
vain things to bring about?

Listeners familiar with the lush, soaring orchestration of the twentieth-century fantasia might find it hard to associate Tallis's tune with rage and fury, but it certainly has a sense of rhetorical immediacy that lifts it beyond the more conventional psalm tunes of its day. This may also be the most rhythmically free piece Tallis ever wrote. Parker's text is in the ubiquitous "common measure" or "common meter," 8.6.8.6., the most frequently used meter in Elizabethan psalms, hymns, and ballads, but the music does not follow its simple iambic pattern at all. Tallis moves freely between phrases of three, four, six, and very often five beats. (Vaughan Williams felt the need to simplify the rhythm in the *English Hymnal*, suppressing all of Tallis's five-beat phrases and nudging the music into more regular form.) The shape of the music is determined by the shape of the text, and even more specifically by the composer's interpretation of that shape. Tallis revisits this sort of rhythmic liberty from time to time in other contexts, but on the whole it is quite foreign to his more elaborate polyphonic style, where the complex ebb and flow of harmony demands a regular alternation of strong and weak beats. *Salve intemerata*, for all its expansive glory, spends almost every moment in strict conformity with an underlying rhythmic pulse. Tallis's third tune does not. His tune also has little in common with the plain jog-trot rhythms of many English metrical psalm tunes, the sort of singing that his more snobbish early-seventeenth-century successors derided as "Geneva jigs" and "Beza's ballets."[11] He takes a very different approach to setting a simple poem in iambic verse. In many ways the closest parallel is with his hymn *O nata lux* (see Chapter 14), although the rhythmic displacement in the Latin piece is somewhat more conventional, never breaking the underlying framework of triple time.

Tallis's harmonization of the third tune is also unusual. In fact it seems to have been colorful enough to confuse John Day and his music typesetters, who did not have all the correct symbols in their font and were clearly not prepared in general for the challenge of working with such a variety of musical scales. The result at this point in the Parker psalter is a bizarre jumble of accidentals, including some apparent absurdities like A-sharp key signatures.[12] It can be difficult at times to figure out what Tallis intended in his original composition, especially in the top part. The outer voices serve as an embellishment of the third-mode tenor melody, which is based on E with the characteristically pungent "Phrygian" semitone above it. Much of the piece unfolds around a subtle interplay of G sharp and G natural. In the Vaughan Williams fantasia, these false relations are played for atmospheric beauty, but Tallis also gave them an abruptness and an edge that are not at all out of keeping with the harsh tone of the psalm.

Parker made a wise choice when he encouraged his readers to try out different musical settings to suit "diversities of tastes." Tallis's eight psalms are not dry textbook illustrations of the eight classic modes, an idealized system that often had little in common with the ways in which real Tudor composers handled melodies and chords. The Parker psalms are not pure diatonic "white-key" compositions without sharps or flats. Accidentals are used freely to make cadences (as in tunes 7 and 8), to help melodies flow more smoothly (as in tunes 1 and 4), and for purely expressive purposes (as in tunes 3 and 6.) These eight tunes provide a flexible resource for psalm-singing in various meters and various moods. In fact Tallis was not the only élite composer of his generation to undertake a project of this sort. John Sheppard composed a larger group of harmonized psalm tunes sometime around 1550, forty-eight in all, built on Sternhold's more familiar English texts. Only the top voice of Sheppard's English psalter has survived. It is found in an early Elizabethan partbook, BL Add. MS 15166, originally one of a set of four, where it is copied together with the top part of Tallis's Parker psalms. The same manuscript also contains a generous selection of anthems, including half a dozen by Tallis. Such a document offers a hint of how these psalms might have been received in their own time: copied into separate partbooks for ease of use by multiple singers, alongside some of the most innovative music to come out of the mid-century English reforms.

How did Parker become acquainted with Tallis's music in the first place? Such a prominent court composer, and such a pillar of the English musical establishment, would have been an obvious choice for someone in Parker's position in the 1560s. It was logical for him to look directly to Elizabeth's court for musical inspiration. He had an almost lifelong bond with the queen which had begun when her mother Anne Boleyn entrusted him shortly before her execution in 1536 with the young girl's spiritual care. By the time his psalm book was published three decades later, she was Supreme Governor of the Church of England and he was her highest-ranking clergyman. Despite their close personal association, they did not always agree on political or religious matters. If anything, she was too conservative for him. She seems to have thought that a married archbishop was somewhat beyond the pale, and the famous anecdote has her speaking to his wife Margaret (née Harleston, from his native Norfolk) in decidedly frosty terms after dinner at their home: "Madam I may not call you, and mistress I am ashamed to call you, so I know not what to call you, but yet I do thank you."[13]

Many of the controversies that plagued Parker during his tenure as archbishop had to do with the everyday furniture of worship, especially with church vestments, which became the subject of long and convoluted disputes. The fierce Elizabethan struggles over "unity of apparel" among the clergy may seem petty in retrospect, but they stood in for much deeper disagreements about reform, authority, and tradition. After several years of exhausting debate Parker said, quite characteristically, that his colleagues found him "too earnest in moderation."[14] He was not a man of extremes, and he seems to have been happiest when he could withdraw from the political battlefield and spend his time with books and manuscripts instead. Lambeth Palace, the official residence of the Archbishop of Canterbury, became an important historical archive and a center of scholarship during the decade and a half Parker spent there. One of his collaborations with John Day was the production of the first ever Anglo-Saxon typeface, which he used in the late 1560s to publish editions of ancient English documents.[15]

Parker's linguistic and antiquarian skills made him an excellent candidate for translating the whole psalter and matching it with a group of high-quality musical settings. In fact he lacked only one qualification: he was not a very good poet. He rather disarmingly uses the actual word "doggerel" on the first page of his preface to the reader, and it can be taken as fair warning. He manages some impressive technical feats of versification—a number of which make it even harder to sing his texts to Tallis's music—but the end results are not much better than the ubiquitous "Sternhold and Hopkins" psalms that were sung in so many pious Elizabethan households. French-speaking Protestant congregations were lucky to have the likes of Clément Marot writing their new metrical psalms. The situation in England was less fortunate. Parker also could not have known that many of his vocabulary choices would quickly become outdated; a line such as (in Tallis's fourth tune) "His face with praise let us prevent: his facts in sight let us denounce" has quite different connotations for the modern singer.

The other obstacle to the full enjoyment of these earliest printed works by Tallis is the way in which they are printed. John Day was eager to take on technical challenges—new fonts, monumental illustrated volumes, specialized diagrams—but his assistants and proofreaders were not always up to the task. His music books are plagued by small mistakes and inconsistencies. The standard of typesetting is often low enough to have been confusing to any amateur musician and annoying to any professional. In Tallis's third tune, for example, the strange constellation of accidentals is only part of the problem. A group of inexperienced singers might have found it difficult even to begin the psalm together, since the three higher parts have an initial rest and the bass is incorrectly told to start right away. The bass part is also given a bizarrely misprinted clef in the last line and, adding insult to injury, a wrong note value during the final cadence of the piece. Similar problems arise in other Day publications containing music by Tallis. The low bass part of *Hear the voice and prayer* (which descends several times to a bottom F) has a rubric declaring that "This bass is for children." *If ye love me* is manipulated to end with some brazen consecutive fifths that serve no musical purpose. Tallis also joins the roster of distinguished composers who were plagiarized either by Day or by his music arranger Thomas Caustun: the last section of Tallis's large Te Deum reappears, with a thin veneer of strategic editing, as part of a service by Caustun printed in Day's 1565 collection of English church music.[16] Almost every work by Tallis that appears in one of Day's prints is mangled in one way or another.

Tallis's contemporaries seem to have noticed a general lack of quality control in these books. John Wolfe, another Elizabethan music printer, complained about "the false printing and evil paper which the said

John Day useth."[17] The composer Thomas Whythorne (who served in Archbishop Parker's private chapel at one point and even set two of Parker's English psalms to music) recalled a heated exchange in the early 1570s with Day, who had just printed one of Whythorne's song-books and was not selling it as quickly as he would have liked: "At my return again to London, I went to my printer to know of him how my music went away out of hands, and he told me that it was not bought of him so fast as he looked for. Then I told him that I thought that it was two causes that he sold them not as yet very fast. The first was because he had printed music heretofore the which was very false printed, and therefore it was a discredit to that which should follow in print hereafter."[18] (The second cause, Whythorne said, was lack of proper advertising.) Some surviving copies of Day's "very false printed" materials from the 1560s have been furnished with handwritten corrections. Most have been left uncorrected, leaving us to wonder who used the books and how they might have dealt with the various flaws in them.[19]

Placing music in the hands of a printer was not a guarantee of increased accuracy, much less of the composer's direct involvement, although both of those advantages will emerge in the next chapter as Tallis and Byrd begin supervising the publication of their own sacred songs. What the act of printing could accomplish right away was the distribution of music to a larger audience than any network of manuscript copies could have allowed. As soon as Tallis's English sacred

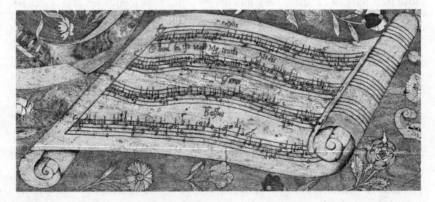

Figure 13.2   Tallis, *O Lord in thee is all my trust*, detail from Eglantine Table at Hardwick Hall. National Trust Images. Reproduced by permission.

works started to appear in print, they left the control of a handful of well-placed professionals and became available to a much broader range of musicians in church and at home. One of the most impressive surviving sources of Tallis's music is an indirect result of that process. Unlike all the other musical documents discussed in this book, it is not written or printed on paper. It is crafted in fine inlaid woodwork. This is a copy of the elegant little song *O Lord in thee is all my trust*, worked into an Elizabethan tabletop (Figure 13.2) at Hardwick Hall.[20] That particular piece of music circulated widely during the later sixteenth century in the printed forms sold by Day. Here it has quite literally found its way into the physical fabric of a house. These domestic musicians chose to make Tallis's music their own in an unusual manner by having it set permanently into a piece of luxury furniture, but other copies of *O Lord in thee is all my trust*, in its various versions, were just as present in printed form in hundreds (if not thousands) of less stately homes. Those printed copies were robust, popular, reasonably priced, and eminently accessible. By the end of the 1560s, Tallis's psalms and anthems had entered the age of mechanical reproduction.

CHAPTER FOURTEEN

The Cantiones *of* 1575

THE WORD "MOTET" FIRST APPEARED IN PRINT IN ENGLAND IN 1570. It is easy to miss because it is not actually in a book of motets. It occurs in the preface to a collection of French songs, the *Recueil du mellange d'Orlande de Lassus*, produced in London by the publisher Thomas Vautrollier. Vautrollier was a Huguenot refugee who had recently come to England, bringing a beautiful French music font with him. In his preface to the *Recueil du mellange*, he speaks about harmony and concord: "Harmony is represented in a lively way in a musical motet *[dans un motet musical]*, where, under the guidance of one part, the other parts hold to such a measure that, although they are all diverse among themselves, they are not discordant in any way." The musical technique he is discussing here is what a modern reader might call imitation or fugal exposition: one voice of a "musical motet" leads the way with a distinctive theme, and the other parts take up that theme in a lively, diverse, and harmonious fashion. Vautrollier is using these musical terms as an extended metaphor for political harmony in England. In his metaphor, Queen Elizabeth turns out to be the "one part" that gives form and guidance to the others.[1] Elizabeth was often the object of extravagant allegory and symbolism during her life. Authors compared her to the phoenix, the moon, the goddess Minerva, and many other colorful figures. Here she is being compared to something more obscure, but, in a way, much more down-to-earth: the leading entry in an imitative motet.

Tallis. Kerry McCarthy, Oxford University Press (2020). © Oxford University Press.
DOI: 10.1093/oso/9780190635213.001.0001.

In 1575, five years after Vautrollier used this metaphor, he published a book of motets by Tallis and Byrd.[2] This time the entire production was dedicated to Elizabeth, who had just granted the two composers a monopoly for the printing and importation of music. The title page (Figure 14.1) and the rest of the prefatory material does not use the word "motet" at all. The music is described in other terms.

> Songs which from their text are called sacred,
> in five and six parts,
> by the English authors Thomas Tallis and William Byrd,
> Gentlemen and Organists of the private chapel
> of the Queen's most serene Majesty.

We have come a long way from the scribe's terse note in the manuscript Harley 1709 (see Chapter 8) that there are "23 anthems in this book." This title page sets the mood for the rest of the publication: the focus here is on identity, courtly prestige, and the art of careful circumlocution. The book is not given the typical Renaissance title *Cantiones sacrae*, "sacred songs." It is named *Cantiones quae ab argumento sacrae*

Figure 14.1   Title page of the *Cantiones*, from the copy now at Trinity College Dublin (OLS 192.n.40). Reproduced by permission of the Board of Trinity College Dublin, the University of Dublin.

vocantur, "songs which from their text are called sacred." An English-Latin dictionary published in 1570 by the Oxford lexicographer Peter Levens defines *argumentum* as "a ditty of a song."[3] "Ditty" has taken on a different meaning in our own day, but among Elizabethan musicians it simply meant the verbal text that went with a piece of music. Byrd, writing in 1588, referred to the extra verses of a strophic song as "the rest of the ditty."[4] Thomas Watson, writing in 1590, described the translation method of his *Italian Madrigals Englished* as "not to the sense of the original ditty, but after the affection of the note."[5] The pieces in Vautrollier's book are "called sacred" because of their words, their ditty, their *argumentum.* This is an unusual way to talk about a collection of motets. It suggests several issues that may have been in the minds of the compilers, including the lack of precedents in England for such an anthology, a lingering uncertainty about the proper uses of religious music, and (perhaps most important of all) the fact that a number of these pieces were completely refitted with new texts before they went to press.[6]

The title page of the 1575 *Cantiones* goes out of its way to identify the composers as "English." The word has appeared before in publications such as the Parker psalter, where the title page declares that the contents have been put "into English meter," but here the authors themselves are named by nationality. They are also described as organists and gentlemen of the Queen's private household: not just accomplished musicians, but also distinguished by their royal service. The following page is taken up by a long dedicatory epistle from the two composers to Elizabeth, offering their music directly to her and praising her musical judgment in extravagant terms. It is the only musical dedication of the sixteenth century that speaks entirely in the first person plural. If Tallis and Byrd wrote this text themselves, at least one of them was well-versed in the arts of both courtly diplomacy and elegant humanist Latin. It is remarkable to see two Englishmen speaking to their own sovereign in a foreign language (albeit one that she read, wrote, and spoke fluently: she was still able to dazzle her court in the 1590s with a brilliant extemporaneous Latin speech in reply to a rude Polish ambassador who had come to harangue her about her foreign policy).[7] The composers' joint statement to her in the *Cantiones* is not just a personal letter to a patron. It is also a public performance for a much wider

audience. Tallis and Byrd invoke the learned authorities of their day—
"philosophers, mathematicians, architects of public affairs . . . poets,
natural scientists"—and launch a preemptive argument against "the bit-
terest enemy of the name of Music."[8] Like other Renaissance courtiers,
they are always anticipating objections, keeping escape options open,
and weighing the possibility of disfavor or failure. Their letter is followed by laudatory poems from other authors, speaking in praise of
music and in defense of English composers, who now dare to appear on
the international stage for the first time.

Luckily for all involved, this book of sacred songs is not in need of
much defense. It is a collection of first-rate music produced to a high
standard. Vautrollier did elegant work with his Pierre Haultin font and
his team of imported staff. He had been given a permit in 1574, just a
year earlier, to employ six "strangers" (foreigners) in his London work-
shop; the composers themselves also appear to have been involved at
several stages, from preliminary editing to last-minute troubleshoot-
ing.[9] The publication required the setting of a total of ninety large
blocks of type, each producing four pages of music. Almost half of
those large blocks were given stop-press corrections: in other words,
changes and improvements were still being made to them even after
the printing process had started.[10] There was an ongoing effort to make
the books easier to use, with constant adjustments to small details such
as the placement of accidentals, the direction of note stems, and the
numbering and indexing of pieces. Vautrollier and his staff were not
just creating an attractive book; they expected their book to be put to
practical use, and they clearly wanted that practical use to result in as
faithful a rendition of the music as possible. A few features, such as the
painstakingly thorough provision of leading-note sharps at cadences
and the very close attention paid to the underlay of the text, seem to
suggest that their target audience was the keen amateur singer rather
than the seasoned professional who knew the unspoken rules and was
used to sorting out such matters without much conscious thought.[11]

Tallis contributed sixteen pieces to the *Cantiones*. (His large bipartite
motet *Suscipe quaeso Domine* is indexed as two separate items, bringing
his official total to seventeen, like Byrd's.) Publishing such a substantial group of motets in 1575 was a fundamentally different endeavor
for him than it was for Byrd. He had thirty years' more experience

in composing, although that was not necessarily an advantage in the political climate of Elizabethan England. Most of his existing Latin-texted music had no place in an anthology that was dedicated to the head of the Church of England and issued in a tense atmosphere of international diplomacy. The rules of the game start to become clear as soon as we notice what is *not* in the collection. There is no music associated with any part of the Mass. There are no references to the Virgin Mary. There is no veneration or invocation of other saints. Those three considerations exclude almost every Latin-texted piece we have discussed so far in this book. If Tallis was simply gathering his best works, it is hard to imagine why he would have ignored something like his splendid six-voice *Videte miraculum*—"Behold the miracle of the Mother of God"—which, fortunately, was preserved in manuscript (see Chapter 15) by a private Elizabethan collector.

Once Tallis had picked his way through the ideological minefield of his existing works, what was left to publish? His sixteen contributions tell a complex story. Four or five of them appear to be versions of older liturgical pieces based on traditional pre-Reformation chants. These ritual works are adapted for use as free-standing motets, with texts reshuffled as necessary and passages of plainsong quietly removed or ignored. A number of other items by Tallis also seem to be older compositions that were revised and reworked for his anthology. *O sacrum convivium, Absterge Domine*, and the two settings of *Salvator mundi* all went through complex editorial journeys on their way to Vautrollier's print shop. These pieces are best known in their 1575 form, but they have also survived in a confusing tangle of other Latin, English, and textless versions, sometimes across many decades.[12] By the mid-1550s, the evergreen *O sacrum convivium* had already moved past its origins as an instrumental fantasia (see Chapter 9) and was being sung to its Latin words in a public procession; this tells us, among other things, that what we think of as Tallis's mature motet style was firmly in place by then.[13] Some of this music seems to have originated as an abstract contrapuntal fabric with no words at all, a luxury textile that could be tailored into various shapes as Tallis or his patrons desired. It is no great surprise to see the final results described in 1575 as "songs which from their text are called sacred." Byrd also did this sort of thing once in a while—his *Laudate pueri* turns out to be a Latin texting of an instrumental work—but almost all of his *Cantiones* seem to have been printed in their uncomplicated original state. Tallis was in a different situation. He was working through a diverse portfolio, drawing on as wide a range of music as possible and adjusting it to fit the needs of his new venue.

Not all of Tallis's works in this collection have such a convoluted history. Some of them are indeed just sacred songs, freely composed for devotional use. A number of pieces appear for the first time in the *Cantiones* without any trace of previous existence or revision: these include the nimble *O nata lux* with its rich, dissonant final cadence, and the supremely confident *Derelinquit impius*, composed on a text closely associated with Tallis's patron Henry Fitzalan, earl of Arundel (see Chapter 16).[14] Much of this material seems to have been newly written for inclusion in the *Cantiones*. The three pieces printed at the end of the book—*In ieiunio et fletu*, *Suscipe quaeso*, and *Miserere nostri*—are perhaps the most surprising of all. To judge from these motets, which were entirely unknown before their appearance in 1575, Tallis's musical imagination was stronger than ever at this late stage in his career.

The text of *In ieiunio et fletu* has to do with fasting and weeping, but Tallis avoids most of the traditional clichés of the penitential motet. This piece gets its effect from its rich and unusual harmonies. It exists in a state of flux: wandering back and forth around the circle of fifths, taking in major chords on E flat and A flat, on A natural and E natural, exploring the edges of the sixteenth-century tonal system and the spaces in between them. It has almost as broad a tonal compass as the motets of the *Prophetiae Sibyllarum* by Lassus, another great work of Renaissance chromaticism. The main difference is in the rate of harmonic change. Lassus revels in constant bold juxtapositions of remote chords, while Tallis generally prefers a gradual harmonic drift that leads the voice and ear to entirely unexpected places. The Elizabethan poet Spenser wrote late in life about the formidable goddess Mutability, who stood before the assembled court of heaven and claimed the highest place of all.[15] Tallis's motet is a study in mutability. Change reigns supreme, at least until the music settles into its relatively stable final section. The strangeness of *In ieiunio et fletu* is reinforced by its unusually low pitch. The deep bass part descends regularly to a bottom D, and the three middle voices are crowded into a baritone register just above it.

It is a sound-world that Tallis never pursued anywhere else to the same extent, although a few moments in his Lamentations (see Chapter 15) have a similar resonance. The very low notation of *In ieiunio* may have been purely pragmatic—writing the same music a fourth or a fifth higher would have required even more exotic chords with more sharps or flats—but Tallis must also have seen (and heard) the effects he could get from such an unusual set of voices. What he is cultivating here is a mannerist style, ready to go to extremes for the sake of heightened musical expression.[16]

Suscipe quaeso, the next piece in the collection, is a substantial motet for seven voices. Tallis brings in the seven parts gradually at the beginning, sometimes in leisurely pairs, sometimes one at a time, with the low bass (as so often in his music) reserved for last. This sort of elegant imitative exposition is what Vautrollier seems to have had in mind when he described the harmonious unfolding of a "musical motet." The whole thing owes a great deal to the style of northern European composers such as Clemens and Gombert, both of whom are named in the prefatory material to the *Cantiones*. Their music was circulating in England at the time and would have been well-known to Tallis. Their influence is audible in various details of *Suscipe quaeso*, such as the many cadences that are thickened and intensified by extra dissonances. It is also present in the general principle of the music: maximum variation within a consistently quite thick musical texture. Most of the voices are singing most of the time. There are none of the elaborate trio sections that break up a piece such as *Salve intemerata*. It is (surprisingly) the much younger Byrd who appears with the sparse, old-fashioned trios, just a few pages later, in his even more substantial motet *Tribue Domine*.

A persistent story has linked *Suscipe quaeso* with the ceremonies of Counter-Reformation penance that took place when England temporarily reconciled with the Pope in the mid-1550s. The idea is appealing, but it does not stand up well under scrutiny. Recycling an old work of public Catholic propaganda in a book dedicated to Elizabeth, head of the Church of England, would have been in poor taste at best and politically disastrous at worst. The primary impetus behind this motet seems to be something different. Like Byrd's *Tribue Domine*, which is a setting of words attributed to St. Augustine, *Suscipe quaeso* is built on a text associated with one of the ancient Church Fathers: in this case the

Synonyma de lamentatione animae peccatricis, a monologue by St. Isidore of Seville (c. 560–636) "on the lamentation of a sinful soul."[17] This was a highly unusual source for the text of a sixteenth-century motet. Tallis, like Byrd, seems to have been interested (or encouraged by a patron) in choosing words that went back in history, before the sectarian disruptions of the Middle Ages and Renaissance, to the era of undivided Christianity. What they have produced here are two new votive antiphons for a post-Reformation age. In fact Byrd's half of the pairing is much more archaic and nostalgic than Tallis's half.

The very last item in the book is another seven-part piece, Tallis's *Miserere nostri Domine*. In a publication designed to impress with technical skill, this complex canon is perhaps the most impressive work of all. Elizabethan musicians liked to write and perform canons. George Waterhouse, one of Tallis's late-sixteenth-century successors in the Chapel Royal, composed and collected more than a thousand of them on a single theme.[18] The core of *Miserere nostri* is an extraordinary four-voice canonic structure, printed with a set of short rubrics which explain how it works:

- "Four parts in one." (Four separate voices sing the same melody.)
- "Canon at the unison." (All four voices start on the same note.)
- "It multiplies by two." (The four voices sing the melody at four different rates of speed: with note lengths in their original form, multiplied by a factor of 2, by a factor of 4, and by a factor of 8.)
- "By ascent and descent." (Two of the voices sing the melody in inversion, with upward intervals in place of downward and vice versa.)

The slowest-moving part of the quartet spends half a minute holding its first note alone. While that one very long note is being sustained, the fastest-moving part sails through everything the slowest-moving part will sing in the whole piece. Meanwhile, the other two parts are proceeding at their own individual speeds. Above this whole interlocking construction, two high voices sing a much simpler unison canon, one following the other closely at the distance of just a few seconds. A freely composed seventh voice completes the seven-part texture. *Miserere nostri* is an imposing display of learned counterpoint, but it is such a successful work because it also makes a beautiful sound, even to the casual listener who might have little or no idea of its arcane inner workings.

There is a hint that Tallis and Byrd might actually have collaborated on this grand finale.[19] The principal part of the four-voice canon, the one with the original (shortest) note lengths and the fullest version of the melody, is attributed to Byrd in every surviving copy of the *Cantiones*, while the other six parts are always attributed to Tallis. The anomaly was not corrected at any point during the editing and printing process, despite plenty of opportunities to make changes. If the most important part of this showpiece was consistently given the wrong composer's name, that is the most embarrassing uncorrected error in the whole collection. It is intriguing to see Byrd's name on the leading voice of the canon, because the real achievement of *Miserere nostri* is contained in that one part: writing a single melody that will harmonize simultaneously with itself in four very different forms. It is conceivable that Byrd might even have come up with the central idea of this piece, then given it to Tallis in the form of a puzzle, to decipher with the help of rubrics and embellish with additional voices. (Sixteenth-century musicians in the Sistine Chapel cultivated the competitive writing and solving of clever canons as part of their group identity. It is not hard to imagine Gentlemen of the Chapel Royal doing the same.[20]) Byrd seems to have been more interested than Tallis in this sort of complex process. Byrd's equally sonorous motet *Quomodo cantabimus*, for example— also the fruit of a musical collaboration with an older musician, in this case with the Habsburg choirmaster Philippe de Monte—uses a similar method of inversion, with one voice singing a part right side up while another sings it, at a slight time lag, upside down.[21] The simple, transparent canon at the unison in the two uppermost parts of *Miserere nostri* is much more characteristic of what Tallis did in a number of his own works. Whether or not the two composers worked together on the music of this final piece, its verbal text may well be a hint at their broader collaboration. The most popular raw material for Elizabethan canons, including all 1,163 by the industrious Waterhouse, was the traditional chant *Miserere mihi Domine*: "have mercy on me, O Lord." The text of *Miserere nostri Domine* is similar, but it recalls the unusual first person plural of Tallis's and Byrd's dedicatory preface: "have mercy on *us*."

The composers make one more joint statement in their book of *Cantiones*. This statement is not addressed to the Almighty or to Queen

Elizabeth; it is addressed to us, the readers. It is a brief Latin poem, just six lines long, printed at the end of the volume after the last notes of *Miserere nostri.*

The authors of the songs to the reader.

We commend these first fruits to you, friendly reader,
as a woman, weak after childbirth,
commits her infant to the trust of a nurse:
for them, instead of milk, there will be the favor of your countenance.
Supported by this, they will dare to promise a great harvest.
Lacking this, they will fall by the honor of the scythe.[22]

With this striking and unexpected metaphor, the composers entrust their work to the good will of their readers. A very different image can be seen elsewhere in the book: the dedicatory epistle begins with a

Figure 14.2   Initial letter from the dedicatory preface of the *Cantiones,* addressed to Queen Elizabeth. Christ Church, Oxford. Reproduced by permission.

large, ornately printed initial letter S (Figure 14.2) that shows the grue-
some mythological figure of Saturn devouring his own child. Much
of the surviving documentation seems to suggest that their firstborn
"infant," the *Cantiones* of 1575, did not come to a good end. It is easy
to conclude that these motets were a commercial failure which finished
Tallis's public career on a note of disappointment and left Byrd unwilling to venture back into publishing for a long time. They certainly
never attempted another joint project of this sort; in fact the next document they addressed to the Queen, two years later, was a letter begging
for money to help support Tallis, who is "now very aged," and Byrd,
who has "fallen into debt and great necessities."

One important piece of evidence regarding the aftermath of the
project is found in an inventory made in 1583, detailing the contents
of Henry Bynneman's bookshop in London.[23] The inventory includes
"books of Byrd's and Tallis's music, in number seven hundred and seventeen," with a total value of £44 14s, a considerable sum of money
that was almost twice Tallis's annual salary at the peak of his active
career in the Chapel Royal. What is sitting on Bynneman's shelves
may simply be a large overstock of *Cantiones*, having failed to sell in
the eight years since their publication. A typical Elizabethan print run
was about a thousand copies, so 717 copies would likely have been a
large part of the original edition. If the price in the inventory can be
trusted, these books were three times as expensive per page as a typical book of English poetry sold in Bynneman's shop, and fifty percent
more expensive per page even than a Greek-Latin lexicon that used
multiple fonts in different languages.[24] A collection of motets was not a
sumptuous luxury item, but it was an unusually specialized book that
required many hours of expert work at all stages of production. Such an
expensive assessment would not be out of place.

It is also possible that some or even all of the "books of Byrd's and
Tallis's music" in the shop were actually *other* composers' music from
foreign countries, imported by Byrd and Tallis under the sweeping
terms of their music monopoly.[25] A rich hoard of that sort would suggest a successful venture into the international music trade, not a sad
tale of two failed entrepreneurs. In any case, the large amount of money
tied up in this inventory is a reminder that printed music was not a
particularly liquid asset. Owning £44 14s in polyphony was less useful

than owning £44 14s in gold or fine textiles or shipbuilding equipment. It is no surprise that the two composers petitioned the Queen (successfully, as it turns out) for a more consistent source of income in the form of rent on royal lands.[26]

Tallis and Byrd entered the printing trade in 1575 with a great deal of fanfare, including statements in various introductory poems that these sacred songs would be "dispersed among foreign peoples" and "published throughout the whole world." The *Cantiones* did not make their authors internationally famous, at least not for several more centuries. They seem not to have circulated much outside England at all, despite isolated hints that a few copies crossed the Channel: the collection was offered for sale in 1578 at the Frankfurt book fair, and one of Byrd's contributions to it, *O lux beata Trinitas*, appears in a late-sixteenth-century manuscript in Breslau (now Wrocław in modern-day Poland), a document which has apparently been lost since the Second World War.[27]

This music had a complicated afterlife, whether or not three-quarters of the copies in fact ended up unsold in a prestigious London bookshop. Elizabethan and Jacobean musicians chose to adapt a number of the *Cantiones* to texts in English, making them suitable for public use in church. Those reworkings are more or less all taken from the relatively conservative first half of the book; there were no attempts, as far as we know, to make Tallis's more experimental pieces such as *In ieiunio et fletu* or *Suscipe quaeso* into respectable English anthems.[28] At least some people clearly appreciated the *Cantiones* in their original form. John Baldwin had a full copy bound together with his own handwritten partbooks, which was high praise from such an opinionated and demanding collector. Henry Ediall, a skilled musician who served as a secretary to the Paget household, reported that singers met there in the late 1570s to perform "songs of Mr. Byrd and Mr. Tallis"—quite likely a reference to their newly published motets, or at least to the general sort of material that was collected in the anthology.[29] The Pagets were part of a tightly knit social (and musical) circle that would support Byrd in tricky political circumstances and produce Tallis's epitaph (see Chapter 17) just a few weeks after his death. The *Cantiones* were published with a heavy gloss of international ambition ("fearing the shores and voices of no nation"), but they seem to have been best received closer to home.[30]

CHAPTER FIFTEEN

John Baldwin's Partbooks

S HAKESPEARE'S GARRULOUS MISTRESS QUICKLY ONCE REMINDED
Falstaff of the time "when the Prince broke thy head for liking his
father to a singing-man of Windsor."[1] We owe much of our knowledge
of Tudor music to one particular singing-man of Windsor: the prolific
scribe John Baldwin, tenor lay clerk at St. George's Chapel and later
Gentleman of the Chapel Royal. He copied 421 identifiable pieces of
music in a variety of formats, from a bespoke presentation manuscript
of Byrd's secular keyboard works (My Lady Nevell's Book) to a careful
completion of some damaged pre-Reformation masses (the Forrest-
Heyther set).[2] At Windsor he was paid regularly "for the copying of
sacred songs," presumably church music in English, but most of the
surviving sources in his handwriting betray what seems to have been
his greatest personal interest: the preservation of complex Latin-texted
works, generally of very high quality.[3]

One of Baldwin's manuscript collections is an elegant set of partbooks now in the library of Christ Church, Oxford (Mus. 979–983).
This collection includes fifteen pieces by Tallis. Eight of them are ritual
works based on chant melodies. The rest are an eclectic group spanning much of Tallis's life, from the early *Salve intemerata* to the apparently quite mature Lamentations. The trajectory of Baldwin's career
gave him access to an impressive range of musical sources, possibly
including the Chapel Royal's own (now lost) collections of Latin liturgical music, and he made the most of the opportunity. He described

Tallis. Kerry McCarthy, Oxford University Press (2020). © Oxford University Press.
DOI: 10.1093/oso/9780190635213.001.0001.

another of his own manuscripts as "a storehouse of treasure," but the description applies just as well to the Christ Church partbooks. His distinctive identity as a scribe—equal parts antiquarian, connoisseur, and magpie—is a thread connecting us to a beautiful and specialized repertory, much of which would otherwise have vanished.

Baldwin chose to copy the Christ Church books on commercially printed blank manuscript paper that was the same size as the 1575 *Cantiones* and was probably issued under the same publishing license.[4] He clearly saw the two anthologies as complementary, and he went out of his way not to copy any music that was already present in the *Cantiones*. The single exception is Tallis's setting of *Dum transisset Sabbatum*, which Baldwin included conspicuously in his manuscript alongside the two classic early-sixteenth-century settings of the same text by John Taverner that launched the tradition of the great Tudor responsories. Otherwise there are no duplicates between the two collections. At a moment when English sacred music was beginning its glacially slow transition (which would not be completed for several centuries) from a culture of manuscript copying to a culture of commercialized print, Baldwin saw and understood the possibilities of both.

The core repertory of Baldwin's partbooks, and the really unique part of them, is a large group of liturgical works from the final years of the Latin rite in England. Baldwin rescued a substantial number of five-voice and six-voice liturgical pieces from oblivion, much as the anonymous Gyffard scribes (see Chapter 11) did for their more modest four-voice counterparts. English musicians of Tallis's generation, unlike most of their contemporaries on the Continent, appear to have spent a good deal of energy on music for the hours of the Divine Office (including the long and complicated service of matins in the very early morning) as well as on music for the Mass. Tallis himself played an important role in creating that repertory—though apparently not as important as the role played by his prolific colleague Sheppard, who left a large hoard of hymns and responsories for the Office, including more than thirty which are found only in Baldwin's partbooks. Baldwin is so familiar with Sheppard's work that he sometimes refers to him simply by the letter *S*. The index in his partbooks, which he left incomplete at his death, begins with the five-voice and six-voice works of Sheppard before continuing on to a handful of other composers. He never got around to indexing Tallis's music, but it is clear from the content of the books that he held it in high esteem.

Tallis and Sheppard served together as Gentlemen of the Chapel Royal during the brief restoration of Catholic worship in the mid-1550s, and they seem to have collaborated to some extent (then if not earlier) in producing Latin liturgical music.[5] They rarely set the same texts. In fact the surviving repertory shows some signs of having been a carefully assembled cycle that covered important events of the church year. It was a somewhat abbreviated year: all of this seasonal music, without exception, was written for the span of about seven months between All Saints' Day on the first of November and the feast of Corpus Christi in late May or June. That corresponds with the annual schedule of the Tudor court (see Chapter 5), which effectively adjourned each year for the monarch's summer travels and reassembled in October. The full Chapel Royal was not required to be in residence during the summer months, which would explain the total absence of liturgical works for important events such as the mid-August feast of the Assumption.[6]

Baldwin's partbooks include a group of eight pieces by Tallis in this ceremonial tradition:

> Responsories
> *Videte miraculum* (Candlemas)
> *Dum transisset Sabbatum* (Easter)
> *Loquebantur variis linguis* (Pentecost)
> *Homo quidam fecit coenam magnam* (Corpus Christi)
>
> Hymns
> *Adesto nunc propitius* (even-numbered verses of *Salvator mundi Domine*) (Christmastide)
> *Haec Deum caeli* (even-numbered verses of *Quod chorus vatum*) (Candlemas)
> *Tu fabricator omnium* (even-numbered verses of *Iesu salvator saeculi*) (Eastertide)
> *Solemnis urgebat dies* (even-numbered verses of *Iam Christus astra ascenderat*) (Pentecost)

This is music for five, six, or seven voices, some of it quite substantial. Each piece is based on a chant melody, set in evenly-measured notes in a single part while the other voices weave a continuous web of polyphony around it. This technique helped to avert what could have been a serious problem with the survival of these works. Baldwin's set of partbooks, like so many of the sets we have seen, is not preserved intact. There were originally six books, of which only five remain. Fortunately, many of the parts in the missing volume—the tenor book, Baldwin's own voice part—were traditional plainsong melodies which can easily be recovered from contemporary sources. Tallis's responsories and hymns are monumental elaborations on those chants. The world of this music is the world of the old *Antiphonale* (see Chapter 7), further enriched with complex polyphony, as illuminators added layers of pigment and gold leaf to already ornate liturgical books.

One of the most memorable pieces in Baldwin's collection is Tallis's six-voice responsory *Videte miraculum*. Figure 15.1 shows the beginning of the top part in Baldwin's distinctive handwriting. The text, with roots reaching back to the fourth century, is a meditation on the miracle of the virgin birth.[7] We have already seen the chant on an illustrated page of the *Antiphonale*, Figure 7.2, designated for vespers on the eve (1 February) of Candlemas. Unlike Tallis's small four-voice responsories in the Gyffard partbooks, *Videte miraculum* does not set the sections of the piece that are entrusted to a select group of skilled solo cantors. Here Tallis takes the more modern approach, favored among English composers by the mid-sixteenth century, of setting the words sung by

Figure 15.1 *Videte miraculum*, detail of treble part, in the Baldwin Partbooks (Oxford, Christ Church, Mus. 982, f. 100v). Christ Church, Oxford. Reproduced by permission.

the whole choir. The whole choir in this case may well have been the full musical ranks of the Chapel Royal, assembled in the presence of the monarch for the great festival that marked the conclusion of the extended Christmas season.[8]

Tallis's setting of *Videte miraculum* is made up of three large sections of six-voice polyphony, alternating with passages of unison chant and gradually trimmed down with each repetition until only the final section is sung by itself. This process results in a large work, lasting nine or ten minutes even at a reasonably brisk tempo; it also offers the opportunity to hear some of the music several times and reflect on it in different contexts. The complex shape of the piece can be represented in tabular form:

[chant] [A] [B] [C] [chant] [B] [C] [chant] [C]

The underlying chant melody is never absent from the polyphonic sections of *Videte miraculum*, not for a single moment. It marches along in steady semibreves, providing Tallis with a number of restrictions and a number of opportunities. The first thing it offers him is a non-negotiable tonal center, with the distinctive and quite un–modern semitone just above the final E on which the plainsong ultimately comes to rest. Tallis did not shy away from E-based or "Phrygian" modes in his music. In this regard he was unlike some other sixteenth-century English composers, including Byrd, who was a great admirer of what his predecessor William Cornysh had called "subtle semitones" but who almost never built a whole piece around this sort of scale.[9] Tallis seems to have welcomed it, whether it was imposed or freely chosen. The "Phrygian" scale with its characteristic flat second degree is central to a wide range of his works, from the Lamentations to *Salve intemerata* to the famous third tune of the Parker psalter. *Videte miraculum* is an example of this tonal arrangement in its purest form.

Another thing provided by the core melody of *Videte miraculum* is a regular rate of harmonic change, an underlying harmonic rhythm. Tallis responds to this framework at the beginning of the piece by setting up a regular series of dissonances against the steadily moving chant, generally falling on every other semibreve. The dissonances are quite often the poignant major-seventh suspensions involving E and F which are directly suggested by the plainsong. There are ten of those suspensions in the earliest part of the piece alone, from the opening bars through the words *concepit virgo*. The effect is haunting. It also has a sense of inevitability about it, a sense that can be experienced by finding a good recording and simply singing along with the slow-moving plainsong as the other five parts unfold around it. It is the closest we will ever come to hearing this particular melody, and its inherent musical possibilities, as Tallis himself heard it.

The musical shape of the whole piece is implicitly linked with the contour of the chant: not just the lingering around semitones in the first part, but also the urgently repeated higher notes in the central section, which Tallis uses as the scaffolding for an unexpected chordal gesture at *stans onerata* and an invocation of great intensity on the name of Mary. A single exceptional B-flat in the chant leads to a brief but colorful shift of tonality. When the chant offers an attractive bass line, as it does near the end at *quae se nescit*, Tallis does not hesitate to give the bass part a lengthy rest and let the plainsong take over its duties. He adapts little fragments of the plainsong and works them into the other parts. (He pursues this technique much further with some other pieces in Baldwin's collection: the entire second half of the sunny and extroverted *Homo quidam*, his responsory for Corpus Christi, is based on an unusually promising imitative figure contained in the chant.) This is music written in a strict traditional style, but it is not music written by a person with his hands tied. It is as full of freedom, flexibility, and invention as anything Tallis ever composed.

Videte miraculum belongs to a tradition of chant-based liturgical music that had already been going on for many generations in England. This piece is not too far removed in spirit from the eleventh-century *organa super responsoria* (polyphonic elaborations of responsory melodies) in the Winchester Troper, a collection that includes a setting of the very same chant. In some ways it is just an unusually elaborate and stylized version of something that took place, to varying degrees, in thousands of pre-Reformation churches: vocal improvisation "upon the plainsong," the art of singing impromptu counterpoint against a familiar melody. To practice this art successfully, singers had to respond to the plainsong and create attractive and fluent lines that merged well with it. Once again, a useful witness to the living tradition is found in the Waltham Abbey manuscript (see Chapter 3), with its counterpoint lessons by the fifteenth-century composer Leonel Power. Just one thing is missing from Power's systematic guide to harmonizing chant melodies: he makes absolutely no mention of any kind of dissonance. Musicians who use his method will produce a euphonious fabric of thirds, sixths, tenths, and rather little else. The luxurious and relentless suspensions in the first part of *Videte miraculum* come from a different world. This is an expressive device used by Continental musicians of Tallis's generation, composers such as Morales, Crecquillon, and Gombert. They most often used it for texts of penitence and lament. For Tallis, it meant something else: it signified mystery.

Another responsory in Baldwin's collection expresses a very different mood. *Loquebantur variis linguis* is sung at vespers on the feast of Pentecost. Tallis may well have chosen the rich seven-voice texture as a symbolic representation of the seven gifts of the Holy Spirit. In any case it effectively depicts the clamor of the apostles as they try out their new gift of preaching in various languages. The music is littered with false relations and dissonant notes sounding against their resolutions. When seven independent voices are in play in this style, one of them will almost inevitably cause some contrapuntal mischief. (Morley criticizes the resulting rough discord as an archaic "fashion" of the earlier sixteenth century and says that it was "devised to be foisted in at a close [a cadence] amongst many parts . . . for though the song were of ten or more parts, yet would that point serve for one."[10]) Baldwin admired the glorious noise of *Loquebantur* enough to copy it twice; it appears in score format in his "commonplace book," now RM 24.d.2 in the British Library. He may well have been interested in seeing the inner workings of Tallis's polyphony by viewing all seven parts on a single page. He also copied out a number of other substantial works in score along with it, including Marenzio's ten-voice madrigal *Basti fin qui le pene*, excerpts from Byrd's ten-voice Great Service, and the eight-voice motets exchanged by Byrd and Philippe de Monte.

Baldwin's collection of Latin liturgical music includes a group of hymns by Tallis which are closely linked to his responsories. The hymn *Quod chorus vatum*—the text invokes the chorus of Old Testament prophets who foretold the birth of Christ—is, like the responsory *Videte miraculum*, music for vespers on the eve of Candlemas. The two pieces are meant to be sung in immediate succession. Tallis follows standard

Tudor practice by setting only the even-numbered verses of the hymn; the first words of his setting are not actually *Quod chorus vatum* but *Haec Deum caeli*, the beginning of the second verse. The odd-numbered verses would either have been sung to their original plainsong, elaborated upon at the organ, or improvised upon in simple polyphony.[11] Tudor keyboard settings of hymn verses, including the few surviving examples by Tallis himself (see Chapter 9), give us some idea of how this alternation would have sounded in practice.

The plainsong melodies used in Tallis's hymns are straightforward, usually with just one or two notes per syllable. They would have been familiar tunes to many sixteenth-century musicians. Tallis always gives them prominence by setting them in the highest voice. (In *Iam Christus astra ascenderat*, the plainsong also appears in a lower voice, three beats later: he discovered that this particular tune could be made to form a clever canon with itself, given some judicious manipulation of note values and rests.) With the melody safely in place in the uppermost part, Tallis can experiment with various accompaniments and harmonizations. One of his most beautiful hymn settings is the final verse of *Quod chorus vatum*, where the bass sings a sevenfold ostinato, the same elegant little melody (with slight variations) miraculously made to interlock with each of the seven phrases of the chant in turn.

All of Tallis's Latin hymns include at least one verse in triple time. This often means an alternation of short and long notes in the plainsong melody, in step with the iambic meter of so many traditional Latin hymns. This was a powerful idea: using triple time to reflect the natural swing of poetry. It may even have had some underlying affinity with the way pre-Reformation English musicians sang these plainsong hymns in everyday practice.[12] In any case Tallis clearly found the technique rewarding, because he went on to use it in very different circumstances. It resurfaces in the 1560s in several of his English-language tunes for Archbishop Parker, and in his popular hymn *O Lord in thee is all my trust*, which became a classic in more than a century's worth of English metrical psalters, harmonized by generations of musicians including Kirbye, Peerson, Ravenscroft, and Playford.[13] This distinctive triple meter also reappears in a new form in the 1575 *Cantiones* with *O nata lux*, which makes no reference at all to plainsong and dispenses with convention by setting only the first verse of its hymn text. By that point in Tallis's career, the traditional setting of hymns had taken on a life of its own.

One of the most impressive works copied by Baldwin is linked to the old liturgical tradition in a different way. Tallis's *Lamentations of Jeremiah* use a text and a musical form drawn from the services of Holy Week. He appears to have been the progenitor of a local tradition of setting these gloomy words to music: he is the oldest English composer to have written polyphonic Lamentations, and almost certainly the first, followed by a distinguished and varied group that includes Byrd, Robert White, Osbert Parsley, and John Mundy, the son of Tallis's Chapel Royal colleague William Mundy. Tallis chose to set the opening section of the book of Lamentations, divided into two separate "lessons" (readings), as sung at the nighttime service of Tenebrae that launches the most intense and serious three days of the liturgical year. Various Elizabethan composers set other portions of the book, but they never returned to the verses set by Tallis; those lines seem to have been considered his own property. His Lamentations show an unusually expressive side of his musical style. The low pitch and closely woven harmonies are a perfect fit for the verbal images of weeping, solitude, captivity, and exile. The first of the two "lessons," *Incipit lamentatio*, is especially striking in the way it migrates around the sixteenth-century tonal system. The opening musical gesture is focused on E, the final cadence lands firmly on a chord of E major, and the central section (*Plorans ploravit*) is in B-flat a tritone away, the remotest point in a long journey away from home.

John Baldwin, the singing-man of Windsor, seems to have fancied himself as something of a poet as well as a music copyist. He ended one of his manuscripts with a sixty-line poem, dated 25 July 1591, in a rustic emulation of the fashionable alexandrine meter used by poets such as Sidney and Spenser.

> Read here, behold, and see, all that musicians be,
> What is enclosed herein: declare I will begin.
> A storehouse of treasure this book may be said,
> Of songs most excellent, and the best that is made,
> Collected and chosen out of the best authors,
> Both stranger and English born . . .[14]

These are not unlike the words that Robert Dowland (son of the famous lutenist and composer) used in his *Musical Banquet*, which he called a "variety of delicious Airs, collected out of the best Authors in English, French, Spanish, and Italian."[15] Baldwin's tastes were eclectic in the best sense of the word. They extended to music that was no longer politically suitable for public performance, from the Eton Choirbook and the votive antiphons of Fayrfax to the liturgical hymns and responsories that Tallis wrote during the final flourishing of the Latin rite in England. He was certainly eager to study contemporary works such as Marenzio's madrigals and Byrd's newly-minted Great Service, but much of his energy was spent on what his own generation would have considered "early music."

Baldwin's enthusiasm for older music was not just a private quirk of one scribe who seems to have had access to the Chapel Royal archives. It was part of a tendency that ran through much of Elizabethan society. Baldwin was a close contemporary of the tireless antiquarian and historian William Camden, whose stated purpose was to "restore Britain to its antiquities and its antiquities to Britain."[16] (The early-seventeenth-century satirist Thomas Earle, in turn, skewered the "Antiquary" as "a man strangely thrifty of time past" who "loves all things, as Dutchmen do cheese, the better for being moldy and worm-eaten."[17]) Even a musician such as Morley, who could hardly be accused of rejecting modern fashions, reached back into the theoretical riches of the fifteenth and early sixteenth centuries when he compiled his *Plain and Easy Introduction*. Baldwin's collections of music can be traced to the same impulse, which was one of the great triumphs of Elizabethan culture: the triumph of memory over political fortune.

CHAPTER SIXTEEN

Three Monuments

T HIS CHAPTER IS ABOUT TALLIS'S THREE MOST MONUMENTAL
works: the mass *Puer natus est nobis*, the votive antiphon *Gaude
gloriosa*, and the forty-voice motet *Spem in alium*. He seems to have
delighted in extremes of scale, both large and small. His 1575 anthology
features a number of elegant little pieces such as *In manus tuas*, some of
which barely take up a few lines of music in the original partbooks.
Such pieces are built on the same principle as the visual art of Tudor
court miniaturists such as Levina Teerlinc (who served under the same
four sovereigns as Tallis) and Nicholas Hilliard: fine workmanship on a
tiny canvas. The works in this chapter are at the other end of the continuum. They are unusually generous in their dimensions and almost
inexhaustible in their detail. They have come down to us in an assortment of late sources—almost all dating from after Tallis's death—so we
are left to solve some puzzles about their origins.

Tallis's seven-voice *Puer natus* mass remained more or less undiscovered until the middle of the twentieth century, when it was pieced
together from private copies made in the 1590s by the country gentleman Edward Paston and his prolific team of music scribes.[1] There
is nothing in those documents to point us to the original context of
the mass, which is unfortunate because it may be the most enigmatic
piece Tallis ever composed.[2] The tenor part of the mass, the fifth voice
from the top in the rich seven-voice texture, consists entirely of the
Christmas chant *Puer natus est nobis* ("Unto us a child is born"). Many

Tallis. Kerry McCarthy, Oxford University Press (2020). © Oxford University Press.
DOI: 10.1093/oso/9780190635213.001.0001.

other works by Tallis use a plainchant tenor, but those tenors are all arranged in a very simple, traditional way. This one is different. It turns out to be governed by a strange and unexpected code. The duration of each note is determined by the vowel to which it is sung in the original chant, with A (as in **na**tus) equal to one unit of length, E (as in pu**er**) equal to two units, I equal to three, O equal to four, and U equal to five. The unit is initially equivalent to a semibreve. In the course of the mass, it changes to various other note values, either longer or shorter. Things become even more complicated for the tenor in the second half of the mass: the chant is sung backwards in the Sanctus, the numerical code is inverted in the Benedictus (with the vowel U now producing the shortest notes), and the melody is radically redistributed in the last Agnus, with a complex interlocking scheme of notes that leaves the tune unrecognizable.

If Tallis ever did anything else as esoteric as this, he hid it so well that it has never been discovered. His method in the *Puer natus* mass recalls some unusually elaborate English works from the beginning of the six-teenth century, in which the tenor part is a cantus firmus organized according to complex rules or riddles—pieces such as Fayrfax's mass *O quam glorifica*, an arcane construction that appears originally to have involved the use of black, red, blue, and green notation.[3] In fact what we see in the surviving copies of the *Puer natus* tenor is most likely a dumbed-down resolution of something that was originally notated in a highly cryptic manner. This tendency toward the cryptic seems to have been common in academic demonstration pieces such as the *O quam glorifica* mass, which was submitted for Fayrfax's doctorate. Another product of the same English academic culture is the anonymous mass *O quam suavis* from around 1500, which survives in the Cambridge University Library in its original presentation manuscript, full of learned rubrics to be deciphered by the singers.[4] Even more tellingly, that mass is copied alongside an anonymous motet (*Ave regina caelorum*) that uses a code almost identical to the one later used by Tallis, in which the vowels A through U in the text of the tenor part produce five note values of increasing length.[5] There is no direct evidence that Tallis ever attended a university or sought a degree, but the structure of his own mass shows a close affinity with the *musica speculativa* that was cultivated at Oxford and Cambridge. Vowel codes of this type were not unique to music. They were popular among students of philosophy, who used them to learn and remember the syllogisms of Aristotelian logic. They also occur in the works of Tudor authors such as John Skelton, who hid behind them in a couple of politically delicate poems, and Humfrey Baker, who (like a number of late medieval scribes before him) offered them to help his readers perform mathematical tricks.[6]

The tenor part of the *Puer natus* mass recalls the arcane academic music of the early sixteenth century. The other six voices of the mass certainly do not. This may be a learned piece, but it has very little in common with the works of Doctor Fayrfax; it is playing by a different set of stylistic rules. There are no florid verses for small groups of soloists, no complex rhythms, no extremes of range, and almost no other devices that are characteristic of the past two generations of large-scale English church music. The mass shares its basic texture and scoring with Tallis's motet *Suscipe quaeso* (see Chapter 14): most of the seven voices are singing most of the time. At the core of this thick texture is the cantus firmus, sustained by the tenor in long (sometimes extremely long) notes, while the other voices weave a continuous web of shorter phrases around it. The effect in much of the mass, especially in the hypnotic setting of the Agnus Dei, is of large slabs of sound adorned with repetitive decoration. This music has a close parallel in an architectural feat such as the coffered Tudor ceiling of the Chapel Royal in St. James's Palace (see Chapter 6), with its interlocking recursive patterns stretching from wall to wall (Figure 16.1).[7]

When might Tallis have written such an impressive work? Its eccentric style does not point strongly to any specific decade. Knowing Tallis's taste for musical experimentation, he could easily have undertaken the project on his own, but it may well have been a commission or a ceremonial work for a special occasion.[8] One popular and well-explored theory points to an origin near the end of 1554, when Queen Mary was said to be pregnant with an heir. Her Spanish husband Philip had recently imported a large group of his own musicians, who sang mass together in early December with Mary's Chapel Royal. What could be a better fit for that festive winter special than a huge seven-voice setting of "Unto us a child is born"? The major flaw in this scenario is that the two choirs sang their joint service on 2 December, the first Sunday of Advent. Using an iconic Christmas chant when

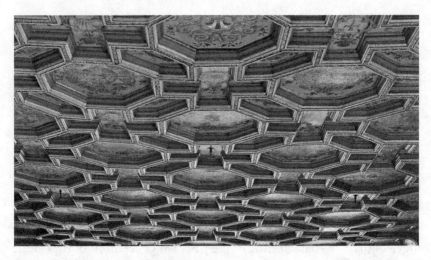

Figure 16.1   Detail from Chapel Royal ceiling in St. James's Palace, 1540. Royal Collection Trust / All Rights Reserved. Reproduced by permission.

the preparatory season of Advent had barely begun would have been a major breach of religious protocol under a regime that took such things very seriously indeed. Tallis also included an elaborate Gloria, a part of the mass that was not sung in Advent. It is appealing to link the *Puer natus* theme more generally to the news of the queen's apparent pregnancy, but that news was still dangerously uncertain, and it turned out to be false. Choosing to celebrate the successful birth of a *puer* (a reference to a specifically male child, after all) would have been jumping several steps ahead of reality. If Tallis or his patrons wanted to draw attention to the political implications of *Puer natus*, they could also have chosen some approach other than encoding the melody and burying it inaudibly in the depths of such a complex work. Renaissance composers, in England and elsewhere, were not generally so subtle when they wished to flatter monarchs and their dynastic ambitions. A more typical approach can be found in a piece such as Fayrfax's antiphon *Lauda vivi*, which features a crystal-clear threefold repetition of the name of "illustrious Henry the Eighth."

If the *Puer natus* mass was ever sung by an international group at court, it would have seemed equally eccentric to English, Spanish, and Flemish musicians. It does not sound particularly "Tudor" at all. It does not sound particularly "Continental" either, although its musical fabric is not unlike some of the more elaborate sonic tapestries woven by Willaert, Gombert, or Clemens. Perhaps its closest kinship is with another of Tallis's seven-voice works, *Miserere nostri*, where long-held notes and moving parts interlock in a slowly unfolding harmonic process. It may also have been intended, like *Miserere nostri*, to impress the cognoscenti with its unusually complex structure. The roots of this approach run very deep in Tallis's musical background: the Waltham Abbey manuscript he owned, for example, includes a fair amount of speculative and even esoteric material alongside its practical guides to sight-reading, notation, and improvisation. One anonymous chapter links musical proportions to the use of various colors of ink, as the original tenor of *O quam glorifica* seems to have done, and as Tallis's older contemporary John Tucke did in great detail when he studied and taught at Oxford in the early sixteenth century.[9] Another section of the Waltham manuscript waxes cosmic: "The seven spheres of the seven planets revolve with the sweetest harmony . . . Just as the universe is adorned by seven tones, and our music by seven notes, the framework of our body is united by seven modes when the body with its four elements is joined to the soul with its three powers, reconciled naturally by musical art. Thus man is called a microcosm, that is, a little universe."[10] The English music theorist Walter Odington also wrote at length about the music of the spheres. Odington's theories did not find their way into the Waltham collection—they are preserved in other English manuscripts of the same generation—but he comes closest to Tallis's working methods when he describes a way of composing melodies "according to their vowels": syllables with the vowel A are given the lowest pitch, syllables with the vowel E are a tone higher, and so forth.[11] Whether or not Tallis was influenced by specific examples of this kind, he was engaging in the same sort of speculative play when he wrote his seven-part mass on *Puer natus*.

Another monumental piece by Tallis is *Gaude gloriosa*, the largest of his votive antiphons in praise of the Virgin Mary. It outdoes all the others in sheer scale, with more unusual combinations of voices and bolder musical gestures. It takes twice as many people to sing this piece as it does to sing *Salve intemerata*, since almost all of the vocal lines are divided at various points. Whoever originally performed it must have had skill, stamina, institutional prestige, financial support, and an impressive architectural space to fill with music. The text is a series of nine invocations to the Virgin, each beginning with the word *Gaude* ("Rejoice" or "Hail"). Some of the most ancient Marian devotions, in the churches of both the East and the West, take a similar form. Canterbury Cathedral had a set of seven stained glass windows showing the seven joys of the Virgin, each with an inscription (unfortunately not the words set to music by Tallis) beginning *Gaude Maria*.[12] Those windows were present when Tallis sang there. They stayed in place until the Puritan preacher Richard Culmer climbed a ladder in 1643 and knocked them out with a pike. At the priory of Great Malvern in Worcestershire, a similar set of *Gaude* windows, installed around 1500, has survived intact and can still be seen today: eleven rather than seven, each with its own *Gaude* inscription, the last a splendid golden centerpiece of Mary being taken up to heaven by two formidable grisaille angels (Figure 16.2).[13] The large contrasting marker beads in medieval rosaries were called "gauds," and wills and household inventories from pre-Reformation England reveal that the gauds were often made of bright and showy materials such as gold, silver, or crystal. The English word "gaudy" can be traced back to the use of such glittering devotional objects. *Gaude gloriosa* expresses the same ideals in sound.

Tallis uses the ninefold structure of the *Gaude gloriosa* text to create musical variety. Each *Gaude*, as in the elaborate Malvern windows, is a vignette presented in new colors. (Tallis does not treat this as a strict rule: there is some enjambment and slippage between sections.) The entire second half of the piece is a study in sharply contrasting scorings, including the *pièce de résistance* of Tudor vocal orchestration, four intertwining high voices combined with low bass—a device that was pioneered by Taverner in his *Corona spinea* mass and used occasionally by the next generation of musicians to adorn works in the highest style.[14] Tallis indulges in some extremes of range, notably in the final Amen, where the treble line is suddenly confronted with a top A that seems to appear out of nowhere. This can be a challenge at the end of an eighteen-minute piece, especially if the performers have chosen upward transposition. *Gaude gloriosa* is also one of the extremely rare places where Tallis cultivated the naive word-painting typical of so many other Renaissance composers. There is sudden upward leaping of

Figure 16.2   Detail from *Gaude* windows at Great Malvern Priory, ca. 1500. Photograph from author's collection.

a seventh, a ninth, and a tenth at *adepta es thronum* ("you have attained the throne"), the growling of very low notes at *potestate diabolica* ("the power of the devil"), and a vociferous full choir entrance in mid-sentence at the word *omnia* ("all things"). There is nothing esoteric or inward-looking about this music. It is a work of magnificent display.

It is hard to tell exactly when *Gaude gloriosa* was written. Votive antiphons had already been popular for decades when Tallis began his career, and he could have composed this one at any time before traditional devotions to the Virgin were banned in the late 1540s. He could also have composed it when such devotions were restored for a few years in the mid-1550s. There was a lot of grand music-making in church during Queen Mary's reign, and Tallis's younger colleague William Mundy was cultivating this kind of work in the 1550s with his memorable *Vox patris caelestis*.[15] If *Gaude gloriosa* was also composed then, it was one of the very last pieces of its kind. English composers, even those working in the most conservative environments, had already begun turning their attention to other types of large-scale music as the first half of the sixteenth century went on. The big votive antiphon was gradually becoming a formal, ceremonial garment for the most special occasions, not a piece for routine everyday wear. *Gaude gloriosa* was somewhat old-fashioned when it was first sung, whether Tallis wrote it as an ambitious young musician or as a well-established member of the royal household.

There is a hint that it might have been composed relatively early in Tallis's life. In the 1970s, a fragmentary sixteenth-century copy of one of the two contratenor parts was found during building renovations at Corpus Christi College, Oxford.[16] The small booklet had been used as filler to reinforce a damaged wall. There are two unusual things about this fragment. First, it is set rather clumsily to English words which are completely unrelated to the original Latin. (The job of adapting the music to this new English text was almost certainly not done by the composer himself.) Second, some of the music in this single part varies from what is found in all other surviving sources of *Gaude gloriosa*. The part takes over whole phrases from the other contratenor line, sings many notes that are incompatible with the standard version of the work, and generally shows signs of having belonged to a separate and perhaps earlier version of the piece. The differences between these two versions are not the sort of changes introduced by meddlesome singers and copyists; they are the sort of changes made by a composer during a large-scale process of rewriting.

The mystery is compounded by the nature of the English text (*See, Lord, and behold*), which turns out to have been the work of Catherine Parr, the last and in many ways most fortunate wife of Henry VIII.[17] It was first printed in 1544 and circulated widely for the rest of the century as a popular devotional text. It is (rather surprisingly) Parr's translation of a Latin prayer by John Fisher, who had been executed less than a decade earlier for refusing to comply with Henry's plans for the Church of England. The words are bellicose and somewhat paranoid, well suited to the tense atmosphere during the last years of Henry's reign. If this English adaptation of *Gaude gloriosa* was made in the mid-1540s, when the new English text was fresh off the press and politically relevant, Tallis's original piece was already written by then. If the English version was made by a later musician with a taste for flamboyant polyphony and forceful devotional poems, its unusual musical variants still reveal *Gaude gloriosa* as a piece that Tallis had time to compose, release to the public, return to at some point, and revise thoroughly for continued use.

Wherever the English version of *Gaude gloriosa* came from, it is an important part of Tallis's story because it is proof that his contemporaries valued his music enough to adjust it to radically changing circumstances. Whether the retexting was done in response to a demand for a public ceremonial work in English in the 1540s or a demand for sophisticated devotional music that good Elizabethan Protestants could sing at home, it took some real effort to produce. Adapting *Gaude gloriosa* to a whole new text and writing it all out by hand would have taken a solid week's work, and it is no less challenging to sing in English than it is to sing in Latin. This music was not thrown out for being old-fashioned. In fact it was treasured for being old-fashioned. The archaic sound of the great votive antiphons, which unfolds here on the largest possible scale, was something that at least some people wanted to keep in their musical repertory as long as possible. Tallis himself seems to have prepared this work for performance with its original Latin text in at least two different situations. One of those situations could easily have been the new foundation of Canterbury Cathedral in 1541, with its ambitious and ostentatiously conservative musical program that seems to have included the singing of a votive antiphon every evening.[18] Another of those situations may well have been the restored Chapel Royal ceremonies during the exciting international exchanges of the mid-1550s. We can only imagine what Cabezón and de Monte thought of the piece if they ever heard it.

The forty-voice motet *Spem in alium* is Tallis's most monumental work of all, far beyond the scale of anything written by any other Tudor composer. Here he takes the traditional English five-part scoring and multiplies it by eight. The basic outline of the piece can be summed up quickly enough. Tallis begins by bringing in each of the forty voices one by one. The sound gradually makes its way through the choir like a wave, followed by the sudden full entrance of all forty parts together. Another wave of sound takes shape, now moving in the opposite direction. Once all forty voices have come into play again, there is an unexpected break in the whole musical fabric, and it then develops into a complex series of rapid-fire exchanges among four sets of ten parts. Each of those sets of ten is equivalent to the full strength of the Chapel Royal or the leading cathedral choirs of Tallis's day: a double-choir arrangement with five parts to a side. *Spem in alium* is conceived on such a massive scale that a ten-part ensemble of that sort is just one building block in an even larger edifice. After another moment of silence and a completely unanticipated shift from C major to A major, the music unwinds into a forty-part coda in grand style.

Many of Tallis's more experimental works leave us wishing for some kind of story: why they were written, where they were sung, and (not least) what people thought of them at the time. We are lucky to have a story for *Spem in alium*. It is told by Thomas Wateridge, a law student in London, who heard the tale in 1611 and wrote it down in his notebook.

> In Queen Elizabeth's time there was a song sent into England of 30 parts (whence the Italians obtained the name to be called the Apices of the world) which being sung made a heavenly harmony. The Duke of _____, bearing a great love to music, asked whether none of our Englishmen could set as good a song, and Tallis, being very skillful, was felt to try whether he would undertake the matter, which he did, and made one of 40 parts which was sung in the long gallery at Arundel House, which so far surpassed the other that the Duke, hearing of the song, took his chain of gold from off his neck and put it about Tallis's neck, and gave it him: which song was again sung at the Prince's coronation.[19]

This is a colorful anecdote, but it does not seem entirely untrustworthy. The "Prince's coronation" was the investiture of James VI's elder son Henry as Prince of Wales in June 1610 at Whitehall Palace (see Chapter 6), an occasion on which an English-texted version of *Spem in alium* was in fact sung. Wateridge tells the story the following year. He is unsure of the original patron's identity, but he chooses to leave a blank space in his notebook ("The Duke of _____") rather than inventing something. A performance "in the long gallery at Arundel House" suggests that the nobleman involved may have been Henry Fitzalan, nineteenth earl of Arundel, whose London residence was Arundel House. Fitzalan was a great patron of music and the dedicatee of Vautrollier's first musical publication in 1570, the book of French songs whose preface (see Chapter 14) compared Queen Elizabeth to the leading voice in *un motet musical*. He assembled a large musical collection which at his death in 1580 was inherited (along with his splendid country palace of Nonsuch) by his son-in-law John, Lord Lumley. Lumley was, not surprisingly, the earliest known owner of a copy of *Spem in alium*: an inventory of his books at Nonsuch made in 1596 includes an item described as "a song of forty parts, made by Mr. Tallis."

Wateridge's anecdote refers to an impressive Italian song "of 30 parts" which was sung in England, prompting an eager patron to see if any local composer could match it. There is no known 30-part Italian piece fitting that exact description, but there was an Italian musician who visited England "in Queen Elizabeth's time" with a 40-part work in hand.[20] Alessandro Striggio, court composer to the Medici in Florence, made a grand tour of Europe in 1567 with his 40-voice mass *Ecco sì beato giorno*.[21] The mass was sung to great acclaim at the Bavarian and French courts. Striggio wrote a letter to Francesco de' Medici from Paris in May 1567: "I thought that . . . since I am near England, a week's journey away, I would go and visit that kingdom and those virtuosi in the profession of music there." He later reported that he had "spent two weeks in London" and "received an infinite number of favors from Her Majesty."[22] These favors seem to have included a performance of his music. Striggio's 40-voice mass, like his related 40-voice motet *Ecce beatam lucem*, is a mirror image of Tallis's work: rather than eight groups of five singers, there are five groups of eight.[23] It is less harmonically adventurous and less rich in polyphonic detail, but it is a satisfying enough piece of music in its own right, and hearing it sung at court could easily have inspired Tallis to "set as good a song" himself.

Tallis's motet gained new popularity in the early seventeenth century when it was performed with the festive text *Sing and glorify* to celebrate Prince Henry's investiture. After Henry's death, the performance was repeated at the investiture of his younger brother Charles. One of the oldest manuscripts of the piece, now in the musical collection belonging to Gresham College, gives the Latin text *Spem in alium* and two versions of the English *Sing and glorify*, one in honor of Henry and one in honor of Charles.[24] The Gresham College scribe also notes that "these be all the ditties [texts] that ever was made to this song of

40 parts" and "this song was first made to a Latin ditty by Mr. Tho. Tallis." The existence of such a forty-part piece seems to have remained a lively presence in English musical folklore, including an improbable story about John Bull spending a few hours in a locked room with the "Lesson or Song of forty parts" and emerging with forty additional parts of his own making.[25] *Spem in alium* was still being recopied by English scribes in the eighteenth century, but by that point it was more an object of vague admiration than of real musical engagement. It was not actually sung again until the 1830s, when it was given a public sight-reading by members of the Madrigal Society. Reactions to its revival were mixed. A nineteenth-century reviewer writing for the *Spectator* dismissed the motet as a "mistake of a barbarous age." Other critics were more favorable, including one who attended the very first performance and found it "perfectly electrical."[26]

When *Spem in alium* was first performed, most likely in the late 1560s, it seems to have made a strong impression on the people who heard it. Quite apart from Wateridge's gossip about gifts of gold chains (conspicuously absent from Tallis's will a couple of decades later), he tells us plainly that Tallis's piece "far surpassed" its model. Composing in so many parts could have resulted in a display of grandiosity or sheer ballast, piled up in an attempt to outdo a musical competitor. *Spem in alium* is nothing of the sort. It is an exceptionally good piece of music in its own right. It does not appear out of nowhere as a bizarre anomaly among Tallis's works; in fact it gives him a chance to revisit some of his favorite techniques on a much larger scale. The rhetorical power of simultaneous rests in all voices is something he explored in English-texted pieces such as the anthem *Verily, verily, I say unto you*, the melancholy song *Like as the doleful dove*, and the canticles of the Short Service. Applied to forty voices rather than four, these sudden silences take on a new dimension. It is clear from tightly-wound manneristic works such as *In ieiunio et fletu* and the first set of Lamentations that Tallis was well aware of the possibilities of chromatic changes and unexpected chord progressions. He uses only one real chromatic shift in *Spem in alium*, the sudden forty-part chord of A major on the word *respice* ("behold!"), which may well be the most arresting moment in all of his music.

A massive work of this sort calls for careful structural planning, in a somewhat different way from the ornate votive antiphons of Tallis's earlier years. The logic of a motet for eight five-voice choirs has to be vertical as well as horizontal. It would have been very hard to write such a piece at all without thinking at least implicitly in harmonic terms from the bass upward. A forty-first part, an instrumental bass part that always follows the lowest sounding voice, has been transmitted in manuscript along with the rest of *Spem in alium*: the Gresham scribe calls the whole thing "the song of 40 parts with a thorough bass, made by Mr. Tho. Tallis." This bass line might have been added as an aid to Jacobean performances, but it is also distinctly possible that it was part of Tallis's original concept. Similar written-out bass lines were an integral part of other late-sixteenth-century pieces on a very large scale, including Striggio's own mass, various Venetian polychoral works, and a (now lost) forty-voice motet by Lassus.[27] Tallis may well have been thinking in the same terms. If he composed *Spem in alium* with a *basso seguente* part, he was influenced in a profound way by his European colleagues.

The earliest documented performances of Tallis's forty-part motet took place in thoroughly secular and even domestic locations: the long gallery at Arundel House and, a generation later, the banqueting hall at Whitehall Palace. The investiture of the Prince of Wales involved both a formal state ceremony in Parliament and a religious service in chapel, but the "song of 40 parts" was not sung during either of those events. It was sung at the investiture banquet.[28] By this point in English history, the most elaborate polyphony had migrated, more often than not, into the realm of worldly music-making and opulent private spaces. The Tudor architecture of Nonsuch, the (now destroyed) home of the first known copy of *Spem in alium*, is particularly evocative of this sort of performance.[29] The Nonsuch banqueting house was a detached freestanding structure built on an octagonal foundation. The main palace also featured two massive octagonal towers on either end, each with a grand eight-sided room inside. Figure 16.3 shows one of the eight-sided towers in a drawing made by the Flemish artist Joris Hoefnagel on a visit to England in 1568, quite possibly the year that *Spem in alium* was composed and first performed. Whether or not Tallis had those particular physical spaces in mind when he wrote a motet for eight equal choirs in circular motion and close interplay, his large-scale music is the product of a similar imagination. His most monumental pieces are works of architecture in their own right.

Figure 16.3   Detail from *Nonsuch Palace from the South*, Joris Hoefnagel, 1568. Victoria and Albert Museum, London. Reproduced by permission.

CHAPTER SEVENTEEN

Remembrances

TALLIS DIED IN LATE NOVEMBER 1585. THE MUSIC SCRIBE ROBERT Dow records the date as the 23rd, as does the Cheque Book of the Chapel Royal.[1] A related document in the Bodleian Library records it as the 20th.[2] In any case, there was no delay in replacing him: the vacancy created in the Chapel was filled on the 30th by the singer Henry Eveseed, who had been a chorister there as a boy. (Eveseed's son, also named Henry, followed his father into the Chapel but was thrown out in disgrace after a series of unfortunate incidents, including a vicious physical assault on Orlando Gibbons at the choir's annual feast in 1620.[3]) Tallis's age at his death is unknown, although one of the prefatory poems to the *Cantiones* of 1575 was already calling him an "old man" (*senex*), and Dow used the same word to describe the composer in the early 1580s. A letter to the queen in 1577 also described him as "very aged," an assessment which seems to fit well with some hints that he may have withdrawn from active musical life in his last decade. His will, written in the first person in August 1583, makes no comment on his age but declares that he is still "whole in body, of good and perfect memory." Among élite Tudor males who survived childhood and avoided a violent end, average life expectancy could reach as high as seventy.[4] Until some new document is discovered, we can only speculate about Tallis's longevity, but it is not at all unlikely that he lived to eighty, as Byrd and a number of his other Chapel Royal associates did.

Tallis. Kerry McCarthy, Oxford University Press (2020). © Oxford University Press.
DOI: 10.1093/oso/9780190635213.001.0001.

The wills of Thomas and his wife Joan Tallis have survived in full.[5] They both exist only in duplicate copies, filed away in probate records as a matter of official documentation, so they do not bear any original signatures or other original marks. It would be interesting to see how Tallis's signature changed in the decades after he added it to the Waltham music manuscript around 1540, but the only handwriting here is that of an anonymous legal scribe. Elizabethan wills can be challenging texts to interpret, full of legal jargon and convoluted attempts at diplomacy. This is not the case with Tallis's will, which is quite simple and accessible. He had almost no surviving family and only a modest set of arrangements to make. The household goods, large and small, were left as a single bequest to Joan, who listed them in all their colorful variety in her own will a few years later.

Tallis (unlike Byrd at the end of his own life) describes himself as "one of the Gentlemen of her Majesty's Chapel," the first of several references to the Chapel in his will. He makes a brief and generic declaration of faith—"I bequeath my soul unto Almighty God, our Lord and Saviour Jesus Christ, the only redeemer of the world"—once again showing a difference of tone from Byrd, who makes a similar statement but follows it immediately with his much more pointed intention to "live and die a true and perfect member of his holy Catholic Church, without which I believe there is no salvation for me."[6] Tallis gives instructions for his burial in the church of St. Alfege, his parish in Greenwich. St. Alfege was known as a musicians' church: half a dozen other singers of the Chapel Royal had already requested to be buried there, and when parish records start to appear around 1600, they are populated with familiar musical figures such as the younger Alfonso Ferrabosco and members of the Lanier family.[7] Tallis provides for charitable gifts to be given "to the poor people of the same parish" and makes the distinctly traditional choice to have his weekly alms distributed on Fridays. His share of the joint monopoly with Byrd "for the printing of musical books, songs, and ruled paper" is left to Joan; if she dies before the monopoly expires, it passes to "Thomas Byrd, my godson, the son of the aforesaid William Byrd."

"My company, the Gentlemen of her Majesty's Chapel" receive £3 6s 8d "towards their feast." Judging from Elizabethan churchwardens' records (and from Falstaff's bar tab in *Henry IV, Part I*), this gift would have supplied about fifteen gallons of imported wine or an impressive amount of high-quality food.[8] "Their feast" seems to have been the annual Chapel feast that took place in early summer before the singers went their separate ways for the court recess. The event was well-established enough by 1591 to merit a recurring gift of £3 from Elizabeth, recorded that year in a personal letter to her treasurer Thomas Henneage: "to the Gentlemen of our Chapel Royal the sum of three pounds of current money in this our realm, to be taken unto them as of our gift towards their feast, as about this time in former years hath been given unto them out of our treasure."[9] In this particular case, Tallis outdoes his queen in generosity.

Tallis also leaves money to Byrd and his Chapel colleague Richard Granwall, who were the overseers of the will, and to the one blood relative he mentions in the whole document, "my cousin John Sayer dwelling in the isle of Thanet." The name of John Sayer is the only currently available key to Tallis's family origins, so it is worth closer scrutiny.[10] The word "cousin" was often used in Elizabethan documents to describe people we would now call nephews and nieces. (Joan Tallis would follow that exact practice in her will a few years later, calling her own niece "my cousin.") The only person who fits the description in this particular case—a man named John Sayer, living in the 1580s on the Isle of Thanet, on the eastern edge of the county of Kent—was almost certainly a nephew, because he was a full generation younger than Tallis. John Sayer's father has a very well-documented ancestral family tree which contains no Tallises of any sort, so the only likely explanation is that John Sayer's mother, who was named Grace, was the composer's sister.[11] We catch a brief glimpse of Grace in her husband's will, made in 1550. Unlike her brother the musician (whose epitaph declares that "children he had none"), Grace had several sons and daughters. When her husband died, her eldest child, John Sayer, the man who would later receive a bequest from his uncle Tallis, was still underage.[12] The enduring family connection with this younger man suggests that Tallis may have been born or raised in Kent, where the Sayers lived and owned local land on the Isle of Thanet and elsewhere for many generations. In the 1550s, Queen Mary even granted Tallis extra income from a special lease (see Chapter 5) of a manor on Thanet; the location may not be a coincidence.

An origin in Kent would fit well with Tallis's youthful appointment at Dover Priory and his early affiliation with Canterbury. He was apparently not an only child, and, at least judging from his sister Grace's name, he seems to have come from a family with slightly unusual naming practices. Tudor women's names varied somewhat more than men's names, but sixteenth-century records are still dominated by a small handful of recurring favorites such as Alice, Elizabeth, Margaret, and Joan. The name Grace is seen far less often, especially in the early Tudor period. In the largest extant collection of English memorial brasses and brass rubbings from before 1600, there is only one that commemorates a woman named Grace; there are 119 Elizabeths and ninety-one Joans.[13] The other notable Grace of this generation was Thomas Cromwell's short-lived daughter, born not long after 1515. It was a less exotic choice than we see with the splendidly named Morpheta Kingsmill (last abbess of the great Benedictine abbey of Wherwell in Hampshire), or, later on in the century, the Gibbons brothers Orlando and Ferdinando, but it carries a hint of both piety and unconventionality that is not entirely out of place with what little we can discern of Tallis's inborn character.[14]

Tallis's godson Thomas Byrd, seven years old when the will was made, was the closest he had to an heir and was next in line for the printing monopoly. Young Thomas inherited his share of the monopoly a few years later, but he seems to have taken a rather different path. After a short time studying law and the humanities, he went to Spain and entered the English Catholic seminary in Valladolid, then was dismissed after two-and-a-half years "because he was not considered sufficiently suited to this institution."[15] He must have had significant musical training at some point, because by 1602 he was back in England, deputizing as Gresham Lecturer in Music for John Bull, who was (as usual) absent without leave. There is no evidence that he was ever involved at all with the music publishing industry, or with his father's vigorous revival of the monopoly in collaboration with the printer Thomas East.[16]

The other Tallis will, the one made by Joan in 1587 and recopied into the records of the Prerogative Court at her death in 1589, is a longer document that contains a more detailed account of the family's possessions and material circumstances. A few treasures are left to important friends and benefactors. A gilt bowl—gold-plated silver—with a matching cover is left to "Mr. Anthony Roper, Esquire," grandson of Thomas More and son of the musical patron William Roper who had supported the professional singers of London through the difficult years of the Reformation. Like his father and grandfather, Anthony Roper was a Catholic and a prominent lawyer. He also had a serious interest in music, working with the Dutch builder Lodewijk Theewes to create a luxury keyboard instrument for his own home, one that functioned both as a harpsichord for recreational music-making and as an organ for clandestine religious services.[17] Joan Tallis expresses her gratitude to him "in respect of his good favors showed to my late husband and me." She does not specify what these favors were, but it is easy to imagine that they may have included both social and financial assistance.[18] Another gift is self-explanatory: she leaves a large gilt cup, also with a matching cover, to William Byrd, along with three silver spoons for Byrd's son Thomas, "my husband's godson." The most valuable possession of all is her house in Greenwich, which goes to her only surviving blood relative, her niece Joan Payre. An adjacent property which she also owns (her first husband's will, made in the 1550s, called it "the tenement") is left to the musician Richard Granwall.

The recently widowed Joan speaks of Granwall with warmth and affection: "In consideration of the great goodwill and friendship which was between my late husband deceased and Richard Granwall, another of the Gentlemen of her Majesty's Chapel, as also for and in consideration of the continual and tender care he hath had of me ever since my husband's death, I being then very old and unable to take care for things myself, wherein I have found him to deal rather as a natural child toward me than otherwise . . . ." It is clear that Granwall played an important role in the family's life during their later years. He was a younger musician who had joined the Chapel in early spring 1572, just six weeks after Byrd; he and Byrd were always side-by-side on royal livery lists, where musicians were named in strict order of seniority, and they served together as overseers of Tallis's will.[19] In addition to the second property in Greenwich, which was being rented out at the time, Granwall received all the family's furniture and household items, spelled out in detail.

This part of the document offers a unique opportunity to look into Tallis's house and see the objects he used in daily life. There is an assortment of dishes and "a wine quart and a wine pint of the new fashion," as well as two linen tablecloths and six linen napkins. (Nearly all Tudor households of this class had linen napkins: an average of about sixteen, even more in large families or in homes that entertained many visitors at once. Thomas and Joan seem to have kept their social gatherings small.)[20] The kitchen is furnished with a brass pot, two spits for cooking meat, and a set of kettles in various sizes. There is a fire screen in front of the parlor fireplace, a fire shovel, a pair of tongs, and two andirons to support burning logs. There are "two Venice carpets" and "four flowerpots of pewter." There are sheets, towels, and pillowcases, including what Joan calls "two pair of flaxen sheets of mine own spinning." The large bedstead, surrounded by a set of curtains, is made up with a featherbed, a bolster, two pillows, two blankets, and "one coverlet of tapestry of the story of a shepherd." Bed curtains were relatively unusual in Tudor wills: only one out of every six bedsteads was furnished with them.[21] Coverlets with woven narrative tapestries (unlike the more usual dyed, painted, or patterned coverlets) were even rarer. The one described by Joan seems to have been one of the few real luxury items in the house. This sort of coverlet, which took skilled weavers many hundreds of hours to produce, would have been imported from Flanders or northern France; the "story of a shepherd" was quite likely a scene from the life of the shepherd Gombault and his love Macée, an especially fashionable subject in sixteenth-century tapestry. The only disappointment in the household inventory is the complete absence of books, musical instruments, or any other objects hinting at music-making. If such items were kept at home, they must have been distributed or disposed of in some other way.

Thomas and Joan had lived together in this house in Greenwich for several decades. Joan's first husband Thomas Bury, another Gentleman of the Chapel, had left it to her at his death in 1554. There is no direct documentation of her second wedding; in fact one of the most familiar documents having to do with Tallis gives what is obviously a garbled account of this marriage. The epitaph on the composer's gravestone in the church of St. Alfege was lost when the building collapsed in 1710 and was rebuilt from the ground up, but the text of the epitaph has become well-known through a transcription by John Strype, published in 1720 in his new appendix to John Stow's classic Elizabethan *Survey of London*. Strype's text tells us, among other things, that the composer "lived in love full three and thirty years with loyal spouse, whose name yclept [called] was Joan." That statement cannot be taken at face value, since it would mean that Joan married Thomas Tallis in 1552, while Thomas Bury was still very much alive, and that she spent a couple of years married to two people at once—a feat beyond the reach even of Henry VIII, to say nothing of the families of his court musicians.

Fortunately there is a more accurate source of Tallis's epitaph which resolves this and various other infelicities in Strype's transcription.[22] (Strype notes that the text is in "Old Letters" but is not always comfortable reading them: he gives the composer's name as "Gallys" rather than "Tallys," and he is unable even to make out the word "Chapel.") A manuscript now in the Cambridge University Library contains a different version of the epitaph, dated December 1585, the month after Tallis's death.[23] It also includes a final stanza not published by Strype. The scribe (and almost certainly the author as well) is Henry Stanford, a minor Elizabethan literary figure who was employed at the time as household tutor to the Paget family. Stanford's manuscript is a poetic notebook full of verses and epigrams on current events, including an epitaph of his own composition for the tomb of Lady Anne Lee (née Paget) which uses wording extremely similar to Tallis's epitaph. The Pagets were known both for their Catholic sympathies and for their musical connections: at one point their household secretary was even interrogated about a "secret choir" there which sang "songs of Mr. Byrd and Mr. Tallis."[24]

This is the epitaph as it was written down by Henry Stanford in December 1585:

Carmen sepulchro Thomae Tallis in re musica peritissimi incisum
[Poem inscribed on the tomb of Thomas Tallis, most skillful in music]

Entombed here doth lie a worthy wight
Who long time did in music bear the bell.
His name to say it Thomas Tallis hight [was called];
In modest virtuous life he did excel.

And served long time in Chapel with great praise,
Four sovereigns' reigns (a thing not often seen):

I mean King Henry and Prince Edward's days,
In time of Mary and our gracious Queen.

He married was, though children he had none,
And lived in love and liking thirty years
With loyal spouse, whose name yclept was Joan,
Who here entombed him company now bears.

As he had lived, so also did he die,
In patient quiet sort (O happy man);
To God full oft for mercy did he cry,
Wherefore he lives, let death do what he can.

He died the year five hundred eighty five
One thousand and since Christ took mortal weed [clothing].
His fame no doubt for music's skill shall live
Though sisters three have cut his fatal thread.

This older version of the text makes much better sense of Thomas and Joan's marriage: it lasted thirty years, and it began in 1555, the year after Joan was first widowed. (This happened at the height of the brief English Catholic revival that took place during the mid-1550s, definitively excluding any possibility that Thomas had been a member of the clergy who chose to marry—as so many did during the Reformation—in keeping with new evangelical views. Such a gesture would have been not only socially undesirable but illegal at the time.) Unfortunately the restored text of the epitaph offers little else of direct biographical value; there is nothing in it to suggest the composer's birthdate, parentage, education, or non-musical interests. Four rediscovered lines of Tallis's epitaph could change our entire view of his life, but all the extra stanza has to offer us are two already obvious facts: that he died in 1585 and that his fame will live on through his music. The poetic imagery of the last lines is appealing enough, with the three Fates ("sisters three") cutting the "fatal thread" of his lifespan, but they provide no news in terms of biography.

One fascinating detail does emerge near the end. The familiar second-hand version of the epitaph, as given by Strype and often repeated in musical literature since the nineteenth century, describes Tallis as having lived in "mild and quiet sort." Rather few prominent composers in any era could be described as "mild," and in some ways it is a surprising, even discouraging, word to see in this context. It is redolent of the unfortunate term "drab" with which so many literary critics (following C. S. Lewis) dismissed the English poetry of Tallis's generation.[25] It certainly does not fit with the tenacity and fierceness of much of Tallis's surviving music: was a piece such as *Gaude gloriosa* the product of a mild character? Henry Stanford's original text does not call Tallis mild at all. It calls him patient. That word is in much closer harmony with what we know of his long, intrepid, luminous career as a composer.

Robert Dow, who had commemorated Tallis in verse in his final years, also wrote a brief memorial poem for him shortly after his death.[26] Figure 17.1 shows the Latin original. Its central theme is already familiar from Tallis's grave inscription: he is remembered as the venerable old musician who served loyally under four sovereigns. Dow's second line is taken verbatim from one of the introductory poems to the 1575 *Cantiones*, now revisited as a funeral tribute.

> He lived in fame under four monarchs,
> Tallis, an old man worthy of great honor.
> If any musician in their time was to be considered outstanding,
> Tallis was always their chief glory.

Another poem written in response to Tallis's death is *Ye sacred Muses*, perhaps the most memorable of his epitaphs because it was set to music

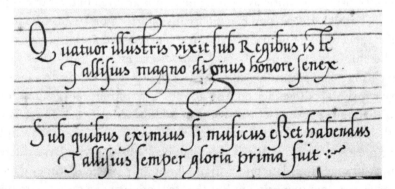

Figure 17.1 Memorial poem for Tallis by the music scribe Robert Dow (Oxford, Christ Church, Mus. 987, no. 42). Christ Church, Oxford. Reproduced by permission.

by Byrd.[27] Whoever wrote this anonymous poem must have been in contact with the international world of learned music-making, because it is an English adaptation of an older lament, *Musae Jovis*, on the death of Josquin. ("Muses, melodious offspring of thrice-great Jove, weep, let the cypress weigh down your locks: Josquin is dead.") This text, unlike the texts from Stanford and Dow, has nothing to do with Tallis's virtues or civic duties. It is simply an expression of grief at the death of a great musician.

> Ye sacred Muses, race of Jove,
> Whom Music's lore delighteth,
> Come down from crystal heavens above
> To earth, where sorrow dwelleth,
> In mourning weeds, with tears in eyes:
> Tallis is dead, and Music dies.

With this handful of funeral poems, we come to the end of the contemporary documents of Tallis's life—the last stop in a journey that began fifty-five years earlier with a brief entry in the accounts of Dover Priory, recording an annual payment to a "player of the organs." These documents show the outline of a long and eventful career, but there are many questions they do not answer. They also tell us almost nothing about Tallis's personality. In the case of a few other composers of his generation, we are lucky enough to catch a vivid glimpse of the human figure behind the music. John Marbeck (see Chapter 10), an exact contemporary of Tallis who wrote some thoroughly traditional pre-Reformation music as a young man, was arrested in the early 1540s for heretical activities and berated by his interrogator: "What the devil made thee meddle with the scriptures? Thy vocation was another way, wherein thou hast a goodly gift, if thou dost esteem it."[28] After some experiments in adapting plainchant to English texts, Marbeck seems to have given up altogether on his "goodly gift" of musical composition. In the preface to one of his works of biblical scholarship, he refers to "the study of music and playing on organs, wherein I consumed vainly the greatest part of my life."[29] This can be compared with Byrd's statement in one of his late publications about "my whole lifetime, which I have worn out in music"; in Byrd's case there is not an ounce of regret, just concern that this work (the magnificent first book of *Gradualia*, as it turns out) should not be unworthy of his old age.[30] There are no surviving words of that sort from Tallis, looking back on his life as a musician in either a positive or a negative way. There are also no hints of religious difficulties of the kind that plagued both Marbeck and Byrd. Tallis was linked to some clandestine Catholics later in life, most notably members of the Roper and Paget households, but for every Catholic associate of his, there were also many who conformed to the Church of England, at court and away from court. Even his close friend Richard Granwall, remembered fondly as an adopted child of the Tallis family in all but name, was happy to enjoy the benefits of property which Elizabeth had seized from a Catholic recusant and given to him.

Flashes of another strong personality can be seen in the life of Tallis's colleague John Sheppard, who was brought to trial in Oxford in 1555 for "arrogance and boasting," "insulting and quarrelsome language," and a "cruel deed" involving the abduction of a boy (presumably a young singer being recruited for his choir) whom he had bound and forcibly hauled more than forty miles.[31] The document recording Sheppard's application for a music degree in 1554 notes that he had "constantly worked with zeal for twenty years and composed many songs."[32] He was indeed an unusually productive and fluent composer, susceptible to few or none of the compositional second thoughts that seem to have preoccupied Tallis at times, and he appears to have had a high opinion of his own achievements: his will, made in some haste at the end of his life, includes a request to be buried in Westminster Abbey with a monument showing "a superscription of the day of my death."[33] Tallis's only instruction for his burial is that he might be laid to rest in his parish church of St. Alfege, with the distribution of forty shillings' worth of bread or money—what he had earned in a whole year as a young organist at Dover—to the poor on the same day. Unlike Sheppard (and again unlike Byrd, who was quite credibly accused of speaking "vile and bitter words"), Tallis is never named in connection with any known controversy or quarrel.[34] Even his epitaph, however well the poet Henry Stanford actually knew him, offers little more than a general portrait of a patient man who seems not to have been drawn in any violent way into the turmoil of his times.

Given the quiet and unspectacular nature of the documents, it is easy to fall into the trap of writing about Tallis in passive terms, as a figure to whom things happened: Tallis as victim of circumstance, of one new regime after another, of endless royal edicts and theological pronouncements. Fortunately this approach does not survive a closer engagement with the astonishing riches of his music. He was much more than a chameleon who took on the colors of his volatile environment, writing with Calvinist severity or with unreconstructed Catholic extravagance as his current monarch demanded. Like the best literary and visual artists of his time, he was at ease with a broad range of styles and could move freely among them while keeping a distinctive voice of his own. Perhaps the closest parallel in Tudor England is found in the work of Holbein, who was equally able to produce life-size portraits of overwhelming grandeur (like the *Ambassadors* sampled on the cover of this book) and miniature devotional images for private use. Tallis was a composer who could create the monumental forty-voice motet *Spem in alium* and the perfect little "tunes" of the Parker psalter at the same stage in his life, perhaps even during the same year. One gift he received from the difficult trajectory of his career was an absolute self-assurance in both the highest styles and the lowest styles, to a degree found among few other musicians of the sixteenth century, or indeed of any century. He did not merely survive constant change; it made him even more resilient and more capable.

Chronology

The left-hand column of this appendix is a list of all known documents of Tallis's life, from his first recorded employment in 1530 until his death in 1585. Each biographical document is paired with an entry in the right-hand column, showing selected historical and cultural events in England at the time when the document was produced. This parallel list of contemporary events is not an exhaustive or continuous timeline of sixteenth-century English history; it is simply offered as context for Tallis's musical career.

Biographical Documents	Contemporary Events
1530–31: Tallis employed as "player of the organs" at Dover Priory (Chapter 1)	1530–31: Publication of *XX [Twenty] Songs*, the earliest surviving printed collection of English polyphonic music; intense controversy regarding the marriage of Henry VIII and Catherine of Aragon
1536–38: Tallis listed among the musicians at the London parish of St. Mary-at-Hill; paid for a total of twelve months' service during these years (Chapter 2)	1536–38: Dissolution of smaller monasteries completed; Anne Boleyn (Henry's second wife) executed; publication of the Ten Articles and Bishops' Book, first official doctrinal statements of the newly independent Church of England; Jane Seymour (Henry's third wife) dies in childbirth
1540: Tallis named as a lay employee of Waltham Abbey at its dissolution; given both "wages" and "rewards" at his departure (Chapter 3)	1540: Birth of William Byrd; dissolution of larger monasteries completed; Anne of Cleves (Henry's fourth wife) divorced; Cromwell executed
1541: Tallis named as the first of twelve singers to be employed as Canterbury Cathedral prepares for its refoundation as a non-monastic church (Chapter 4)	1541: Catherine Howard (Henry's fifth wife) imprisoned and stripped of her royal titles

Biographical Documents	Contemporary Events
1543–44: Tallis first appears among the Gentlemen of the Chapel Royal in a lay subsidy roll, a list compiled for tax purposes (Chapter 5)	1543–44: Death of Hans Holbein; war declared against Scotland and France; weekly Bible reading in English mandated in churches; Catherine Parr (Henry's sixth wife) publishes a long prayer in English which is set to the music of Tallis's *Gaude gloriosa*
1547: Tallis provided with livery for the funeral of Henry VIII and the coronation of Edward VI; seventeenth in seniority among musicians of the Chapel (Chapter 5)	1547: Edward Seymour, Duke of Somerset, named Lord Protector and regent of England under the boy king Edward; injunctions prohibit bell-ringing at services and images in stained glass
1549: Tallis named as an overseer of the will of Richard Pygott, composer and Gentleman of the Chapel (Chapter 5)	1549: First edition of the Book of Common Prayer, provided with music by John Marbeck the following year; first printed English metrical psalter with music; all old books of service music to be "burnt or otherwise defaced or destroyed"
1553: Tallis provided with livery for the funeral of Edward VI and the coronation of Mary; eighth in seniority among musicians of the Chapel (Chapter 5)	1553: Publication of Christopher Tye's *Acts of the Apostles*; the Gentlemen of the Chapel Royal perform an elaborately costumed morality play for the new Queen; Latin services revived and Book of Common Prayer suppressed
1554: Tallis witnesses the will of Thomas Bury, Gentleman of the Chapel (Chapter 5)	1554: Philip of Spain arrives in England with musicians, including Antonio de Cabezón and Philippe de Monte; the Gentlemen of the Chapel and the choir of Winchester Cathedral sing at the royal wedding; death of Philip van Wilder
1555: Tallis marries Joan Bury, Thomas's widow; they subsequently live in her house in Greenwich (Chapter 17)	1555: The Queen is thought to be pregnant with an heir and about to give birth; Ridley, Latimer, and other Protestants burned at the stake
1557: Tallis granted a lease on royal property, shared with his Chapel colleague Richard Bower, providing twenty-one years of supplemental income (Chapter 5)	1557: Publication of *Tottel's Miscellany*, first printed English poetic anthology, including the words of Tallis's song *When shall my sorrowful sighing slack*; severe two-year influenza epidemic begins, during which approximately 10 percent of adult residents of London die; death of Nicholas Ludford

Biographical Documents	Contemporary Events
1558: Tallis provided with livery for the funeral of Mary (Chapter 5)	1558: Birth of Thomas Morley; death of John Sheppard; Matthew Parker becomes Archbishop of Canterbury
1559: Tallis provided with livery for the coronation of Elizabeth; seventh in seniority among musicians of the Chapel (Chapter 5)	1559: Restoration of the Book of Common Prayer; celebration of the Mass suppressed
1561: Tallis named as a witness and overseer of Richard Bower's will, along with William Roper, prominent lawyer and grandson of Thomas More (Chapter 5)	1561: Birth of Peter Philips; Castiglione's *Book of the Courtier* published in English; spire of St. Paul's Cathedral destroyed by lightning strike and fire
1562–74: Tallis named in numerous tax assessments and lay subsidy rolls linked with the Chapel Royal, indicating comfortable financial status and a well-established place among Elizabeth's court musicians (Chapter 5)	1562–74: Births of Shakespeare, John Dowland, Thomas Campion, and John Wilbye; deaths of Tye, Robert Parsons, and Robert White; Alfonso Ferrabosco and (briefly) Alessandro Striggio in England; publication of Parker's psalter with music by Tallis; Byrd joins the Chapel Royal
1575: Tallis and Byrd jointly awarded a monopoly on the printing and importation of music; the two composers publish *Cantiones quae ab argumento sacrae vocantur*, a large collection of music with Latin words (Chapter 14)	1575: Thomas Whythorne finishes writing his musical autobiography; death of Parker
1577: Tallis and Byrd petition Elizabeth for relief from financial losses in their printing venture; granted a twenty-one-year lease on various royal properties (Chapter 5)	1577: Francis Drake begins his circumnavigation of the world aboard the *Golden Hind*
1580: Tallis mentioned in a letter to Byrd by an unidentified "Sugeham," along with "Mr. Blitheman, Mr. More, Mr. Mundy, and the rest, my good friends" (Chapter 5)	1580: Drake completes his circumnavigation of the world; an earthquake causes significant damage in and around London; Jesuit mission to England begins
1583: Tallis makes his last will and testament, witnessed by Byrd (Chapter 17)	1583: Birth of Orlando Gibbons; Philippe de Monte, now employed in Prague, sends his motet *Super flumina Babylonis* to Byrd
1585: Tallis dies in late November; epitaph written, almost certainly by the poet Henry Stanford, who copies it into his private literary anthology in December (Chapter 17)	1585: Settlement of Roanoke in what is now North Carolina, the first attempt to establish a permanent English colony in the New World

List of Works

This list is designed to help the reader locate editions of Tallis's music for singing, playing, listening, and study.

Note: As this book goes to press, a number of pieces are awaiting publication in a future volume of Early English Church Music. These items will complete the critical edition of Tallis's Latin-texted music. Works in this forthcoming EECM group are marked with the symbol §.

Key to Abbreviations

AE	Antico Edition (Nick Sandon, general editor)
CFM	Cantus Firmus Music (Timothy Symons, general editor)
EECM 12	*Thomas Tallis, English Sacred Music*, vol. 1, *Anthems*, ed. Leonard Ellinwood and Paul Doe. Early English Church Music 12, rev. ed. London: Stainer & Bell, 1973.
EECM 13	*Thomas Tallis, English Sacred Music*, vol. 2, *Service Music*, ed. Leonard Ellinwood and Paul Doe. Early English Church Music 13, rev. ed. London: Stainer & Bell, 1974.
EECM 48	*The Gyffard Partbooks*, vol. 1, ed. David Mateer. Early English Church Music 48. London: Stainer & Bell, 2007.
EECM 51	*The Gyffard Partbooks*, vol. 2, ed. David Mateer. Early English Church Music 51. London: Stainer & Bell, 2009.
EECM 56	*Cantiones Sacrae 1575*, ed. John Milsom. Early English Church Music 56. London: Stainer & Bell, 2014.
EECM 64	*Thomas Tallis: Latin Church Music, 1: Mass* Salve intemerata *& Votive Antiphons*, ed. David Skinner. Early English Church Music 64. London: Stainer & Bell, 2021.
FW	*The Fitzwilliam Virginal Book*, ed. J. A. Fuller Maitland and W. Barclay Squire. New York: Dover, 1963.
KW	*Thomas Tallis: Complete Keyboard Works*, ed. Denis Stevens. London: Peters, 1953.
LB	*The Tudor Church Music of the Lumley Books*, ed. Judith Blezzard. Recent Researches in the Music of the Renaissance 65. Middleton, WI: A-R Editions, 1985.

MB 1   *The Mulliner Book*, ed. John Caldwell. Musica Britannica 1, rev. ed. London: Stainer & Bell, 2011.

MB 44   *Elizabethan Consort Music*, vol. 1, ed. Paul Doe. Musica Britannica 44. London: Stainer & Bell, 1979.

OUP   *Tudor Church Music* octavo series, ed. John Milsom. Oxford: Oxford University Press.

TA   *A Tallis Anthology*, ed. John Milsom. Oxford: Oxford University Press, 1992.

TCM 6   *Thomas Tallis*, ed. Percy Buck. Tudor Church Music 6. Oxford: Oxford University Press, 1928.

TP   *The Tallis Psalter: Psalms and Anthems, Canticles, Preces and Responses*, ed. David Skinner. London: Novello, 2013.

WM   *The Wanley Manuscripts*, ed. James Wrightson. Recent Researches in the Music of the Renaissance, 99–101. Middleton, WI: A-R Editions, 1995.

Latin-texted Music

Absterge Domine: EECM 56, p. 27; TCM 6, p. 180

Adesto nunc propitius (even-numbered verses of Salvator mundi Domine): TCM 6, p. 242 §

Alleluia [Ora pro nobis]: EECM 48, p. 67; TCM 6, p. 88

Audivi vocem de coelo: EECM 48, p. 130; TA, p. 1; TCM 6, p. 90

Ave Dei patris filia: EECM 64; AE, ed. David Allinson, no. RCM020; TCM 6, p. 162 (incomplete)

Ave rosa sine spinis: EECM 64; AE, ed. Nick Sandon, no. RCM136; TCM 6, p. 169

Candidi facti sunt: EECM 56, p. 323; TCM 6, p. 186

De lamentatione Ieremiae prophetae (Lamentations II): OUP, ed. Philip Brett (1991, original low pitch; 1995, transposed for SAATB); TCM 6, p. 110 §

Derelinquit impius: EECM 56, p. 217; TA, p. 9; TCM 6, p. 189

Domine quis habitabit: TCM 6, p. 246 §

Dum transisset Sabbatum: EECM 56, p. 227; TCM 6, p. 257

Euge caeli porta: TCM 6, p. 179 §

Gaude gloriosa: EECM 64; CFM, ed. Timothy Symons (2017); TCM 6, p. 123

Haec Deum caeli (even-numbered verses of Quod chorus vatum): TCM 6, p. 261 §

Hodie nobis caelorum rex: EECM 48, p. 138; TCM 6, p. 92

Homo quidam fecit: TCM 6, p. 282 §

Honor virtus et potestas: EECM 56, p. 244; TCM 6, p. 237

Illae dum pergunt (even-numbered verses of Sermone blando angelus): EECM 56, p. 252; TCM 6, p. 193

In ieiunio et fletu: EECM 56, p. 356; TA, p. 28; OUP, ed. Peter le Huray (1969); TCM 6, p. 198

In manus tuas: EECM 56, p. 83; TA, p. 36; OUP, ed. John Milsom (1993); TCM 6, p. 202

In pace in idipsum: CFM, ed. Timothy Symons (2015); EECM 48, p. 142; TCM 6, p. 94

Incipit lamentatio Ieremiae prophetae (Lamentations I): OUP, ed. Philip Brett (1991, original low pitch; 1995, transposed for SAATB); TCM 6, p. 102 §

Laudate Dominum: TA, p. 40; TCM 6, p. 266 §

Loquebantur variis linguis: CFM, ed. Timothy Symons (2015); TCM 6, p. 272 §

Magnificat for four voices: EECM 51, p. 141; TCM 6, p. 64

Magnificat for five voices: TCM 6, p. 73 §

Mass for four voices: EECM 48, p. 73; TCM 6, p. 31

Mass on *Puer natus est nobis*: CFM, ed. Sally Dunkley and David Wulstan (2015) §

Mass on *Salve intemerata*: EECM 64; AE, ed. Nick Sandon, no. RCM134; TCM 6, p. 3

Mihi autem nimis: EECM 56, p. 115; TA, p. 54; TCM 6, p. 204

Miserere nostri: EECM 56, p. 417; TCM 6, p. 207

Nunc Dimittis for five voices: ed. Stephen Rice, in *Epiphany to All Saints for Choirs* (New York: Oxford University Press, 2004), p. 70; TCM 6 p. 85 §

O nata lux: EECM 56, p. 126; TA, p. 74; OUP, ed. Anthony Greening (1969); TCM 6, p. 209

O sacrum convivium: EECM 56, p. 137; TA, p. 77; OUP, ed. John Milsom (1991); TCM 6, p. 210

O salutaris hostia: TA, p. 77; TCM 6, p. 276 §

Procul recedant somnia I (verse 2 of Te lucis ante terminum; melody for Sundays and feast days): CFM, ed. Timothy Symons (2015); EECM 56, p. 305; TA, p. 107; TCM 6, p. 214

Procul recedant somnia II (verse 2 of Te lucis ante terminum; melody for ordinary weekdays): CFM, ed. Timothy Symons (2015); EECM 56, p. 307; TA, p. 110; TCM 6, p. 215

Rex sanctorum: TCM 6, p. 298 (untexted) §

Salvator mundi I: EECM 56, p. 6; OUP, ed. John Milsom (1992); TA, p. 99; TCM 6, p. 216

Salvator mundi II: EECM 56, p. 310; TCM 6, p. 219

Salve intemerata: EECM 64; AE, ed. Nick Sandon, no. RCM134; TCM 6, p. 144

Sancte Deus: EECM 51, p. 182; TCM 6, p. 98

Solemnis urgebat dies (even-numbered verses of Iam Christus astra ascenderat): TCM 6, p. 285 §

Spem in alium: *Spem in alium nunquam habui: A Motet in Forty Parts*, ed. Philip Brett (Oxford: Oxford University Press, 1966); TCM 6, p. 299 §

Suscipe quaeso Domine: EECM 56, p. 364; TCM 6, p. 222

Tu fabricator omnium (even-numbered verses of Iesu salvator saeculi): TCM 6, p. 289 §

Videte miraculum: CFM, ed. Timothy Symons (2015); TCM 6, p. 293 §

English-texted Music

A new commandment: TP, p. 39; EECM 12, p. 19

Benedictus: LB, p. 104; EECM 13, p. 102

Blessed are those that be undefiled: TP, p. 45; EECM 12, p. 1

Fond youth is a bubble (secular version of Purge me, O Lord): MB 1, p. 25 (textless); EECM 12, p. 95

Hear the voice and prayer: TP, p. 57; WM, vol. 99, p. 162; OUP, ed. John Milsom (1993); TA, p. 19; EECM 12, p. 11

If ye love me: TP, p. 62; WM, vol. 100, p. 127; TA, p. 25; EECM 12, p. 16; OUP, ed.
Peter le Huray (1972)
Like as the doleful dove: EECM 12, p. 98
Litany: EECM 13, p. 150
O Lord, give thy Holy Spirit: TP, p. 65; TA, p. 60; OUP, ed. John Milsom (1991);
EECM 12, p. 25
O Lord, in thee is all my trust: TP, p. 69; TA, p. 64; EECM 12, p. 29
O ye tender babes: MB 1, p. 123 (textless); EECM 12, p. 102
Preces (first setting): TP, p. 22; EECM 13, p. 120
Preces (second setting): EECM 13, p. 122
Psalm 119 (selected verses): EECM 13, p. 125
Purge me, O Lord: TP, p. 82; MB 1, p. 38; TA, p. 95; OUP, ed. John Milsom (1991);
EECM 12, p. 40
Remember not, O Lord God: MB 1, p. 67; LB, p. 52; EECM 12, pp. 43 and 111
Responses (first setting): TP, p. 24; EECM 13, p. 144
Responses (second setting): EECM 13, p. 147
Short Service ("Dorian Service"): TP, p. 27 (Magnificat and Nunc Dimittis only);
EECM 13, p. 1
Te Deum "for meanes": EECM 13, p. 78
Tunes for Archbishop Parker's Psalter: TP, p. 2; EECM 13, p. 160
Verily, verily, I say until you: TA, p. 113; OUP, ed. Anthony Greening (1992); EECM
12, p. 51
When shall my sorrowful sighing slack: MB 1, p. 130; EECM 12, p. 106

Instrumental Music

Alleluia [Per te Dei genitrix]: KW, p. 8 (with title "Fantasy")
Clarifica me pater I: MB 1, p. 152; KW, p. 4
Clarifica me pater II: MB 1, p. 153; KW, p. 4
Clarifica me pater III: MB 1, p. 156; KW, p. 5
Ecce tempus idoneum I: MB 1, p. 152; KW, p. 6
Ecce tempus idoneum II: MB 1, p. 157; KW, p. 7
Ex more docti mistico: MB 1, p. 151; KW, p. 8
Fantasia (O sacrum convivium): EECM 56, p. 433
Felix namque I: KW, p. 10; FW, vol. 1, p. 427
Felix namque II: KW, p. 20; FW, vol. 2, p. 1
Gloria tibi trinitas: KW, p. 32
Iam lucis orto sidere: MB 1, p. 134; KW, p. 33
In nomine I: MB 44, p. 38
In nomine II: MB 44, p. 39
Iste confessor: MB 1, p. 158; KW, p.34
Natus est nobis: MB 1, p. 15; KW, p. 40
Point ("A poyncte"): MB 1, p. 155; KW, p. 40
Solfing song: MB 44, p. 63
Veni redemptor I: MB 1, p. 150; KW, p. 41
Veni redemptor II: MB 1, p. 154; KW, p. 42

APPENDIX C

Personalia

For additional names, see the general index at the end of the book. Biographical entries within this appendix are cross-referenced with *q.v.*

Baldwin, John (d. 1615) was a tenor lay clerk of St. George's, Windsor, then from 1598 onward a Gentleman of the Chapel Royal. He was also an expert music scribe who preserved a number of Tallis's unpublished works by making manuscript copies of them. His career in and around the royal household gave him access to an important hoard of earlier musical repertory, including materials used by Tallis and other Chapel musicians during the last years of the Latin rite. One of Baldwin's own songs (*In the merry month of May*, for three voices) was sung in 1591 for Queen Elizabeth I (q.v.); she found it so delightful that she demanded a repeat performance.

Bower, Richard (d. 1561) served the ill-fated Cardinal Wolsey in the 1520s as a singer under the direction of Richard Pygott (q.v.). By 1538 he was a member of the Chapel Royal, where he eventually became Master of the Children and received payments for the choristers' expenses and musical activities. Tallis was an overseer of Bower's will, a duty he shared with William Roper (q.v.), a patron of London musicians and pillar of the mid-sixteenth-century Catholic community. Like Tallis, Bower was buried in his Greenwich parish church of St. Alfege with a brass memorial (now lost).

Bury, Thomas (ca. 1490–1554) was one of Tallis's senior colleagues at court. He was a boy chorister in the prestigious household chapel of Lady Margaret Beaufort, then a young scholar at Eton from 1504 to 1509, and finally a Gentleman of the Chapel Royal, accompanying Henry VIII (q.v.) to the Field of the Cloth of Gold. His widow Joan (q.v. under "Tallis, Joan") inherited his properties in Greenwich and, the year after his death, married Tallis.

Byrd, Thomas (1576–after 1651), younger son of the composer William Byrd (q.v.), was Tallis's godson, almost certainly his namesake, and eventual heir to Tallis's share of the printing monopoly established in 1575. After a brief period spent studying law and the humanities in England, he emigrated to Spain at the age of twenty and entered the English Catholic seminary at Valladolid. He was expelled from the seminary in 1599 "because he was not considered sufficiently suited to this institution." He then returned to England, where he was described as a "professor of the science of music" and appointed in 1602 to deputize for John Bull as Gresham Lecturer in Music.

Byrd, William (1539/40–1623) was the most significant and versatile English composer of the generation after Tallis. He was born in London into a musically inclined family. After a nine-year stint as organist and choirmaster at Lincoln Cathedral, he joined the Chapel Royal in 1572. He shared a publishing monopoly with Tallis, produced a monumental collection of Latin motets with him in 1575, and composed the elegy *Ye sacred Muses* on his death. Byrd's long career was marked by great personal ambition and loyalty to the English Catholic cause. A laudatory poem about the two composers states that Tallis was Byrd's teacher; he certainly had a profound influence on many aspects of the younger man's compositional style.

Cranmer, Thomas (1489–1556) was a leading figure of the English Reformation and architect of the new vernacular liturgy set to music by Tallis. His work on the Book of Common Prayer had a lasting effect on English prose style. During his twenty years as Archbishop of Canterbury, he presided over the sweeping changes that took place in the English church. When the country returned briefly to Catholic practice in the mid-1550s, he was deprived of his office and burnt as a heretic.

Day, John (1521/2–1584) was a successful London printer who published a number of classic Reformation works, including the *Whole Book of Psalms* and *Foxe's Book of Martyrs*. He collaborated extensively with Matthew Parker (q.v.) and, in the 1560s, produced the earliest surviving printed sources of Tallis's music. His music editions were popular but sometimes of questionable accuracy. He left twenty-six children and a valuable (and controversial) monopoly on the printing of psalm books in English.

Dow, Robert (1553–1588) was a scholar, teacher of calligraphy, and music copyist. He became a fellow of All Souls College, Oxford at the age of twenty-two and was still adding to his manuscript collection of music when he died thirteen years later. It is one of the few sets of English Renaissance music partbooks that have survived completely intact. Dow made a note in one of the books, recording the date of Tallis's death as 23 November 1585. He also added short commendatory verses in praise of Tallis, both before and after his death.

Edward VI (1537–1553) was the second of the four sovereigns Tallis served as a member of the Chapel Royal. As the only legitimate son and the immediate successor of Henry VIII (q.v.), he became king at the age of nine. English law placed the realm under the authority of protectors and governors as long as the monarch was under eighteen. The resulting vacuum of power was filled by various strong personalities at court, leading to an era of vehement Protestant reform and, at times, violent unrest. This was the point at which the language of church services changed fully from Latin to English. The young king himself had little time for ornate church music but loved elaborate displays of secular music and dance. Philip van Wilder (q.v.) taught him to play the lute.

Elizabeth I (1533–1603), daughter of Henry VIII (q.v.) and Anne Boleyn, was the last of the four sovereigns Tallis served as a member of the Chapel Royal. Her reign lasted almost half a century. It was an era of relative political stability and the rise of England as a global power; it was also an era during which the arts flourished and literacy rates increased significantly. Elizabeth was a consummate survivor who refused to compromise her authority and independence by marrying. Like her father, she ruled the national church with a firm hand while maintaining a distinct preference for many old-fashioned religious customs.

Fayrfax, Robert (1464–1521) was born on 23 April 1464 around ten o'clock at night, the sixth child of a well-connected gentry family near Peterborough who recorded such things carefully. He served for more than twenty years in the Chapel Royal, where he was the beneficiary of many private gifts and honors. He also held two doctorates, one each from Oxford and Cambridge. His music was highly regarded in his own lifetime and remained popular in Tallis's day, appearing more frequently in manuscripts than the works of any other composer around 1500.

Granwall (or Cranwall), Richard (d. 1607) came to the Chapel Royal in 1572 from King's College, Cambridge. He was a close friend of Tallis, whose wife Joan (q.v.) mentioned "the great goodwill and friendship which was between my late husband deceased and Richard Granwall." He took care of Joan in her old age and inherited much of the couple's property, including their second house in Greenwich. Unlike Byrd (q.v.), who was appointed to the Chapel only six weeks earlier, he remained musically and politically active at court until his death.

Harington, John (ca. 1517–1582) was the earliest known student of Tallis. He grew up in Stepney and may have met Tallis during the composer's time in London, or during his own youthful service at court. His eventful career took him from political scandal and imprisonment in the Tower to an honorable social position as a gentleman and scholar. Elizabeth I (q.v.) was godmother to his son, also named John. John junior noted that his father was "much skilled in music, which was pleasing to the King, and which he learnt in the fellowship of good Master Tallis when a young man."

Henry VIII (1491–1547) was the first of the four sovereigns Tallis served as a member of the Chapel Royal. The political and religious landscape of England changed irrevocably during the latter part of Henry's reign as he established himself as the head of a fully independent national church. He has earned popular notoriety for his ambition and his voracious appetites, but he could also be a discerning, highly effective patron of the arts when it suited him. His dissolution of the English monasteries was responsible for several sharp turns in Tallis's early career. He married six times in a quest for male heirs; a text by his sixth wife Catherine Parr (q.v.) was set to the suitably magnificent music of Tallis's *Gaude gloriosa*.

Heyborne, Ferdinand (alias Richardson; ca. 1559–1618) called Tallis "my great master" in a poem published in 1575. Like the considerably older John Harington (q.v.), who was also a student of Tallis, he was a skilled amateur. He used music as a means of social advancement, eventually becoming such a trusted member of the Privy Chamber that he was carrying private messages on behalf of the Queen. His artistic pursuits (many of them carried out under the name "Richardson") included a dozen keyboard works of his own, the provision of musical exercises for young aristocratic pupils, and some dealings with the Elizabethan music publishing industry.

Heywood, John (1496/97–1578 or later), grandfather of the poet John Donne, began his career as a singer and keyboard player in the service of Henry VIII (q.v.). He was soon noticed as an unusually witty man who had a gift for playwriting and theatrical productions, including a number of plays performed by the boy choristers of the

Chapel Royal and St. Paul's. The most important surviving source of Tallis's keyboard music, a manuscript belonging to Thomas Mulliner (q.v.), contains an inscription referring to Heywood. He and his entire immediate family remained Catholic throughout the sixteenth century, at the cost of considerable material difficulties; the last years of his life were spent in exile in what is now Belgium.

Ludford, Nicholas (ca. 1490–1557) was a singer, organist, and composer who spent his entire known career in London. By the early 1520s he was a member of the Fraternity of St. Nicholas, the London church musicians' guild, and was employed in the church of St. Stephen's, Westminster, where many royal baptisms, weddings, and funerals took place. His music is all Latin-texted, much of it composed on a monumental scale.

Lumley, John (ca. 1533–1609) was a bibliophile and art collector whose library at Nonsuch Palace contained almost three thousand volumes, including important musical works by Tallis and many others. He was the earliest known owner of a copy of Tallis's forty-part *Spem in alium*; his father-in-law Henry Fitzalan, earl of Arundel, may have been involved in commissioning it. Byrd (q.v.) dedicated a book of motets to Lumley in 1591, praising him for his "most intense love towards all the daughters of the Muses and of Science."

Mary I (1516–1558) was the third of the four sovereigns Tallis served as a member of the Chapel Royal. She succeeded the boy king Edward (q.v.) in 1553, despite the violent objections of many who did not want to see a woman or a Catholic on the throne. As the daughter of Catherine of Aragon, she had a strong affinity for Spanish culture. She chose to marry King Philip II of Spain, who brought a large retinue with him to England, including a number of first-rate musicians. One of the first acts of Mary's reign was the complete repeal of all her recent predecessors' religious laws, followed by a series of severe measures taken against heretics. If she and Philip had produced an heir, the course of English history and musical life would have run in a very different direction.

Marbeck (or Merbecke), John (ca. 1505–ca. 1585) was an exact contemporary of Tallis. After his conventional early life as an organist and composer at St. George's Chapel, Windsor, his career took an unexpected turn in the late 1530s when he began collecting new writings by Calvin and other reformers whose ideas were not yet in favor in England. After a narrow escape from burning at the stake, he went on to produce *The Book of Common Prayer Noted*, the first full musical setting of Cranmer's (q.v.) new English liturgy. He retired from active duty as a musician in the early 1570s and devoted the rest of his life to publishing polemical works.

Morley, Thomas (1557/58–1602) was a musical entrepreneur, composer, and theorist. He played a crucial role in the invention of the English madrigal and the transformation of Elizabethan secular music. After the Tallis/Byrd printing monopoly expired in 1596 at the end of its twenty-one-year term, Morley took full advantage of the hiatus and soon held the monopoly himself. While compiling his *Plain and Easy Introduction to Practical Music*, he appears to have consulted the only book known to have belonged personally to Tallis, the Waltham Abbey manuscript of music theory compiled by John Wylde (q.v.)

Mulliner, Thomas (active ca. 1545–1575) was the mid-sixteenth-century scribe who produced a valuable manuscript anthology (British Library Add. MS 30513, the "Mulliner Book") containing most of Tallis's known keyboard works and all of his known secular songs. Very little is known about Mulliner himself, except that he served as organist of Corpus Christi College, Oxford, in the early 1560s, and that he had a connection to John Heywood (q.v.), who served as a witness that the manuscript was indeed Mulliner's own.

Mundy, William (ca. 1528–1591) belonged to a musical family spanning several generations. He began his career in the 1540s as head chorister at Westminster Abbey and joined Tallis in the Chapel Royal in 1564. He was among the very last English composers to work in traditional Latin-texted genres, and among the very first to write verse anthems and other creative settings for the new English rites. Robert Dow (q.v.) was a great admirer of his music.

Paget, Thomas (ca. 1544–1590) was a Catholic nobleman who spent much of his fortune on the cultivation of music and musicians. "Songs of Mr. Byrd and Mr. Tallis" were sung in the Paget household in the 1570s. Thomas Paget and his like-minded brother Charles eventually went into exile on the Continent, taking the composer Peter Philips into their entourage. The poet Henry Stanford (q.v.), who was almost certainly the author of Tallis's epitaph, was a private tutor to Paget's young son at the time of Tallis's death.

Parker, Matthew (1504–1575) was archbishop of Canterbury for the last fifteen years of his life. After a distinguished career as an administrator and theologian, he had hoped to retire to Cambridge to pursue his scholarly interests, but instead he was appointed by the Queen to be her chief prelate. He played a major role in forging an Elizabethan compromise between radical reformers and more traditional-minded groups. His book of English psalms in verse includes a set of "tunes" by Tallis in four-part harmony.

Parr, Catherine (1512–1548) was the sixth and last wife of Henry VIII (q.v.), outliving him at his death in 1547. The music and liturgy of the Chapel Royal made its first forays into the vernacular during her reign. She published an English translation of Latin prayers by John Fisher, including a long English text which was set to the music of Tallis's *Gaude gloriosa*.

Pygott, Richard (d. 1549) was one of the most successful church musicians of his generation in England, celebrated both as a composer and as a trainer of young choristers. He served Wolsey until the cardinal's downfall, then almost immediately joined the royal household. Unlike many older members of the Henrician Chapel Royal, he had a direct personal connection with Tallis, who oversaw his will and received a generous bequest from him.

Redford, John (d. 1547) was the most significant English keyboard composer before Tallis. He was an associate of John Heywood (q.v.), who was, like him, involved in both music and theater. Morley (q.v.) praised Redford for his skill in "breaking" (paraphrasing and ornamenting) plainsong melodies. More than forty of his organ works survive; they form the first English collection of varied and fully written-out organ music for use in church.

Roper, William (ca. 1498–1578) was a lawyer and author, son-in-law of Thomas More. His extensive charitable activities included gifts to English Catholic exiles (including a number of people involved in the book trade) and to the guild of parish musicians in London, who considered him an important benefactor and displayed his portrait prominently in their hall. His younger son Anthony (ca. 1535–1597) had a serious interest in music—he commissioned a luxury keyboard instrument from the Dutch builder Lodewijk Theewes—and was thanked by name in Joan Tallis's (q.v.) will for "good favours showed to my late husband and me."

Sheppard, John (ca. 1515–1558) came to the Chapel Royal from Magdalen College, Oxford. He said in his application for an Oxford degree in 1554 that he had been composing "with zeal" for twenty years; his surviving works include a very large repertory of Latin-texted music, some of it unusually dense and dissonant, and a considerable amount of English church music. He died during the London influenza epidemic of 1557–58, with a request (not granted) to be buried in Westminster Abbey with a monument.

Stanford, Henry (ca. 1552–1616) was a poet and literary tutor who was closely associated with several important Elizabethan families, including the Careys and the Pagets. He was an Anglican priest whose connections to Catholic patrons brought him under political suspicion at various points in his life. His literary notebook includes the earliest and most accurate known version of Tallis's epitaph, dated December 1585; he is almost certainly the author as well as the scribe.

Tallis, Joan (d. 1589) married Thomas Tallis in 1555; the correct date of their wedding is recorded by Henry Stanford (q.v.) They lived together in the house in Greenwich that she had inherited from her first husband Thomas Bury (q.v.), an older member of the Chapel Royal. Her will gives a detailed account of the material goods in a successful Tudor musician's household. She signed it with a mark rather than her full name, perhaps more likely due to her physical decline in old age (a decline noted in the document) than to illiteracy.

Taverner, John (ca. 1490–1545) was a highly influential composer of the generation just before Tallis's. He spent most of his career in and around Lincolnshire, where his family seems to have originated. He dabbled in Lutheranism during his time at Oxford in the 1520s, but there is no supporting evidence for the stories told by John Foxe and other authors about radical Protestant activities. His music (almost all sacred, vocal, and Latin-texted) is characterized by great melodic drive and self-assurance. Tallis clearly knew it and learned from it.

Tunstall, Cuthbert (1474–1559) was an English bishop and scholar who lived through the Reformation at close range: he was present at the Diet of Worms, officiated at the coronation of Edward VI (q.v.), and died under house arrest in London as an octogenarian who was no longer able in good conscience to take the oath of royal supremacy over the Church of England. He wrote the text of Tallis's *Salve intemerata*.

Tye, Christopher (ca. 1505–1573) served as choirmaster of Ely Cathedral from the 1540s onward, but he was also associated with court circles and seems to have had close links to the Chapel Royal. His work spans nearly all the musical styles of mid-sixteenth-century England, from luxurious six-part polyphony to his terse and didactic *Acts of the Apostles*. He was one of the very few Tudor composers who were also clergymen; he was described in the early 1560s as "a Doctor of Music, but without skill in preaching."

Van Wilder, Philip (ca. 1500–1553) was a Flemish musician who spent his entire known career in England, most of it (beginning in 1525/26) at the royal court as a lutenist, music tutor, composer, and curator of instruments. He was paid a considerably higher salary than Tallis and his associates in the royal household chapel. More than forty of his musical works have survived, including some that circulated as far afield as Italy, France, and Germany. He and Tallis wrote closely matched four-voice settings of the prayer *Sancte Deus*.

Vautrollier, Thomas (died 1587) was a French Huguenot printer from Troyes who came to London in the early 1560s. He soon acquired a reputation for elegant printing of difficult materials, including translations and adaptations of Continental works. In 1570 he produced his first book of music, an edition of French chansons by Lassus with the texts bowdlerized to suit pious tastes. In 1575 he printed the *Cantiones sacrae*, the only publication of Tallis's music that was overseen by the composer himself.

Wylde, John (fl. 1425–1450) was precentor (cantor and music director) of Waltham Abbey. He made a manuscript compendium of music theory treatises by various authors. This manuscript is the only known document that bears Tallis's signature; it presumably went with him when the abbey was dissolved in 1540. It is an eclectic collection, including an extremely rare set of written instructions for producing faburden, still the most popular method of musical improvisation in church during Tallis's early years.

APPENDIX D

Select Bibliography

Allinson, David, "Philip van Wilder, Henry VIII's Lost Composer," notes to *Philip van Wilder: Complete Sacred Music*, CD TOCC 0198 (Toccata Classics, 2013).

Allinson, David, *The Rhetoric of Devotion: Some Neglected Elements in the Context of the Early Tudor Votive Antiphon* (PhD dissertation, University of Exeter, 1998).

Apel, Willi, *The History of Keyboard Music to 1700*, tr. Hans Tischler (Bloomington: Indiana University Press, 1972).

Aplin, John. "Cyclic Techniques in the Earliest Anglican Services." *Journal of the American Musicological Society* 35 (1982), 409–35.

Aplin, John, "'The Fourth Kind of Faburden': The Identity of an English Four-Part Style," *Music & Letters* 61 (1980), 260–1.

Aplin, John, "The Origins of John Day's 'Certaine Notes'," *Music & Letters* 62 (1981), 295–9.

Ashbee, Andrew, *Records of English Court Music*, 7 vols. (Aldershot: Scolar, 1986–96).

Ashbee, Andrew, "Groomed for Service: Musicians in the Privy Chamber at the English Court, c.1495–1558," *Early Music* 25 (1997), 193–4.

Ashbee, Andrew, and David Lasocki, *A Biographical Dictionary of English Court Musicians, 1485–1714*, 2 vols. (Aldershot: Ashgate, 1998).

Ashbee, Andrew, and John Harley, *The Cheque Books of the Chapel Royal* (Aldershot: Ashgate, 2000).

Baillie, Hugh, "A London Church in Early Tudor Times," *Music & Letters* 36, no. 1 (1955): 55–64.

Baillie, Hugh, "A London Gild of Musicians, 1460–1530," *Proceedings of the Royal Musical Association* 83 (1956–57): 15–28.

Benham, Hugh, *John Taverner: His Life and Music* (Aldershot: Ashgate, 2003).

Benham, Hugh, "'Stroke' and 'Strene' Notation in Fifteenth- and Sixteenth-Century Equal-Note Cantus Firmi," *Plainsong and Medieval Music* 2 (1993): 153–67.

Bennett, John, "A Tallis Patron?", *Royal Musical Association Research Chronicle* 21 (1988): 41–4.

Bent, Margaret, "New and Little-Known Fragments of English Medieval Polyphony," *Journal of the American Musicological Society* 21 (1968): 137–56.

Bicknell, Stephen, *The History of the English Organ* (Cambridge University Press: Cambridge, 1996).

Blezzard, Judith, *The Tudor Church Music of the Lumley Books*, Recent Researches in the Music of the Renaissance vol. 65 (Madison, WI: A-R Editions, 1985).

Bowers, Roger, "The Chapel Royal, the First Edwardian Prayer Book, and Elizabeth's Settlement of Religion, 1559," *Historical Journal* 43 (2000): 317–44.

Bowers, Roger, *Choral establishments within the English church: their constitution and development, 1340–1542* (PhD dissertation, University of East Anglia, 1976).

Bowers, Roger, "An Early Tudor Monastic Enterprise: Choral Polyphony for the Liturgical Service," in *The Culture of Medieval English Monasticism*, ed. James G. Clark (Woodbridge: Boydell, 2007), 21–54.

Bowers, Roger, "The Liturgy of the Cathedral and its Music, c.1075–1642," in *A History of Canterbury Cathedral*, ed. Patrick Collinson, Nigel Ramsey, and Margaret Sparks (Oxford: Oxford University Press, 1995), 408–50.

Bowers, Roger, "Testwood, Robert (c. 1490–1543)," *Oxford Dictionary of National Biography* (Oxford: Oxford University Press, 2004).

Bowers, Roger, "Thomas Tallis at Dover Priory, 1530–1531," *Early Music* 44 (2016): 197–205.

Bowers, Roger, "The Vocal Scoring, Choral Balance and Performing Pitch of Latin Church Polyphony in England, c. 1500–58," *Journal of the Royal Musical Association* 112 (1986–87): 38–76; reprinted in Bowers, *English Church Polyphony: Singers and Sources from the 14th to the 17th Century* (Aldershot: Ashgate Variorum, 1999).

Bray, Roger, "British Library, R.M. 24.d.2 (John Baldwin's Commonplace Book): An Index and Commentary," *Royal Musical Association Research Chronicle* 12 (1974): 137–51.

Bray, Roger, "John Baldwin," *Music and Letters* 56 (1975): 55–9.

Bray, Roger, ed., *Masses Tecum principium and O quam glorifica*, Robert Fayrfax, Early English Church Music vol. 45 (London: Stainer & Bell, 2004).

Bray, Roger, "Music and the Quadrivium in Early Tudor England," *Music and Letters* 76 (1995): 1–18.

Bray, Roger, "The Part-Books Oxford, Christ Church, MSS 979–983: An Index and Commentary," *Musica Disciplina* 25 (1971): 179–97.

Brett, Philip, ed., *Byrd Edition*, 20 vols. (London: Stainer & Bell, 1970–2004).

Brett, Philip, "Edward Paston (1550–1630): A Norfolk Gentleman and his Musical Collection," *Transactions of the Cambridge Bibliographical Society* 4 (1964); 51–69, reprinted in *William Byrd and his Contemporaries: Essays and a Monograph*, ed. Joseph Kerman and Davitt Moroney (Berkeley and Los Angeles: University of California Press, 2007), 31–59.

Brett, Philip, "Homage to Taverner in Byrd's Masses," in *William Byrd and his Contemporaries: Essays and a Monograph*, ed. Joseph Kerman and Davitt Moroney (Berkeley and Los Angeles: University of California Press, 2007), 8–21.

Brigden, Susan, "Howard, Henry, earl of Surrey (1516/17–1547)," *Oxford Dictionary of National Biography* (Oxford: Oxford University Press, 2004).

Burgess, Clive, and Andrew Wathey, "Mapping the Soundscape: Church Music in English Towns, 1450–1550", *Early Music History* 19 (2000): 1–46.

Butchart, David, "The Letters of Alessandro Striggio: An Edition with Translation and Commentary," *RMA Research Chronicle* 23 (1990): 1–78.

Butler, Katherine, *Music in Elizabethan Court Politics* (Woodbridge: Boydell, 2015).

Caldwell, John, ed., *The Mulliner Book*, Musica Britannica 1 (London: Stainer and Bell, revised ed. 2011).

Carley, James, "Monastic Collections and Their Dispersal," in *The Cambridge History of the Book in Britain*, ed. John Barnard and D. F. Mackenzie (Cambridge: Cambridge University Press, 2002), 339–48.

Cole, Suzanne. "'Often seene, but seldome sung': eighteenth- and nineteenth-century manuscripts of Thomas Tallis's *Spem in alium*," in *Nineteenth-Century British Music Studies*, vol. 2, ed. Jeremy Dibble and Bennett Zon (Ashgate, 2002), 154–68.

Cole, Suzanne. " 'This mistake of a barbarous age': Performances and Perceptions of Tallis's *Spem in alium* in Nineteenth-century England". *Context: A Journal of Music History* 15–16 (1998): 21–31.

Cole, Suzanne, *Thomas Tallis and his Music in Victorian England* (Woodbridge: Boydell, 2008).

Cole, Suzanne, "Who is the Father? Changing Perceptions of Tallis and Byrd in Late Nineteenth-Century England," *Music & Letters* 89 (2008): 1–15.

Collins, David, "A 16th-Century Manuscript in Wood: The Eglantine Table at Hardwick Hall," *Early Music* 4 (1976): 275–9.

Collinson, Patrick, Nigel Ramsey, and Margaret Sparks, eds., *History of Canterbury Cathedral* (Oxford: Oxford University Press, 1995).

Colvin, Howard and Susan Foister, eds., *The Panorama of London circa 1544* (London: London Topographical Society, 1996).

Crankshaw, David, and Alexandra Gillespie, "Parker, Matthew (1504–1575)," *Oxford Dictionary of National Biography* (Oxford: Oxford University Press, 2004).

Day, Timothy. "Tallis in performance," *Early Music* 33 (2005): 683–92.

Dobson, Barrie, "The Monks of Canterbury in the Later Middle Ages, 1220–1540," in *A History of Canterbury Cathedral*, ed. Patrick Collinson, Nigel Ramsey, and Margaret Sparks (Oxford: Oxford University Press, 1995), 69–153.

Doe, Paul, *Tallis*, 2nd ed. (Oxford University Press, 1976).

Doe, Paul, and David Allinson. "Thomas Tallis." *Grove Music Online* (www.oxfordmusiconline.com/subscriber/article/grove/music/27423).

Dumitrescu, Theodor, *The Early Tudor Court and International Musical Relations* (Aldershot: Ashgate, 2007).

Dunkley, Sally, ed., *Thomas Tallis: Mass Puer natus est nobis* (Cantus Firmus Music, 2015).

Easton, Timothy, and Stephen Bicknell, "Two Pre-Reformation Organ Soundboards," *Proceedings of the Suffolk Institute of Archaeology and History* 38 (1995): 268–95.

Ellinwood, Leonard, rev. Paul Doe, *Thomas Tallis: English Sacred Music*, vol. 1, *Anthems*. Early English Church Music 12 (London: Stainer & Bell, 1971).

Fallows, David, "Henry VIII as a Composer," in *Sundry Sorts of Music Books: Essays on the British Library Collections*, ed. Chris Banks, Arthur Searle, and Malcolm Turner (London: British Library, 1993), 27–39.

Fenlon, Iain and Hugh Keyte, "Memorialls of Great Skill: A Tale of Five Cities," *Early Music* 8 (1980): 329–34.

Fenlon, Iain, and Milsom, John, " 'Ruled Paper Imprinted': Music Paper and Patents in Sixteenth-Century England," *Journal of the American Musicological Society* 37 (1984): 139–63.

Flynn, Jane, "The Education of Choristers in England during the Sixteenth Century," in *English Choral Practice, 1400–1650*, ed. John Morehen (Cambridge: Cambridge University Press, 1995), 80–99.

Flynn, Jane, *A Reconsideration of the Mulliner Book (BL Add. MS 30513): Music Education in Sixteenth-Century England* (PhD dissertation, Duke University, 1993).

Foister, Susan, *Holbein and England* (New Haven: Yale University Press, 2004).

Frere, Walter Howard, "Edwardine Vernacular Services Before the First Prayer Book," *Journal of Theological Studies* 1 (1900): 229–46; also in *Walter Howard Frere: A Collection of His Papers on Liturgical and Historical Subjects*, Alcuin Club Collections vol. 35, ed. J.H. Arnold (Oxford: Oxford University Press, 1940), 5–21.

Frere, Walter Howard, and W. M. Kennedy, eds., *Visitation Articles and Injunctions of the Period of the Reformation* (London: Longmans, Green, 1910).

Gaskin, Hilary, *Music Copyists in Late Sixteenth-Century England, with Particular Reference to the Manuscripts of John Baldwin* (PhD dissertation, Cambridge University, 1985).

Haines, Charles Reginald, *Dover Priory* (Cambridge: Cambridge University Press, 1930).

Harley, John, *Thomas Tallis* (Farnham: Ashgate, 2015).

Harley, John, *The World of William Byrd: Musicians, Merchants and Magnates* (Burlington, VT: Ashgate, 2010).

Harman, Alec, ed., *A Plain and Easy Introduction to Practical Music* (London: Norton, 1952).

Harrison, Frank Llewellyn, *Music in Medieval Britain* (London: Routledge, 1958).

Harvey, Barbara, *Living and Dying in England 1100–1540: The Monastic Experience* (Oxford: Clarendon, 1993).

Hughes, Philip, and James Larkin, *Tudor Royal Proclamations* (New Haven: Yale University Press, 1964–69).

Humphreys, David, "Tallis's *Suscipe quaeso*," *Early Music* 28 (2000): 508–9.

Humphreys, David, "Why Did Tallis Compose the *Missa Puer nobis natus est*?", *Musical Times* 157 (2016): 9–15.

Johnstone, Andrew. "Tallis's Service 'of Five Parts Two in One' Re-evaluated," in *Canons and Canonic Techniques, 14th–16th Centuries: Theory, Practice, and Reception History*, ed. Katelijne Schiltz and Bonnie Blackburn (Leuven: Peeters, 2007), 381–405.

Johnstone, Andrew, "Thomas Tallis and the Five-part English Litany of 1544: Evidence of 'the notes used in the king's majesty's chapel'," *Early Music* 44 (2016): 219–32.

Kerman, Joseph. "Byrd, Tallis and the Art of Imitation," in *Write All These Down: Essays on Music* (Berkeley and Los Angeles: University of California Press, 1994), 90–105.

Kerman, Joseph. "The Elizabethan Motet: A Study of Texts for Music," *Studies in the Renaissance* 9 (1962): 273–308.

Kerman, Joseph, *The Masses and Motets of William Byrd* (Berkeley and Los Angeles: University of California Press, 1981).

Kerman, Joseph, "The Missa *Puer natus est* by Thomas Tallis," in *Write All These Down: Essays on Music* (Berkeley and Los Angeles: University of California Press, 1994), 125–38; also in *Sundry Sorts of Music Books: Essays on the British Library Collections Presented to O. W. Neighbour on his 70th Birthday*, ed. Chris Banks, Arthur Searle, and Malcolm Turner (London: British Library, 1993), 40–53.

Kerman, Joseph. "A Tallis Mass." *Early Music* 27 (1999): 669–71.

Kisby, Fiona, "A Mirror of Monarchy: Music and Musicians in the Household Chapel of the Lady Margaret Beaufort, Mother of Henry VII," *Early Music History* 16 (1997): 203–34.

Kisby, Fiona, *The Royal Household Chapel in Early-Tudor London, 1485–1547* (PhD dissertation, Royal Holloway, 1996).

Kisby, Fiona, "Royal Minstrels in the City and Suburbs of Early Tudor London: Professional Activities and Private Interests," *Early Music* 25, no. 2 (1997): 199–219.

Kisby, Fiona, "'When the King Goeth a Procession': Chapel Ceremonies and Services, the Ritual Year, and Religious Reforms at the Early Tudor Court, 1485–1547," *Journal of British Studies* 40 (2001): 44–75.

Le Huray, Peter. *Music and the Reformation in England, 1549–1660* (Cambridge: Cambridge University Press, 1978).

Leaver, Robin, *The Work of John Marbeck* (Appleford: Sutton Courtenay, 1978).

Lloyd, Richard, "Music at the Parish Church of St Mary at Hill, London," *Early Music* 2, no. 2 (1997): 221–6.

Lloyd, Richard, *Provision for Music in the Parish Church in Late-medieval London* (PhD dissertation, Royal Holloway, University of London, 1999), 161–2.

Lockwood, Lewis, "A Continental Mass and Motet in a Tudor Manuscript," *Music and Letters* 42 (1961): 336–47.

MacCulloch, Diarmaid, *Thomas Cranmer: A Life* (New Haven: Yale University Press, 1996).

Marlow, Richard. "Sir Ferdinando Heyborne, alias Richardson." *Musical Times* 115 (1974): 736–9.

Marsh, Dana, *Music, Church, and Henry VIII's Reformation* (DPhil dissertation, Oxford, 2007), 136.

Mateer, David, "Baldwin, John (d. 1615)," *Oxford Dictionary of National Biography* (Oxford: Oxford University Press, 2004).

Mateer, David, "The Compilation of the Gyffard Partbooks," *RMA Research Chronicle* 26 (1993): 19–43.

Mateer, David, "The 'Gyffard' Partbooks: Composers, Owners, Date and Provenance," *Royal Musical Association Research Chronicle* 28 (1995): 21–50.

Mateer, David, ed., *The Gyffard Partbooks, I and II*, Early English Church Music 48 and 51 (London: Stainer & Bell, 2007–2009).

Mateer, David, "Marbeck [Merbecke], John (c. 1505–1585?)," *Oxford Dictionary of National Biography* (Oxford: Oxford University Press, 2004).

Maxim, Christopher, "A Little-Known Keyboard Plainsong Setting in the Fitzwilliam Virginal Book: A Key to Tallis's Compositional Process?," *Early Music* 29 (2001): 275–82.

Maynard, John, *The Parish of Waltham Abbey, Its History and Antiquities* (London: J. R. Smith, 1865).

McCarthy, Kerry, "Evidence of Things Past," *Journal of the Royal Musical Association* 135 (2010): 405–11.

McCarthy, Kerry, "A Late Anthem by Tallis," *Early Music* 44 (2016): 191–5.

McCarthy, Kerry, "Tallis, Isidore of Seville and *Suscipe quaeso*," *Early Music* 35 (2007): 447–50.

McCarthy, Kerry, "Tallis's Epitaph Revisited," *Early Music* 47 (2019): 57–64.

Meech, Sanford, "Three Musical Treatises in English from a Fifteenth-Century Manuscript," *Speculum* 10 (1935): 235–69.

Milsom, John, "The Arcane Colours of Fayrfax," *Early Music* 33 (2005): 523–4.

Milsom, John, "Caustun's Contrafacta," *Journal of the Royal Musical Association* 132 (2007): 1–31.

Milsom, John, "The Culture of Partleaves: Peterhouse and Beyond," in *Music, Politics and Religion in Early Seventeenth Century Cambridge: The Peterhouse Partbooks in Context*, ed. Scott Mandelbrote (forthcoming).

Milsom, John, ed., *The Dow Partbooks* (DIAMM Publications, 2010).

Milsom, John, *English Polyphonic Style in Transition: A Study of the Sacred Music of Thomas Tallis* (PhD dissertation, University of Oxford, 1983).

Milsom, John, "English-Texted Chant Before Merbecke," *Plainsong and Medieval Music* 1 (1992): 77–92.

Milsom, John, "A New Tallis Contrafactum," *Musical Times* 123 (1982): 429–31.

Milsom, John, "The Nonsuch Music Library," in Chris Banks, Arthur Searle, and Malcolm Turner, eds., *Sundry Sorts of Music Books: Essays on the British Library Collections Presented to O. W. Neighbour on his 70th Birthday* (London, 1993), 146–82.

Milsom, John, "Tallis, Byrd and the 'Incorrected Copy': Some Cautionary Notes for Editors of Early Music Printed from Movable Type," *Music & Letters* 77 (1996): 348–67.

Milsom, John. "A Tallis Fantasia." *Musical Times* 126 (1985): 658–62.

Milsom, John, "Tallis, the Parker Psalter, and Some Known Unknowns," *Early Music* 44 (2016): 207–18.

Milsom, John, "Tallis's First and Second Thoughts," *Journal of the Royal Musical Association* 113 (1988): 203–22.

Milsom, John, *Thomas Tallis & William Byrd: Cantiones Sacrae 1575*, Early English Church Music vol. 56 (London: Stainer & Bell, 2014).

Milsom, John, "William Mundy's 'Vox patris caelestis' and the Accession of Mary Tudor," *Music and Letters* 91 (2010): 1–38.

Monson, Craig. "'Throughout All Generations': Intimations of Influence in the Short Service Styles of Tallis, Byrd and Morley," in *Byrd Studies*, ed. Alan Brown and Richard Turbet (Cambridge: Cambridge University Press, 1992), 83–111.

Morehen, John, "The English Anthem Text," *Journal of the Royal Musical Association* 117 (1992): 62–85.

Moroney, Davitt, "Alessandro Striggio's Mass in Forty and Sixty Parts," *Journal of the American Musicological Society* 60 (2007): 1–69.

Moroney, Davitt. *"Under Fower Sovereygnes":* Thomas Tallis and the Transformation of English Polyphony (PhD dissertation, University of California, Berkeley, 1980).

Nichols, John Gough, ed., *The Diary of Henry Machyn, Citizen and Merchant-Taylor of London* (London: Camden Society, 1848).

Nixon, Howard, "Day's Service Book, 1560–1565," *British Library Journal* 10 (1984): 1–31.

Oastler, Christopher Lewis, *John Day, the Elizabethan Printer* (Oxford: Oxford Bibliographical Society, 1975).

Page, Daniel, *Uniform and Catholic: Church Music in the Reign of Mary Tudor* (PhD dissertation, Brandeis University, 1996).

Payne, Ian, "A Tale of Two Counties: The Biography of Thomas Tallis (c.1505–85) Revisited," *Transactions of the Leicestershire Archaeological and Historical Society* 88 (2014): 85–100.

Phillips, Peter, *English Sacred Music 1549–1649* (Oxford: Gimell, 1991).

Phillips, Peter, "Sign of Contradiction: Tallis at 500," *Musical Times* 146 (2005): 7–15.

Phillips, Peter. "Treble or Soprano? Performing Tallis," *Early Music* 33 (2005): 495–502.

Quitslund, Beth, "The Psalm Book," in *The Elizabethan Top Ten: Defining Print Popularity in Early Modern England* (Farnham: Ashgate, 2013), 203–11.

Quitslund, Beth, *The Reformation in Rhyme: Sternhold, Hopkins and the English Metrical Psalter, 1547–1603* (Aldershot: Ashgate, 2008).

Rayment, Louise, "The Sixteenth-Century School at St. Mary-at-Hill, London," *London Journal* 41, no. 2 (2016): 111–27.

Rice, Stephen. "Reconstructing Tallis's Latin *Magnificat* and *Nunc dimittis*," *Early Music* 33 (2005): 647–58.

Rimbault, Edward, ed., *The Old Cheque-book: Or Book of Remembrance, of the Chapel Royal* (London, 1872).

Rose, Malcolm. "The History and Significance of the Lodewijk Theewes Claviorgan," *Early Music* 32 (2004): 577–93.

Rosendale, Timothy, "'Fiery toungues': Language, Liturgy, and the Paradox of the English Reformation," *Renaissance Quarterly* 54 (2001): 1142–64.

Sandon, Nick, "The Henrician Partbooks at Peterhouse, Cambridge," *Proceedings of the Royal Musical Association* 103 (1976–77): 106–40.

Sandon, Nick, *The Henrician Partbooks Belonging to Peterhouse* (PhD dissertation, University of Exeter, 1983, revised 2009).

Sandon, Nick, notes to Blue Heron BHCD 1008, *The Lost Music of Canterbury: Music from the Peterhouse Partbooks* (2018).

Sandon, Nick, "The Manuscript London, British Library Harley 1709," in Susan Rankin and David Hiley, eds., *Music in the Medieval English Liturgy* (Oxford: Clarendon, 1993), 355–79.

Schofield, Bertram, "The Manuscripts of Tallis's Forty-Part Motet," *Musical Quarterly* 37 (1951): 176–83.

Scott, Heather Gilderdale, "The Royal Window (c. 1485) at Canterbury Cathedral and the Magnificat Window (c. 1500) at Great Malvern Priory (Worcs.): Dynastic Rivalry in Late Medieval England?," in *Medieval Art, Architecture and Archaeology at Canterbury*, ed. Alixe Bovey, Conference Transactions of the British Archaeological Association no. 35 (Leeds: Maney, 2013), 228–44.

Searle, William George, *Christ Church, Canterbury. I. The chronicle of John Stone, monk of Christ Church 1415–1471. II. Lists of the deans, priors, and monks of Christ Church Monastery* (Cambridge: Cambridge Antiquarian Society, 1902).

Select Documents of English Constitutional History, ed. George Burton Adams and H. Morse Stephens (London: Macmillan, 1914).

Shaw, Anthony, *The Compendium Compertorum and the Making of the Suppression Act of 1536* (PhD dissertation, University of Warwick, 2003).

Skinner, David, "'Deliuer me from my deceytful ennemies': A Tallis Contrafactum in Time of War," *Early Music* 44 (2016): 233–50.

Smith, Jeremy, *Thomas East and Music Publishing in Renaissance England* (Oxford: Oxford University Press, 2003).

Smith, Jeremy, "Unlawful Song: Byrd, the Babington Plot and the Paget Choir," *Early Music* 38 (2010): 497–508.

Stevens, Denis, "A Musical Admonition for Tudor Schoolboys," *Music and Letters* 39 (1957): 49–52.

Stevens, Denis, "A Songe of Fortie Partes, Made by Mr. Tallys," *Early Music* 10 (1982): 171–81.

String, Tatiana, "A Neglected Henrician Decorative Ceiling," *Antiquaries Journal* 76 (1996): 139–51.

Sweeny, Cecily, "John Wylde and the Musica Guidonis," *Musica Disciplina* 29 (1975): 43–59.

Thurley, Simon, "The Cloister and the Hearth: Wolsey, Henry VIII and the Early Tudor Palace Plan," *Journal of the British Archaeological Association* 162 (2009): 179–95.

Thurley, Simon, *Houses of Power* (London: Bantam, 2017).

Thurley, Simon, *The Royal Palaces of Tudor England: Architecture and Court Life 1460–1547* (New Haven: Yale University Press, 1993).

Turbet, Richard, "A Selective Bibliography of Writings about Tudor Music 1992–2007: For John Harley on his Eightieth Birthday," *Fontes Artis Musicae* 55 (2008): 340–62.

Turbet, Richard, "Tudor Music: A Selective Bibliography of Writings 2008–2019," *NEMA Newsletter* 5 (2020).

Wegman, Rob, *The Crisis of Music in Early Modern Europe, 1470–1530* (New York: Routledge, 2005).

Williamson, Magnus, "Affordable Splendour: Editing, Printing and Marketing the Sarum Antiphoner (1519–20)," *Renaissance Studies* 26 (2012): 60–87.

Williamson, Magnus, *The Eton Choirbook: Facsimile with Introductory Study* (Oxford: DIAMM Publications), 2010.

Williamson, Magnus, *The Eton Choirbook: Its Institutional and Historical Background* (DPhil dissertation, Oxford University, 1997, rev. 2009).

Williamson, Magnus, "The Fate of Choirbooks in Protestant Europe," *Journal of the Alamire Foundation* 7 (2015): 117–31.

Williamson, Magnus, "The International Face of Tudor Music," *Early Music* 37 (2009): 467–9.

Williamson, Magnus, ed., *John Sheppard, III: Hymns, Psalms, Antiphons, and Other Latin Polyphony*, Early English Church Music vol. 54 (London: Stainer & Bell, 2012).

Williamson, Magnus, "Liturgical Polyphony in the Pre-Reformation English Parish Church: A Provisional List and Commentary," *Royal Musical Association Research Chronicle* 38 (2005): 1–43.

Williamson, Magnus, "Queen Mary I, Tallis's *O sacrum convivium* and a Latin Litany," *Early Music* 44 (2016): 251–70.

Willis, Jonathan, *Church Music and Protestantism in Post-Reformation England: Discourses, Sites and Identities* (Farnham: Ashgate, 2010).

Winters, William, *Ecclesiastical works of the Middle Ages; or, historical notices of early manuscripts formerly belonging to the ancient monastic library of Waltham Holy Cross* (Waltham Abbey: Winters, 1877).

Winters, William, *The History of the Ancient Parish of Waltham Abbey or Holy Cross* (Waltham Abbey: Winters, 1888).

Wizeman, William, *The Theology and Spirituality of Mary Tudor's Church* (Aldershot: Ashgate, 2006).

Woodfield, Ian, "'Music of Forty Several Parts': A Song for the Creation of Princes," *Performance Practice Review* 7 (1994): 54–64.

Wridgway, Neville, *The Choristers of St. George's Chapel, Windsor Castle* (Slough: Luff, 1980); unpublished revised edition (April 2002) in typescript in the Chapel Archives.

Wrightson, James, *The Wanley Manuscripts*, Recent Researches in the Music of the Renaissance 99–101 (Madison, WI: A-R Editions, 1995).

Wulstan, David, "Where there's a Will: New Light on John Sheppard," *Musical Times* 135 (1994): 25–7.

Youings, Joyce, *The Dissolution of the Monasteries* (London: Allen and Unwin, 1971).

Notes

Preface

1 Suzanne Cole, *Thomas Tallis and his Music in Victorian England* (Woodbridge: Boydell, 2008), 81.
2 Charles Reginald Haines, *Dover Priory* (Cambridge: Cambridge University Press, 1930), 314.
3 Susan Foister, *Holbein and England* (New Haven: Yale University Press, 2004), 214–22.
4 John Milsom, "Tallis's First and Second Thoughts," *Journal of the Royal Musical Association* 113 (1988): 203–22.
5 *The Dow Partbooks*, ed. John Milsom (Oxford: DIAMM Publications, 2010), 37: *Talis es et tantus Tallisi musicus, ut si fata senem auferrent musica muta foret.*
6 John Harley, *Thomas Tallis* (Farnham: Ashgate, 2015).

Chapter One

1 *A Discourse of Sea-Ports, principally of the port and haven of Dover* (London, 1700); reprinted in *The Harleian Miscellany, or a collection of scarce, curious, and entertaining pamphlets and tracts, as well in manuscript as in print* (London, 1744), 4:294.
2 Roger Bowers, "Thomas Tallis at Dover Priory, 1530–1531," *Early Music* 44, no. 2 (May 2016): 197–205.
3 British Library Add. MS 25107; Charles Reginald Haines, *Dover Priory* (Cambridge: Cambridge University Press, 1930), 443–68.
4 Mary Bateson, "Archbishop Warham's Visitation of Monasteries," *English Historical Review* 6, no. 21 (January 1891), 22.
5 BL Add. 25107, f. 5r.
6 Philip Butterworth, *Magic on the Early English Stage* (Cambridge: Cambridge University Press, 2005), 10–11.
7 Haines, *Dover Priory*, 314.
8 Haines, *Dover Priory*, 420.
9 Jane Flynn, *A Reconsideration of the Mulliner Book (BL Add. MS 30513): Music Education in Sixteenth-Century England* (PhD dissertation, Duke University, 1993), 124–5.
10 Bowers, "Thomas Tallis at Dover Priory," 203.
11 Roger Bowers, "The Musicians of the Lady Chapel of Winchester Cathedral Priory, 1402–1539," *Journal of Ecclesiastical History* 45 (1994), 218, fn. 20; reprinted in *English Church Polyphony* (Aldershot: Ashgate, 1999), 5:218.
12 Rob Wegman, *The Crisis of Music in Early Modern Europe, 1470–1530* (New York: Routledge, 2005), 164.
13 Rob Wegman, "Obrecht and Erasmus," *Journal of the Alamire Foundation* 3 (2011): 110.

14 Joyce Youings, *The Dissolution of the Monasteries* (London: Allen and Unwin, 1971), 224–5.

15 Roger Bowers, "An Early Tudor Monastic Enterprise: Choral Polyphony for the Liturgical Service," in *The Culture of Medieval English Monasticism*, ed. James G. Clark (Woodbridge: Boydell, 2007), 34.

16 George G. Perry, "The Visitation of the Monastery of Thame, 1526," *English Historical Review* 3 (1888): 713.

17 Thomas Cooper, *Thesaurus Linguae Romanae et Britannicae* (London, 1565).

18 Bowers, "An Early Tudor Monastic Enterprise," 44; Bowers, "The Musicians and Liturgy of the Lady Chapels of the Monastery Church," in *Westminster Abbey: The Lady Chapel of Henry VII*, ed. T. W. T. Tatton-Brown and Richard Mortimer (Woodbridge: Boydell, 2003), 51–2.

19 Haines, *Dover Priory*, 319–21.

20 Anthony Shaw, *The Compendium Compertorum and the Making of the Suppression Act of 1536* (PhD dissertation, University of Warwick, 2003), 227.

21 Bateson, "Archbishop Warham's Visitation," 24–5.

22 Henry Ellis, ed., *Original Letters Illustrative of English History* (London: Richard Bentley, 1846), 3:165; James Gairdner, ed., *Letters and Papers Foreign and Domestic of the Reign of Henry VIII* (London: Longmans, 1886), 9: 226.

23 Haines, *Dover Priory*, 115–20.

Chapter Two

1 *The Panorama of London circa 1544*, ed. Howard Colvin and Susan Foister (London: London Topographical Society, 1996).

2 James Howell, *Londinopolis, an historicall discourse or perlustration of the city* (London, 1657), f. M3r.

3 Geoffrey Bullough, *Narrative and Dramatic Sources of Shakespeare* (London: Routledge, 1973), 362; *The True Chronicle History of King Leir and His Three Daughters* (London, ca. 1590), lines 1022–23.

4 James Peller Malcolm, *Londinium Redivivum* (London, 1803), 3:481.

5 Richard Lloyd, "Music at the Parish Church of St Mary at Hill, London," *Early Music* 25, no. 2 (1997): 221–6; John Harley, *The World of William Byrd: Musicians, Merchants and Magnates* (Farnham: Ashgate, 2010), 32–7.

6 London Metropolitan Archives, P69/MRY4/B/005/MS01239/001/003 (hereafter *LMA*), f. 681r, 693v; *The Medieval Records of a London City Church: St. Mary at Hill, 1420–1559*, ed. Henry Littlehales (London: Early English Text Society, 1905), 375, 380.

7 Hugh Baillie, "A London Church in Early Tudor Times," *Music & Letters* 36, no. 1 (1955): 61.

8 *LMA*, f. 681r; Littlehales, 375.

9 *LMA*, f. 613v, 678v, 690v; Littlehales, 358, 372, 377.

10 *LMA*, f. 498r, 612v; Littlehales, 322, 358.

11 *LMA*, f. 498r; Littlehales, 322.

12 Louise Rayment, "The Sixteenth-Century School at St. Mary-at-Hill, London," *London Journal* 41, no. 2 (2016): 111–27.

13 *LMA*, f. 497r–509v; Littlehales, 321–8.

14 *LMA*, f. 690r; Littlehales, 377.

15 *LMA*, f. 498r; Littlehales, 322.

16 *LMA*, f. 588r; Littlehales, 351.

17 John Foxe, *Actes and Monuments*, 8, *K. Henry. 8. Troubles at London about the vj. Articles* (London, 1570).

18 *London and Middlesex Chantry Certificate 1548*, ed. C. J. Kitching (London: London Record Society, 1980), 5–6.

19 Fiona Kisby, "Royal Minstrels in the City and Suburbs of Early Tudor London: Professional Activities and Private Interests," *Early Music* 25, no. 2 (1997): 209.

20 Magnus Williamson, "Liturgical Polyphony in the Pre-Reformation English Parish Church: A Provisional List and Commentary," *Royal Musical Association Research Chronicle* 38 (2005): 1–43.

21 Clive Burgess and Andrew Wathey, "Mapping the Soundscape: Church Music in English Towns, 1450–1550," *Early Music History* 19 (2000): 13–17.

22 Baillie, "A London Church," 56–7.

23 Hugh Baillie, "A London Gild of Musicians, 1460–1530," *Proceedings of the Royal Musical Association* 83 (1956–57): 15–28.

24 *The Bede Roll of the Fraternity of St. Nicholas*, ed. Norman James and Valerie James (London: London Record Society, 2004).

25 *LMA*, f. 678v–695r; Littlehales, 372–80.

26 *LMA*, f. 693r; Littlehales, 379.

27 Charles Wriothesley, *A Chronicle of England*, ed. William Douglas Hamilton (London: Camden Society, 1875), 1: 81.

28 Diarmaid MacCulloch, *Thomas Cranmer: A Life* (New Haven: Yale University Press, 1996), 162–4, 242–51.

29 P. L. Hughes and J. F. Larkin, *Tudor Royal Proclamations: The Early Tudors, 1485–1553* (New Haven: Yale University Press, 1964), 274.

30 Roger Bowers, "An Early Tudor Monastic Enterprise: Choral Polyphony for the Liturgical Service," in *The Culture of Medieval English Monasticism*, ed. James G. Clark (Woodbridge: Boydell, 2007), 53.

31 Richard Lloyd, *Provision for Music in the Parish Church in Late-Medieval London* (PhD dissertation, Royal Holloway, University of London, 1999), 161–2.

Chapter Three

1 TNA E117/11/24, fo. 14r; William Winters, *The History of the Ancient Parish of Waltham Abbey or Holy Cross* (Waltham Abbey: Winters, 1888), 125.

2 TNA E322/252: "*unanimi assensu et consensu ac spontanea voluntate.*"

3 TNA E117/11/24, fo. 20v.

4 TNA E117/11/24, fo. 9v, 21r.

5 Miriam Gill, "Monastic Murals and *Lectio* in the Later Middle Ages," in *The Culture of Medieval English Monasticism*, ed. James G. Clark (Woodbridge: Boydell, 2007), 66.

6 This disappointing error is found in Kerry McCarthy, *Byrd* (Oxford: Oxford University Press, 2013), 4.

7 John F. Pound, *Poverty and Vagrancy in Tudor England*, 2nd ed. (London: Longman, 1986), 18.

8 Barbara Harvey, *Living and Dying in England 1100–1540: The Monastic Experience* (Oxford: Clarendon Press, 1993), 175.

9 Bodleian MS Ashmole 1495, f. 3r.

10 Kerry McCarthy and John Harley, "From the Library of William Byrd," *Musical Times* 150, no. 4 (2009): 17–30.

11 William Winters, *Ecclesiastical Works of the Middle Ages; or, Historical Notices of Early Manuscripts Formerly Belonging to the Ancient Monastic Library of Waltham Holy Cross* (Waltham Abbey: Winters, 1877), 65–6.

12 James P. Carley, "Monastic Collections and Their Dispersal," in *The Cambridge History of the Book in Britain*, ed. John Barnard and D. F. Mackenzie (Cambridge: Cambridge University Press, 2002), 341; Alan Coates, *English Medieval Books: the Reading Abbey Collections from Foundation to Dispersal* (Oxford: Clarendon Press, 1999), 122–4.

13 Theodor Dumitrescu, *The Early Tudor Court and International Musical Relations* (Aldershot: Ashgate, 2007), 202–8; Magnus Williamson, "The International Face of Tudor Music," *Early Music* 37 (2009): 467–9.

14 Cecily Sweeny, "John Wylde and the Musica Guidonis," *Musica Disciplina* 29 (1975): 43–59.

15 Sanford B. Meech, "Three Musical Treatises in English from a Fifteenth-Century Manuscript," *Speculum* 10 (1935): 235–69.

16 Tim William Machan, "Speght's 'Works' and the Invention of Chaucer," *Text* 8 (1995): 159–60.

17 M. D. Knowles and Thurston Dart, "Notes on a Bible of Evesham Abbey," *English Historical Review* 79 (1964): 775–8.

18 E. A. Webb, *The Records of St. Bartholomew's Priory and St. Bartholomew the Great, West Smithfield* (London: H. Milford, 1921), 1:256; John Maynard, *The Parish of Waltham Abbey, Its History and Antiquities* (London: J. R. Smith, 1865), 44.

19 *Letters and Papers, Foreign and Domestic, Henry VIII*, vol. 11, *July–December 1536*, ed. James Gairdner (London: Her Majesty's Stationery Office, 1888), 26.

Chapter Four

1 William George Searle, *Christ Church, Canterbury. I. The chronicle of John Stone, monk of Christ Church 1415–1471. II. Lists of the deans, priors, and monks of Christ Church Monastery* (Cambridge Antiquarian Society, 1902), 11 ("*inter omnes religiosos regni excellentissimam vocem habuit*"); 12 ("*suo tempore organista praecipuus . . . omnem cantum organicum in ecclesia disposuit et gubernavit*").

2 Roger Bowers, *Choral Establishments Within the English Church: Their Constitution and Development, 1340–1542* (PhD dissertation, University of East Anglia, 1976), 4073–4; Bowers, "The Liturgy of the Cathedral and its Music, c.1075–1642," in *A History of Canterbury Cathedral*, ed. Patrick Collinson, Nigel Ramsey, and Margaret Sparks (Oxford: Oxford University Press, 1995), 419.

3 Bowers, "The Liturgy of the Cathedral and its Music," 426.

4 Barrie Dobson, "The Monks of Canterbury in the Later Middle Ages, 1220–1540," in *A History of Canterbury Cathedral*, ed. Patrick Collinson, Nigel Ramsey, and Margaret Sparks (Oxford: Oxford University Press, 1995), 153.

5 Canterbury Cathedral Archives DCc/DE/164, unfoliated.

6 Bowers, "The Liturgy of the Cathedral and its Music," 421, 427.

7 Nick Sandon, *The Henrician Partbooks Belonging to Peterhouse, Cambridge* (DPhil dissertation, Exeter, 1983, revised 2009), 133–7.

8 Sandon, *The Henrician Partbooks*, 133.

9 Canterbury Cathedral Archives DCc/MA40, f. IV.

10 John Harley, *The World of William Byrd: Musicians, Merchants and Magnates* (Burlington, VT: Ashgate, 2010), 143–4.

11 *Statutes of the Realm* (London, 1810–1825), no. 728 (31 Henry VIII c. 9); *Enactments in Parliament: 37 Edward III–13 Anne*, ed. Lionel Lancelot Shadwell (Oxford: Clarendon, 1912), 124.

12 Arthur Francis Leach, *Educational Charters and Documents 598 to 1909* (Cambridge: Cambridge University Press, 1911), 456–7.

13 Leach, *Educational Charters*, 464–9.

14 John Strype, *Memorials of the Most Reverend Father in God, Thomas Cranmer* (London, 1694), 109.

15 Diarmaid MacCulloch, *Thomas Cranmer: A Life* (New Haven: Yale University Press, 1996), 285.

16 *Portiforium secundum usum Sarum noviter impressum et a plurimis purgatum mendis. In quo nomen Romano pontifici falso ascriptum omittitur, una cum aliis que christianissimo nostri regis statuto repugnant* (London, 1541), STC 15834.

17 W. H. Frere and W. P. M. Kennedy, *Visitation Articles and Injunctions of the Period of the Reformation* (London: Longmans, Green, 1910), 2:386.

18 Patrick Collinson, "The Protestant Cathedral," in *A History of Canterbury Cathedral*, ed. Patrick Collinson, Nigel Ramsey, and Margaret Sparks (Oxford: Oxford University Press, 1995), 160–1.

19 Frere and Kennedy, *Visitation Articles*, 2:140–6.

20 Sandon, *The Henrician Partbooks*, 128–30; Sandon, notes to Blue Heron BHCD 1008, *The Lost Music of Canterbury: Music from the Peterhouse Partbooks* (2018).

21 George Joye, *The defence of the mariage of preistes* (Antwerp, 1541), STC 21804, f. C4v.

22 Bowers, "The Liturgy of the Cathedral and its Music," 436–7.

Chapter Five

1 National Archives E179/69/36; Andrew Ashbee, *Records of English Court Music*, vol. 7, *1485–1558* (Aldershot: Scolar, 1993), 91–2. Second copy with slight variants in National Archives E179/69/37; Ashbee, *Records*, 7:92–3. Additional incomplete copy, not including the section with Tallis's name, in National Archives E179/69/35; Ashbee, *Records*, 7:89–91.

2 Roger Schofield, *Taxation Under the Early Tudors 1485–1547* (Oxford: Blackwell, 2004), 13–15.

3 Fiona Kisby, "Royal Minstrels in the City and Suburbs of Early Tudor London: Professional Activities and Private Interests," *Early Music* 25, no. 2 (1997): 199–219.

4 David Fallows, "Henry VIII as a Composer," in *Sundry Sorts of Music Books: Essays on the British Library Collections*, ed. Chris Banks, Arthur Searle, and Malcolm Turner (London: British Library, 1993), 27.

5 John Harley, *Thomas Tallis* (Farnham, Ashgate, 2015), 58–9, 147–8.

6 Amy Louise Erickson, *Women and Property in Early Modern England* (London: Routledge, 1993), 161.

7 David Wulstan, "Where There's a Will: New Light on John Sheppard," *Musical Times* 135 (1994): 25–7.

8 Henry Ellis, ed., *Original Letters Illustrative of English History* (London: Richard Bentley, 1846), 2:49; Frank Llewellyn Harrison, *Music in Medieval Britain* (New York: Praeger, 1958), 171.

9 Harley, *Tallis*, 58; Pygott, *Missa Veni sancte spiritus*, ed. Nick Sandon, Antico Edition RCM119, 1993, rev. 2018.

10 Nick Sandon, *The Henrician Partbooks Belonging to Peterhouse, Cambridge* (DPhil dissertation, Exeter, 1983, revised 2009), 2:108–11.

11 Andrew Ashbee and David Lasocki, *A Biographical Dictionary of English Court Musicians, 1485–1714* (Aldershot: Ashgate, 1998), I: 220–1.

12 Fiona Kisby, "A Mirror of Monarchy: Music and Musicians in the Household Chapel of the Lady Margaret Beaufort, Mother of Henry VII," *Early Music History* 16 (1997): 217–18.

13 Harley, *Tallis*, 96.

14 Reginald H. Adams, *The Parish Clerks of London* (London: Phillimore, 1971), xiii.

15 John Bennett, "A Tallis Patron?," *Royal Musical Association Research Chronicle* 21 (1988): 41–4.

16 John Harley, *The World of William Byrd: Musicians, Merchants and Magnates* (Burlington, VT: Ashgate, 2010), 126–7.

17 Ashbee, *Records of English Court Music* VII, 105; VII, 130; VI, 3.

18 Charles William Wallace, *The Evolution of the English Drama Up to Shakespeare* (Berlin: Reimer, 1912), 94–5; Meg Twycross, "The Widow and Nemesis: Costuming Two Allegorical Figures in a Play for Queen Mary Tudor," *Yearbook of English Studies* 43 (2013): 262–80.

19 National Archives, Patent Rolls C66/1129; full transcription in Richard Turbet, *William Byrd: A Guide to Research* (New York: Garland, 1987), 325–7.

20 John Milsom, *Thomas Tallis & William Byrd: Cantiones Sacrae 1575*, Early English Church Music 56 (London: Stainer & Bell, 2014), x.

21 John Harley, *William Byrd: Gentleman of the Chapel Royal* (Aldershot: Ashgate, 1999), 65.

22 Jeremy Smith, *Thomas East and Music Publishing in Renaissance England* (Oxford: Oxford University Press, 2003), 185, fn. 72.

23 Ashbee, *Records of English Court Music* VI, 38.

24 Milsom, *Cantiones*, xxi: "Communemque mihi tecum sic orno magistrum."

25 St. George's Chapel Archives and Chapter Library, SGC XI.D.15, one page only; transcribed on p. 183 of the typescript of Neville Wridgway's unpublished revised edition (April 2002) of *The Choristers of St. George's Chapel, Windsor Castle* (Luff, 1980), also in the Chapel Archives; reference kindly provided by David Mateer.

26 Westminster Abbey Muniment Room MS 37045, f. 3r; John Harley, "New Light on William Byrd," *Music and Letters* 79 (1998): 478, fn. 10.

27 Joseph Kerman, *The Masses and Motets of William Byrd* (Berkeley and Los Angeles: University of California Press, 1981), 59–61.

28 Bodleian Library MS Wood D.19(4); transcribed in Richard Turbet, *William Byrd: A Guide to Research* (New York: Garland, 1987), 330.

29 John Harington, *Nugae Antiquae*, ed. Henry Harington (London, 1769), 132–3.

30 Harington, *Nugae Antiquae*, 134; Harington, *A new discourse of a stale subject, called the metamorphosis of Ajax* (London, 1596), f. Biii v.

31 Oliver Neighbour, "Music Manuscripts of George Iliffe from Stanford Hall, Leicestershire, Including a New Ascription to Byrd," *Music and Letters* 88 (2007), 430–2.

32 Edward Rimbault, ed., *The Old Cheque-book: Or Book of Remembrance, of the Chapel Royal, from 1561–1744* (London: Camden Society, 1872), 73.

33 Harley, *Tallis*, 14.

34 Rimbault, *The Old Cheque-book*, 71–2.

35 Andrew Johnstone, "Thomas Tallis and the Five-part English Litany of 1544: Evidence of 'the notes used in the king's majesty's chapel'," *Early Music* 44 (2016): 219–32.

36 David Skinner, "'Deliuer me from my deceytful ennemies': A Tallis Contrafactum in Time of War," *Early Music* 44 (2016): 238.

37 Diarmaid MacCulloch, *Thomas Cranmer* (New Haven: Yale University Press, 1996), 330–1.

38 Fiona Kisby, "'When the King Goeth a Procession': Chapel Ceremonies and Services, the Ritual Year, and Religious Reforms at the Early Tudor Court, 1485–1547," *Journal of British Studies* 40 (2001): 71–4.

39 John Strype, *Historical Memorials* (London, 1721), 2, part 1:25.

40 Francis Aidan Gasquet, *Edward VI and the Book of Common Prayer* (London: Hodges, 1890), 147; John Aplin, "The Survival of Plainsong in Anglican Music: Some Early English Te-Deum Settings," *Journal of the American Musicological Society* 32 (1979): 251–2.

41 Charles William Wallace, *The Children of the Chapel at Blackfriars, 1597–1603* (Lincoln, NE: University of Nebraska Press, 1908), 63.

42 *John Sheppard, III: Hymns, Psalms, Antiphons, and Other Latin Polyphony*, ed. Magnus Williamson, *Early English Church Music* vol. 54 (London: Stainer & Bell, 2012), xiii.

43 *The Chronicle of Queen Jane and of Two Years of Queen Mary*, ed. John Gough Nichols (London: Camden Society, 1850), 142.

44 John Edwards, "Spanish Religious Influence in Marian England," in *The Church of Mary Tudor*, ed. Eamon Duffy and David Loades (Aldershot: Ashgate, 2006), 211–13; John Edwards, "Corpus Christi at Kingston upon Thames: Bartolomé Carranza and the Eucharist in Marian England," in *Reforming Catholicism in the England of Mary Tudor: The Achievement of Friar Bartolomé Carranza*, ed. John Edwards and Ronald Truman (Aldershot: Ashgate, 2005), 139–51.

45 Roger Bowers, "The Chapel Royal, the First Edwardian Prayer Book, and Elizabeth's Settlement of Religion, 1559," *Historical Journal* 43 (2000): 321–4.

46 Harley, *Tallis*, 147.

47 Bowers, "The Chapel Royal," 342.

48 Raphael Holinshed, *The firste volume of the chronicles of England* (London, 1577), f. 76v.

49 Shropshire Archives LB/15/1/225, fo. 3r–6r; Alan Smith, "Elizabethan Church Music at Ludlow," *Music & Letters* 49 (1968): 108–21.

50 Magnus Williamson, "The Fate of Choirbooks in Protestant Europe," *Journal of the Alamire Foundation* 7 (2015): 126–7.

51 Fiona Kisby, *The Royal Household Chapel in Early-Tudor London, 1485–1547* (PhD dissertation, Royal Holloway, 1996), 88.

52 Kisby, *Royal Household Chapel*, 199.

53 Stephen Bicknell, *The History of the English Organ* (Cambridge: Cambridge University Press, 1996), 45.

54 Ellis, *Original Letters,* 49–50; Harrison, *Music in Medieval Britain*, 171.

55 Harley, *Tallis*, 147–8.

56 Rimbault, *The Old Cheque-book*, 123.

57 Harley, *The World of William Byrd*, 143–4.

58 *Calendar of the Cecil Papers in Hatfield House,* vol. 24, *Addenda, 1605–1668* (London: Her
Majesty's Stationery Office, 1976), 142.

Chapter Six

1 Simon Thurley, *The Royal Palaces of Tudor England: Architecture and Court Life 1460–1547*
(New Haven: Yale University Press, 1993), 75–8.

2 Thurley, *Royal Palaces of Tudor England,* for Hampton Court (Figure 1, p. vi; Figure 97,
p. 76; back endpapers), Richmond (Figure 32, p. 25; Figure 43, p. 32), and Greenwich
(front endpapers; Figure 67, p. 49); Thurley, *Houses of Power* (Bantam, 2017), for
Whitehall (pp. 138–39).

3 Fiona Kisby, *The Royal Household Chapel in Early-Tudor London, 1485–1547* (PhD dissertation, Royal Holloway, 1996), 317.

4 Fiona Kisby, " 'When the King Goeth a Procession': Chapel Ceremonies and Services,
the Ritual Year, and Religious Reforms at the Early Tudor Court, 1485–1547," *Journal
of British Studies* 40 (2001): 61–3.

5 Lucy Wooding, *Henry VIII,* 2nd ed. (London: Routledge, 2015), 49; *Letters and Papers,
Foreign and Domestic, Henry VIII,* vol. 3, *1519–1523,* ed. J. S. Brewer (London: Her Majesty's
Stationery Office, 1867), 467.

6 Kisby, " 'When the King Goeth a Procession'," 49.

7 Peter McCullough, *Sermons at Court* (Cambridge: Cambridge University Press, 1998),
13; Thurley, *Houses of Power,* 316.

8 Thurley, *Royal Palaces of Tudor England,* 66–7.

9 Thurley, *Royal Palaces of Tudor England,* 220–4 and 230.

10 Kisby, "When the King Goeth a Procession," 60.

11 Simon Thurley, "The Cloister and the Hearth: Wolsey, Henry VIII and the Early
Tudor Palace Plan," *Journal of the British Archaeological Association* 162 (2009): 190.

12 *Calendar of State Papers Relating To English Affairs in the Archives of Venice,* vol. 6,
1555–1558, ed. Rawdon Brown (London: Public Record Office, 1877), 147; Magnus
Williamson, "Queen Mary I, Tallis's *O sacrum convivium* and a Latin Litany," *Early
Music* 44 (2016): 260.

13 Simon Thurley, *Hampton Court: A Social and Architectural History* (New Haven: Yale,
2004), 101–2.

14 J. W. Blench, "John Longland and Roger Edgeworth, Two Forgotten Preachers of the
Early Sixteenth Century," *Review of English Studies* 5 (1954): 127.

15 Thurley, *Royal Palaces of Tudor England,* back endpapers.

16 A. R. Myers, ed., *The Household of Edward IV: The Black Book and the Ordinance of 1478*
(Manchester: Manchester University Press, 1959), 135.

17 Kisby, *The Royal Household Chapel in Early-Tudor London,* 346.

18 *A Collection of Ordinances and Regulations for the Government of the Royal Household*
(Society of Antiquaries, 1790), 200.

19 *A Collection of Ordinances,* 212; Andrew Ashbee, ed., *Records of English Court Music,* vol.
7, *1485–1558* (Aldershot: Scolar), 417.

20 *A Collection of Ordinances,* 208; Ashbee, *Records of English Court Music,* 7:417.

21 Simon Thurley, *Royal Palaces of Tudor England,* 27–31.

22 Fiona Kisby, *The Royal Household Chapel in Early-Tudor London,* 547; Gordon Kipling,
ed., *The Receyt of the Ladie Kateryne* (Oxford: Early English Text Society, 1990), 72–3.

23 *I diarii di Marino Sanuto*, vol. 20 (Venice, 1887), col. 266; Roger Bowers, "The Vocal Scoring, Choral Balance and Performing Pitch of Latin Church Polyphony in England, c. 1500–58," *Journal of the Royal Musical Association* 112 (1986–87), 50, n28; reprinted in Bowers, *English Church Polyphony: Singers and Sources from the 14th to the 17th Century* (Aldershot: Ashgate Variorum, 1999), III, also 50, note 28.

24 Thurley, *Royal Palaces of Tudor England*, Plan 11, 258.

25 G. W. Bernard, *The King's Reformation: Henry VIII and the Remaking of the English Church* (New Haven: Yale, 2005), 151–2.

26 John Strype, *Ecclesiastical Memorials* (Oxford, 1822), 3, part 1:48.

27 Thurley, *Houses of Power*, 350.

28 Simon Thurley, "Whitehall Palace and Westminster 1400–1600: A Royal Seat in Transition," in *The Age of Transition: The Archaeology of English Culture 1400–1600*, ed. David Gaimster and Paul Stamper (Oxford: Oxbow, 1997), 93–103; *Statutes of the Realm* (London, 1817), 3:668 (28 Henry VIII c. 12.)

29 David Skinner, "'At the Mynde of Nicholas Ludford': New Light on Ludford from the Churchwardens' Accounts of St Margaret's, Westminster," *Early Music* 22 (1994): 393–413; Fiona Kisby, "Music and Musicians of Early-Tudor Westminster," *Early Music* 23 (1995): 22–40.

30 Simon Bradley and Nikolaus Pevsner, *The Buildings of England: London*, vol. 6, *Westminster* (New Haven: Yale, 2003), 231–2.

31 Donald O'Connell, "Medieval Choir Stalls in Parish Churches," in *King's Lynn and the Fens: Medieval Art, Architecture and Archaeology*, ed. John McNeill (London: Routledge, 2008), 242; Tim Tatton-Brown and Richard Mortimer, eds., *Westminster Abbey: The Lady Chapel of Henry VII* (Woodbridge: Boydell, 2003), 203; Robert G. Arns and Bret E. Crawford, "Resonant Cavities in the History of Architectural Acoustics," *Technology and Culture* 36 (1995): 104–35.

32 Howard Colvin, *The History of the King's Works, 1485–1660, Part II* (London, 1963), 315.

33 Thurley, *Houses of Power*, 273–4.

34 McCullough, *Sermons at Court*, 46–7.

35 Diarmaid MacCulloch, *The Boy King: Edward VI and the Protestant Reformation* (Berkeley and Los Angeles: University of California Press, 2002), 23.

36 John Harley, *Thomas Tallis* (Farnham: Ashgate, 2015), 146–7.

37 Tatiana String, "A Neglected Henrician Decorative Ceiling," *Antiquaries Journal* 76 (1996): 139–51.

38 Diarmaid MacCulloch, *Thomas Cromwell: A Revolutionary Life* (New York: Viking, 2018), 512–13.

39 Elizabeth Ann Culling, *The Impact of the Reformation on the Tudor Royal Household* (PhD dissertation, Durham, 1986), 74.

40 Kisby, *The Royal Household Chapel in Early-Tudor London*, 317.

41 Harley, *Tallis*, 94–5.

Chapter Seven

1 Magnus Williamson, "Affordable Splendour: Editing, Printing and Marketing the Sarum Antiphoner (1519–20)," *Renaissance Studies* 26 (2012): 60–87.

2 Owain Edwards, "How many Sarum Antiphoners Were There in England and Wales in the Sixteenth Century?," *Revue bénédictine* 99 (1989): 155–80.

3 Clive Burgess and Andrew Wathey, "Mapping the Soundscape: Church Music in English towns, 1450–1550," *Early Music History* 19 (2000): 36.

4 Williamson, "Affordable Splendour," 67, fig. 1: "quorum precium vile est ut nulla vobis excusationis ausa relinquatur."

5 Diarmaid MacCulloch, *Thomas Cranmer: A Life* (New Haven: Yale University Press, 1996), 225; John Wickham Legg, ed., *Breviarium Romanum a Francisco Cardinali Quignonio editum* (Cambridge: Cambridge University Press, 1888), xx: "Accedit tam perplexus ordo, tamque difficilis precandi ratio, ut interdum paulo minor opera in inquirendo ponatur, quam cum inveneris in legendo."

6 Roger Bowers, *Choral Establishments within the English Church: Their Constitution and Development, 1340–1542* (PhD dissertation, University of East Anglia, 1976), 2016–22.

7 *Sane sunt membris res calide mense decembris.—Lotio sit vana sed vasis potatio cara.—Sit tepidus potus frigore contrarie totus.*

8 John Gough Nichols, ed., *Two Sermons Preached by the Boy Bishop* (London: Camden Society, 1875), xxv–xxvi.

9 William Peter Mahrt, "Responsory Prosae and the Post-Christmas 'Choir Solemnities' at Salisbury Cathedral," *Plainsong and Medieval Music* 25 (2016): 27–36.

10 Fiona Kisby, "'When the King Goeth a Procession': Chapel Ceremonies and Services, the Ritual Year, and Religious Reforms at the Early Tudor Court, 1485–1547," *Journal of British Studies* 40 (2001): 71, fn. 134.

11 Susan Brigden, "Youth and the English Reformation," *Past and Present* 95 (1982): 50–1.

12 *The Diary of Henry Machyn, Citizen and Merchant-Taylor of London*, ed. John Gough Nichols (London: Camden Society, 1848), 121.

13 Jane Flynn, *A Reconsideration of the Mulliner Book (BL Add. MS 30513): Music Education in Sixteenth-Century England* (PhD dissertation, Duke University, 1993), 574–6.

14 Francis Lee Utley, "The Choristers' Lament," *Speculum* 21 (1946): 194–202.

15 Jane Flynn, *Reconsideration*, 560–1.

16 Paul Vincent Sullivan, *Ludi Magister: The Play of Tudor School and Stage* (PhD dissertation, University of Texas, Austin, 2005), 35–55.

17 John Stanbridge, *Vulgaria Stanbryge* (London, 1515), STC 23196, f. C5r; Robert Whittinton, *Vulgaria Roberti Whitintoni Lichfeldiensis* (London, 1520), STC 25570, f. H1v; Stanbridge, f. C4r; William Horman, *Vulgaria uiri doctissimi Guil. Hormani Caesariburgensis* (London, 1519), STC 13811, f. 87r; Stanbridge, f. B4r.

18 Stanbridge, f. B4r; Stanbridge, f. C4v; Horman, f. 13r; Horman, f. 11v; Horman, f. 107v.

19 Horman, f. 107r.

20 *Psalmes, Sonets and Songs (1588)*, ed. Jeremy Smith, *Byrd Edition* (London: Stainer & Bell, 2004), 12:xliii.

21 Horman, f. 281v.

22 Gottfried von Bülow, "Diary of the Journey of Philip Julius, Duke of Stettin-Pomerania, Through England in the Year 1602," *Transactions of the Royal Historical Society* 6 (1892): 26–9.

23 Philip Hughes and James Larkin, *Tudor Royal Proclamations* (New Haven: Yale University Press, 1964–69), 1:175.

24 MacCulloch, *Cranmer*, 535.

25 Terence Bailey, *The Processions of Sarum and the Western Church* (Toronto, 1971), 16.

26 Theodor Dumitrescu, *The Early Tudor Court and International Musical Relations* (Aldershot: Ashgate, 2007), 34.

27 Legg, ed., *Breviarium Romanum a Francisco Cardinali Quignonio editum*, xxi: "ut vix aetas hominum ad earum rationem perdiscendam sufficerit."

28 Robert Saltwood, *A comparison bytwene.iiij. byrdes, the Larke, the Nyghtyngale, the Thrusshe & the Cucko, for theyr syngynge who shuld be chauntoure of the quere* (John Mychel, ca. 1533–34), STC 21647, f. B2v.

Chapter Eight

1 Nicholas Sandon, "The Manuscript London, British Library Harley 1709," in Susan Rankin and David Hiley, eds., *Music in the Medieval English Liturgy* (Oxford: Clarendon Press, 1993), 355–79.

2 John D. Bergsagel, "The Date and Provenance of the Forrest-Heyther Collection of Tudor Masses," *Music and Letters* 44 (1963), 240–8, and John Milsom, ed., *The Forrest-Heather Partbooks*, Renaissance Music in Facsimile no. 15 (New York: OMI, 1986).

3 *Musical Times* 45 (July 1904), 443; British Library, Cotton MS Vespasian A. xxv, f. 141v.

4 Rob Wegman, *The Crisis of Music in Early Modern Europe, 1470–1530* (New York: Routledge, 2005), 173.

5 Nick Sandon, *The Henrician Partbooks Belonging to Peterhouse, Cambridge* (DPhil dissertation, Exeter, 1983, revised 2009), 1:17.

6 Harrison, *Music in Medieval Britain*, 431.

7 *Visitation Articles and Injunctions of the Period of the Reformation*, ed. Walter Howard Frere and W. M. Kennedy (Alcuin Club, 1910), 3:22–3.

8 Frank Llewellyn Harrison, *Music in Medieval Britain* (New York: Praeger, 1958), 81 and 295.

9 David Allinson, *The Rhetoric of Devotion: Some Neglected Elements in the Context of the Early Tudor Votive Antiphon* (PhD dissertation, University of Exeter, 1998), 1:207–13.

10 As first pointed out by Jason Smart; see William Wizeman, *The Theology and Spirituality of Mary Tudor's Church* (Routledge, 2006), 223; Cuthbert Tunstall, tr. Thomas Paynell, *Certaine godly and deuout prayers* (London, 1558), f. D.ii r–D.iii r.

11 *A Life of John Colet*, ed. J. H. Lupton (London, 1887), 291–304; John B. Gleason, *John Colet* (Berkeley and Los Angeles: University of California Press, 1989), 179–84.

12 Thomas Starkey, *A preface to the Kynges hyghnes* (London, 1536), f. A.i r (*To the Reders*).

13 Desiderius Erasmus, ed. Richard Taverner, *Prouerbes or adagies* (London, 1539), f. D.i v.

14 Dana Marsh, *Music, Church, and Henry VIII's Reformation* (DPhil dissertation, Oxford, 2007), 136; Roger Bowers, "Testwood, Robert (c.1490–1543)," *Oxford Dictionary of National Biography* (Oxford: Oxford University Press, 2004).

15 Thomas Wilson, *The arte of rhetorique* (London, 1553), f. Q.iii r.

16 *I diarii di Marino Sanuto*, vol. 20 (Venice, 1887), col. 266; Roger Bowers, "The Vocal Scoring, Choral Balance and Performing Pitch of Latin Church Polyphony in England, c. 1500–58," *Journal of the Royal Musical Association* 112 (1986–87), 50, n28; reprinted in Bowers, *English Church Polyphony: Singers and Sources from the 14th to the 17th Century* (Aldershot: Ashgate Variorum, 1999), 3:50, n28.

17 Nick Sandon, *The Henrician Partbooks Belonging to Peterhouse* (PhD dissertation, University of Exeter, 1983, revised 2009), 96; Oxford, Bodleian Library, MS Lat.

Liturg. e. 10., f. 24 v.: "xxiii die mensis Aprilis viz in festo Sancti Georgi martyris circa hora decima ad nocte Anno domini M CCCCmo lxiiii."

18 Letters and papers, Foreign and Domestic of the Reign of Henry VIII (London: Her Majesty's Stationery Office, 1864–1932), vol. 2, part 2, no. 1473.

19 Magnus Williamson, "Royal Image-Making and Textual Interplay in Gilbert Banaster's 'O Maria et Elizabeth'," Early Music History 19 (2000): 237, fn. 1.

20 Magnus Williamson, The Eton Choirbook: Its Institutional and Historical Background (DPhil dissertation, Oxford University, 1997, rev. 2009); Williamson, The Eton Choirbook: Facsimile with Introductory Study (Oxford: DIAMM Publications), 2010.

21 Magnus Williamson, "The Fate of Choirbooks in Protestant Europe," Journal of the Alamire Foundation 7 (2015): 126–7.

22 John Milsom, "The Culture of Partleaves: Peterhouse and Beyond," in Music, Politics and Religion in Early Seventeenth Century Cambridge: The Peterhouse Partbooks in Context, ed. Scott Mandelbrote (forthcoming).

23 Edgar Hoskins, Horae Beatae Mariae Virginis: Or, Sarum and York Primers (London: Longmans, Green & Co, 1901), 134.

24 Ballads from Manuscripts, ed. Frederick Furnivall (London: Ballad Society, 1868–72), 1:391; Stewart James Mottram, Empire and Nation in Early English Renaissance Literature (Woodbridge: Boydell, 2008), 86–7.

25 Sandon, The Henrician Partbooks Belonging to Peterhouse, 258 and 262.

Chapter Nine

1 The Mulliner Book, ed. John Caldwell, Musica Britannica 1, revised ed. (London: Stainer and Bell, 2011).

2 Francis Knights, "Thomas Mulliner's Oxford Career," The Organ 75 (1996): 132–5.

3 Jane Flynn, A Reconsideration of the Mulliner Book (British Library Add. MS 30513): Music Education in Sixteenth-Century England (PhD dissertation, Duke University, 1993): 84–96.

4 Magnus Williamson, "English Organ Music, 1350–1550," in Studies in English Organ Music, ed. Iain Quinn (Abingdon: Routledge, 2018), 97–121.

5 Thomas Morley, A Plaine and Easie Introduction to Practicall Musicke (London, 1597), 90; ed. R. Alec Harman (London: Norton, 1952), 169.

6 Jane Flynn, "The Education of Choristers in England during the Sixteenth Century," in English Choral Practice, 1400–1650, ed. John Morehen (Cambridge: Cambridge University Press, 1995), 80–99.

7 Magnus Williamson, "Playing the Organ, Tudor-style: Some Thoughts on Improvisation, Composition and Memorisation," in Aspects of English Keyboard Music Before 1630, ed. David Smith (Abingdon: Routledge, 2019), 99–122.

8 Morley, Plaine and Easie Introduction, 96; ed. Harman, 177.

9 John Harley, Thomas Tallis (Farnham: Ashgate, 2015), 208–9.

10 Thomas O. Sloane, "Schoolbooks and Rhetoric: Erasmus's Copia," Rhetorica: A Journal of the History of Rhetoric 9 (1991): 113–29.

11 Willi Apel, The History of Keyboard Music to 1700, trans. Hans Tischler (Bloomington: Indiana University Press, 1972), 158.

12 Christopher Maxim, "A Little-Known Keyboard Plainsong Setting in the Fitzwilliam Virginal Book: A Key to Tallis's Compositional Process?," Early Music 29 (2001): 275–82.

13 Timothy Easton and Stephen Bicknell, "Two Pre-Reformation Organ Soundboards," *Proceedings of the Suffolk Institute of Archaeology and History* 38 (1995): 268–95.

14 Reconstructed in 2000–1 by Martin Goetze and Dominic Gwynn for the Early English Organ Project; recorded on *More sweet to hear: Organs & Voices of Tudor England* (OXCD-101), The Choir of Gonville & Caius College, Cambridge, Geoffrey Webber and Magnus Williamson.

15 British Library, Royal MS 18 D II, f. 199r; Ewald Flügel, "Kleinere Mitteilungen aus Handschriften," *Anglia* 14 (1892): 478.

16 Giles Farnaby, *Canzonets to Fowre Voyces* (London, 1598), f. 4r; Anne Daye and Jennifer Thorp, "English Measures Old and New: Dulwich College MS. XCIV/f.28," *Historical Dance* 4 (2018): 28.

17 John Milsom, *English Polyphonic Style in Transition: A Study of the Sacred Music of Thomas Tallis* (DPhil dissertation, University of Oxford, 1983): 24.

18 Denis Stevens, "A Musical Admonition for Tudor Schoolboys," *Music and Letters* 39 (1957): 49–52.

19 British Library, Additional MSS 30480-4, the "Hamond" partbooks; *Mulliner Book*, ed. Caldwell, 38–9 and 243.

20 Oxford, Bodleian Library, Tenbury MS 958, 18–19.

21 Richard Edwards, *The Paradise of Dainty Devices* (1576), no. 107; ed. Hyder Edward Rollins (Harvard, 1927), 107.

22 Morley, *Plaine and Easie Introduction*, 166; ed. Harman, 275.

23 Rollins, *Paradise*, 4.

24 *Mulliner Book*, ed. Caldwell, 254.

25 Susan Brigden, "Howard, Henry, earl of Surrey (1516/17–1547)," *Oxford Dictionary of National Biography* (Oxford: Oxford University Press, 2004).

26 John Milsom, "Tallis's First and Second Thoughts," *Journal of the Royal Musical Association* 113 (1988): 214–17.

27 British Library, Additional MS 31390.

28 Morley, *Plaine and Easie Introduction*, 179; Harman, 293.

29 John Milsom, "A Tallis Fantasia," *Musical Times* 126 (1985), 658–62; John Milsom, *Thomas Tallis & William Byrd: Cantiones Sacrae 1575*, Early English Church Music 56 (Stainer & Bell, 2014), 128.

30 Oliver Neighbour, *The Consort and Keyboard Music of William Byrd* (London: Faber, 1978), 29–31.

31 Edinburgh University Library, MS La. III. 483, fo. 73r and 74r.

32 *Enchiridion musices Nicolai Wollici Barroducensis* (Paris, 1512), f. Aiii r: "Ah pater in celis precibus si flecteris ullis / da precor inceptis splendida vela meis / Explorare queam: que sunt gratissima musis / da dextram misero virgo serena mihi."

Chapter Ten

1 Lewis Lockwood, "A Continental Mass and Motet in a Tudor Manuscript," *Music and Letters* 42 (1961): 336–47.

2 Nick Sandon, *The Henrician Partbooks Belonging to Peterhouse* (PhD dissertation, University of Exeter, 1983, revised 2009), 68–9.

3 Nick Sandon, "The Henrician Partbooks at Peterhouse, Cambridge," *Proceedings of the Royal Musical Association* 103 (1976–77): 106–40.

4 Peterhouse, Perne Library, MSS 31 (Contratenor), 32 (Bassus), 40 (Triplex) and 41 (Medius); formerly Cambridge, University Library, Peterhouse MSS 471–4.

5 Bonnie Blackburn, "Johannes Lupi and Lupus Hellinck. A Double Portrait," *Musical Quarterly* 59 (1973): 547–83.

6 Robert Fayrfax, *Masses Tecum principium and O quam glorifica*, ed. Roger Bray, *Early English Church Music* vol. 45 (London: Stainer & Bell, 2004); John Milsom, "The Arcane Colours of Fayrfax," *Early Music* 33 (2005): 523–4.

7 Isobel Preece, review of Thomas Forrest Kelly, *Plainsong in the Age of Polyphony*, in *Journal of the Royal Musical Association* 118 (1993): 305: "Bone Deus, quantum ocij boni hisce temporibus in Anglia et Scotia in una missa cantanda inaniter conterunt."

8 Philip Brett, "Homage to Taverner in Byrd's Masses," in *William Byrd and his Contemporaries: Essays and a Monograph,* ed. Joseph Kerman and Davitt Moroney (Berkeley and Los Angeles: University of California Press, 2007), 8–21.

9 Magnus Williamson, review of Theodor Dumitrescu, *The Early Tudor Court and International Musical Relations*, in *Early Music* 37 (2009): 468.

10 Lockwood, "A Continental Mass and Motet," 345.

11 Sandon, *The Henrician Partbooks Belonging to Peterhouse*, 3.

12 David Mateer, "Marbeck [Merbecke], John (c. 1505–1585?)," *Oxford Dictionary of National Biography* (Oxford: Oxford University Press, 2004).

13 Robin Leaver, *The Work of John Marbeck* (Appleford: Sutton Courtenay, 1978), 25.

14 Dana Marsh, *Music, Church, and Henry VIII's Reformation* (DPhil dissertation, Oxford, 2007), 136; Roger Bowers, "Testwood, Robert (c. 1490–1543)," *Oxford Dictionary of National Biography* (Oxford: Oxford University Press, 2004).

15 Hugh Aston, *Gaude virgo mater Christi* (= *Gaude mater matris Christi*), Peterhouse no. 69; Fayrfax, *O Maria Deo grata* (= *O Albane Deo grate*), Peterhouse no. 7; Taverner, *O Christe Jesu pastor bone* (= *O Wilhelme pastor bone*), Peterhouse no. 37.

16 Sandon, *The Henrician Partbooks*, 128–30; Sandon, notes to Blue Heron BHCD 1008, *The Lost Music of Canterbury: Music from the Peterhouse Partbooks* (2018).

Chapter Eleven

1 British Library, Add. MSS 17802–5; *The Gyffard Partbooks, I and II*, ed. David Mateer, *Early English Church Music* vols. 48 and 51 (London: Stainer & Bell, 2007–9).

2 Joseph Kerman, *The Masses and Motets of William Byrd* (Berkeley and Los Angeles: University of California Press, 1981), 59–61.

3 David Mateer, "The Compilation of the Gyffard Partbooks," *RMA Research Chronicle* 26 (1993), 19.

4 D. J. Keene and Vanessa Harding, "St. Pancras Soper Lane 145/36," in *Historical Gazetteer of London Before the Great Fire: Cheapside* (London: London Centre for Metropolitan History, 1987), 782–90.

5 Hugh Benham, *John Taverner: His Life and Music* (Aldershot: Ashgate, 2003), 132.

6 Caroline M. Barron and Marie-Hélène Rousseau, "Cathedral, City and State, 1300–1540," in *St. Paul's: The Cathedral Church of London, 604–2004*, ed. Derek Keene, Arthur Burns, and Andrew Saint (New Haven: Yale University Press, 2004), 43.

7 Theodor Dumitrescu, *The Early Tudor Court and International Musical Relations* (Aldershot: Ashgate, 2007), 84–6.

8 Andrew Ashbee, "Groomed for Service: Musicians in the Privy Chamber at the English Court, c.1495–1558," *Early Music* 25 (1997): 193–4.

9 Francis Galpin, *Old English Instruments of Music: Their History and Character*, 2nd ed. (London: Methuen & Co., 1911), 292–8.

10 Katherine Butler, "'By Instruments her Powers Appeare': Music and Authority in the Reign of Queen Elizabeth I," *Renaissance Quarterly* 65 (2012): 359–60; Katie Nelson, "Love in the Music Room: Thomas Whythorne and the Private Affairs of Tudor Music Tutors," *Early Music* 40 (2012): 22.

11 Laurie Stras, "*Voci pari* Motets and Convent Polyphony in the 1540s: The *materna lingua* Complex," *Journal of the American Musicological Society* 70 (2017): 617–96.

12 David Allinson, "Philip van Wilder, Henry VIII's Lost Composer," notes to *Philip van Wilder: Complete Sacred Music*, CD TOCC 0198 (Toccata Classics, 2013): 5.

13 Magnus Williamson, "Liturgical Polyphony in the Pre-Reformation English Parish Church: A Provisional List and Commentary," *RMA Research Chronicle* 38 (2005): 12.

14 Andrew Ashbee, *Records of English Court Music*, vol. 7: *1485–1558* (Aldershot: Scolar, 1993), 272 and 277.

15 Margaret Bent, "New and Little-Known Fragments of English Medieval Polyphony," *Journal of the American Musicological Society* 21 (1968): 149–50; Hugh Benham, "'Stroke' and 'Strene' Notation in Fifteenth- and Sixteenth-Century Equal-Note Cantus Firmi," *Plainsong and Medieval Music* 2 (1993): 153–67.

16 Stefan Scot, ed., *John Sheppard, IV: The English Sacred Music*, Early English Church Music (forthcoming).

17 Thomas Morley, *A Plain and Easy Introduction to Practical Music*, ed. Alec Harman (New York: Norton, 1952), 291.

18 Patrick Macey, "Josquin as Classic: *Qui habitat, Memor esto*, and Two Imitations Unmasked," *Journal of the Royal Musical Association* 118 (1993): 1–43.

19 David Mateer, "The 'Gyffard' Partbooks: Composers, Owners, Date and Provenance," *Royal Musical Association Research Chronicle* 28 (1995): 40.

20 Mateer, "The 'Gyffard' Partbooks," 29–37.

21 Mateer, "The 'Gyffard' Partbooks," 34.

22 Kerry McCarthy, "Evidence of Things Past," *Journal of the Royal Musical Association* 135 (2010): 405–11.

Chapter Twelve

1 *An Act for Uniformity of Service and Administration of the Sacraments throughout the Realm* (2 & 3 Edw. 6 c 1); *Select Documents of English Constitutional History*, ed. George Burton Adams and H. Morse Stephens (London: Macmillan, 1914), 274.

2 Charles Wriothesley, *A Chronicle of England During the Reigns of the Tudors*, ed. William Douglas Hamilton, vol. 1 (London: Camden Society, 1875), 83; John Aplin, "The Survival of Plainsong in Anglican Music: Some Early English Te-Deum Settings," *Journal of the American Musicological Society* 32 (1979): 251.

3 John Strype, *Historical Memorials* (London, 1721), 2, part 1: 25.

4 Wriothesley, *Chronicle*, 187.

5 John Milsom, "English-Texted Chant Before Merbecke," *Plainsong and Medieval Music* 1 (1992), 77–92.

6 Diarmaid MacCulloch, *Thomas Cranmer* (New Haven: Yale University Press, 1996), 504–5.

7 Judith Blezzard, *The Tudor Church Music of the Lumley Books*, Recent Researches in the Music of the Renaissance 65 (Madison: A-R Editions, 1985); James Wrightson, *The Wanley Manuscripts*, Recent Researches in the Music of the Renaissance 99–101 (Madison: A-R Editions, 1995).

8 Oxford, Bodleian Library, Mus. Sch. e. 420–2.

9 Wrightson, *Wanley Manuscripts* I, RRMR 99:xiii.

10 *The Cambridge History of the English Language*, vol. 3, *1476–1776*, ed. Roger Lass (Cambridge: Cambridge University Press, 1999), 570.

11 Timothy Rosendale, "'Fiery toungues': Language, Liturgy, and the Paradox of the English Reformation," *Renaissance Quarterly* 54 (2001): 1142–64.

12 John Milsom, "Caustun's Contrafacta," *Journal of the Royal Musical Association* 132 (2007): 1–31.

13 Kerry McCarthy, "A Late Anthem by Tallis," *Early Music* 44 (2016): 191–5.

14 British Library, Royal Appendix 74–6.

15 David Humphreys, "Secular Melodies in the Lumley Partbooks," *Early Music* 22 (1994): 191.

16 John Aplin, "'The Fourth Kind of Faburden': The Identity of an English Four-Part Style," *Music & Letters* 61 (1980): 260–1.

17 John Milsom, "English Polyphonic Style in Transition: A Study of the Sacred Music of Thomas Tallis" (DPhil dissertation, Oxford, 1983), vol. 2, appendix 2.3:5–6.

18 John Milsom, "Tallis's First and Second Thoughts," *Journal of the Royal Musical Association* 113 (1988): 203–22.

19 Walter Howard Frere, "Edwardine Vernacular Services Before the First Prayer Book," *Journal of Theological Studies* 1 (1900): 229–46; also in *Walter Howard Frere: A Collection of His Papers on Liturgical and Historical Subjects*, Alcuin Club Collections 35, ed. J. H. Arnold (Oxford: Oxford University Press, 1940), 5–21.

20 Magnus Williamson, preface to *John Sheppard (d. 1558/9), The Second Service "in F fa ut": Magnificat and Nunc dimittis* (Oxford: Oxford University Press, 2004).

21 Nigel Davison, review of *Tallis: English Sacred Music I and II*, (Early English Church Music vols. 12 and 13), *Music & Letters* 56 (1975): 226.

22 Suzanne Cole, "Who is the Father? Changing Perceptions of Tallis and Byrd in Late Nineteenth-Century England," *Music & Letters* 89 (2008), pp. 1–14.

23 Suzanne Cole, *Thomas Tallis and his Music in Victorian England* (Woodbridge: Boydell, 2008), pp. 37–9.

Chapter Thirteen

1 Beth Quitslund, "The Psalm Book," in *The Elizabethan Top Ten: Defining Print Popularity in Early Modern England* (Farnham: Ashgate, 2013), 203–11.

2 John Aplin, "The Origins of John Day's 'Certaine Notes'," *Music & Letters* 62 (1981): 295–9; Howard M. Nixon, "Day's Service Book, 1560–1565," *British Library Journal* 10 (1984): 1–31.

3 John Strype, *Annals of the Reformation* (Oxford: Clarendon Press, 1824), 4:613: "dulcissimum otium literarum."

4 Strype, *Annals*, 613: "absolvi psalterium versum metrice lingua vulgari."

5 Jonathan Willis, *Church Music and Protestantism in Post-Reformation England: Discourses, Sites and Identities* (Farnham: Ashgate, 2010), 61–2.

6 Claude Palisca, "The Ethos of Modes during the Renaissance," in *The Emotional Power of Music: Multidisciplinary Perspectives*, ed. Tom Cochrane, Bernardino Fantini, and Klaus R. Scherer (Oxford: Oxford University Press, 2013), 107–8; Hyun-Ah Kim, *The Renaissance Ethics of Music: Singing, Contemplation and Musica Humana* (London: Routledge, 2015), 39.

7 British Library MS Lansdowne 763, fo. 49v: "Quintus Tonus; pre ceteris hillaris et iocundus."

8 Strype, *Annals*, 611: "duris praeceptoribus."

9 Beth Quitslund, *The Reformation in Rhyme: Sternhold, Hopkins and the English Metrical Psalter, 1547–1603* (Aldershot: Ashgate, 2008), 254–6.

10 John Milsom, "Tallis, the Parker Psalter, and Some Known Unknowns," *Early Music* 44 (2016): 216.

11 George Wither, *A Preparation to the Psalter* (London, 1619): 8.

12 Milsom, "Tallis, the Parker Psalter, and Some Known Unknowns," 207–15.

13 A. N. Wilson, *The Elizabethans* (New York: Farrar, Straus, and Giroux, 2011), 69; Edward Wedlake Brayley, *A Concise Account, Historical and Descriptive, of Lambeth Palace* (London, 1806), 80.

14 *Correspondence of Matthew Parker*, ed. J. Bruce and T. T. Perowne, Parker Society vol. 42 (Cambridge: Cambridge University Press, 1853), 173.

15 David J. Crankshaw and Alexandra Gillespie, "Parker, Matthew (1504–1575)," *Oxford Dictionary of National Biography* (Oxford: Oxford University Press, 2004).

16 John Milsom, "Caustun's Contrafacta," *Journal of the Royal Musical Association* 132 (2007): 19–21; Peter Phillips, *English Sacred Music 1549–1649* (Oxford: Gimell, 1991), 392–6.

17 Christopher Lewis Oastler, *John Day, the Elizabethan Printer* (Oxford: Oxford Bibliographical Society, 1975), 24.

18 *The Autobiography of Thomas Whythorne*, ed. James M. Osborn (Oxford: Oxford University Press, 1961), 220.

19 Samantha Arten, The Whole Booke of Psalmes, *Protestant Ideology, and Musical Literacy in Elizabethan England* (PhD dissertation, Duke, 2018), 260–84.

20 David Collins, "A 16th-Century Manuscript in Wood: The Eglantine Table at Hardwick Hall," *Early Music* 4 (1976): 275–9.

Chapter Fourteen

1 Katherine Butler, *Music in Elizabethan Court Politics* (Woodbridge: Boydell, 2015), 33–4; Richard Freedman, *The Chansons of Orlando di Lasso and their Protestant Listeners* (Rochester, NY: University of Rochester press, 2001), 189.

2 John Milsom, *Thomas Tallis & William Byrd: Cantiones Sacrae 1575*, Early English Church Music 56 (London: Stainer & Bell, 2014).

3 Peter Levens, *Manipulus vocabulorum* (London, 1570), f. I.iii: "a dittie of a song: *argumentum, materia*."

4 Jeremy Smith, ed., *Byrd Edition*, vol. 12, *Psalmes, Sonets and Songs (1588)* (London: Stainer & Bell, 2004), xlii.

5 Thomas Watson, *Italian Madrigals Englished (1590)*, ed. Albert Chatterley, Musica Britannica 74 (London: Stainer & Bell, 1999), xix.

6 Milsom, *Cantiones*, xiii–xiv.

7 Janet M. Green, "Queen Elizabeth I's Latin Reply to the Polish Ambassador," *Sixteenth Century Journal* 31 (2000): 987–1008.

8 Milsom, *Cantiones*, xii; Craig Monson, ed., *Byrd Edition*, vol. 1, *Cantiones Sacrae (1575)* (London: Stainer & Bell, 1977), xvii and xxv.

9 Milsom, *Cantiones*, xxiii.

10 John Milsom, "Tallis, Byrd and the 'Incorrected Copy': Some Cautionary Notes for Editors of Early Music Printed from Movable Type," *Music & Letters* 77 (1996), 348–67.

11 Milsom, *Cantiones*, xxvi and 439–40.

12 Milsom, *Cantiones*, 1–81, 128–67, and 308–20.

13 Magnus Williamson, "Queen Mary I, Tallis's *O sacrum convivium* and a Latin Litany," *Early Music* 44 (2016): 251–70.

14 Milsom, *Cantiones*, 215–16.

15 Edmund Spenser, *The Faerie Queene: Book Six and the Mutabilitie Cantos*, ed. Andrew Hadfield and Abraham Stoll (Indianapolis: Hackett, 2007), xviii–xxii and 183–222.

16 James Haar, "Classicism and Mannerism in 16th-Century Music," *International Review of Music Aesthetics and Sociology* 25 (1994): 5–18.

17 Kerry McCarthy, "Tallis, Isidore of Seville and *Suscipe quaeso*," *Early Music* 35 (2007): 447–50.

18 Denis Collins, " 'Sufficient to quench the thirst of the most insaciate scholler whatsoeuer': George Waterhouse's 1,163 Canons on the Plainsong *Miserere*," in *Canons and Canonic Techniques, 14th–16th Centuries: Theory, Practice, and Reception History*, ed. Katelijne Schiltz and Bonnie Blackburn (Leuven: Peeters, 2007), 407–20.

19 Milsom, *Cantiones*, 414–16.

20 Thomas Schmidt-Beste, "A Dying Art: Canon Inscriptions and Canon Techniques in 16th-Century Papal Chapel Repertoire," in *Canons and Canonic Techniques*, ed. Schiltz and Blackburn, 339–58.

21 Joseph Kerman, *The Masses and Motets of William Byrd* (Berkeley and Los Angeles: University of California Press, 1981), 180–2.

22 Monson, *Byrd Edition*, 1:xxii and xxvii; Milsom, *Cantiones*, xxii.

23 Mark Eccles, "Bynneman's Books," *The Library* 12 (1957): 83.

24 Milsom, *Cantiones*, xxix.

25 Milsom, *Cantiones*, xxix–xxx.

26 John Harley, *William Byrd: Gentleman of the Chapel Royal* (Aldershot: Ashgate, 1999), 65–6.

27 John Harley, "New Light on William Byrd," *Music and Letters* 79 (1998): 478; Richard Charteris, *Newly Discovered Music Manuscripts from the Private Collection of Emil Bohn* (Holzgerlingen: American Institute of Musicology, 1999), 255.

28 John Morehen, "The English Anthem Text," *Journal of the Royal Musical Association* 117 (1992): 71–2.

29 Jeremy Smith, "Unlawful Song: Byrd, the Babington Plot and the Paget Choir," *Early Music* 38 (2010): 505–7.

30 Monson, *Byrd Edition*, 1:xvi and xxv; Milsom, *Cantiones*, xviii.

Chapter Fifteen

1 *Henry IV, Part II*, II.i.85–86.

2 David Mateer, "Baldwin, John (d. 1615)," *Oxford Dictionary of National Biography* (Oxford: Oxford University press: 2004); Hilary Gaskin, *Music Copyists in Late Sixteenth-Century England, with Particular Reference to the Manuscripts of John Baldwin* (PhD dissertation, Cambridge University), 1985.

3 Roger Bray, "John Baldwin," *Music and Letters* 56 (1975): 55–9; "The Part-Books Oxford, Christ Church, MSS 979–983: An Index and Commentary," *Musica Disciplina* 25 (1971): 179–97; "British Library, R.M. 24.d.2 (John Baldwin's Commonplace Book): An Index and Commentary," *Royal Musical Association Research Chronicle* 12 (1974): 137–51.

4 Iain Fenlon and John Milsom, "'Ruled Paper Imprinted': Music Paper and Patents in Sixteenth-Century England," *Journal of the American Musicological Society* 37 (1984): 148.

5 Magnus Williamson, ed., *John Sheppard*, vol. 3, *Hymns, Psalms, Antiphons and Other Latin Polyphony*, Early English Church Music 54 (London: Stainer & Bell, 2012), xx.

6 Daniel Page, *Uniform and Catholic: Church Music in the Reign of Mary Tudor* (PhD dissertation, Brandeis University, 1996), 208–13.

7 Henri Barré, "Le sermon pseudo-augustinien App. 121," *Revue des études augustiniennes* 9 (1963): 111–37.

8 Fiona Kisby, "'When the King Goeth a Procession': Chapel Ceremonies and Services, the Ritual Year, and Religious Reforms at the Early Tudor Court, 1485–1547," *Journal of British Studies* 40 (2001): 44–75.

9 Roger Bray, "The Interpretation of Musica Ficta in English Music c. 1490–c. 1580," *Proceedings of the Royal Musical Association* 97 (1970–71): 31.

10 Thomas Morley, *A Plaine and Easie Introduction to Practicall Musicke* (London, 1597): 154.

11 Williamson, ed., *John Sheppard*, 3:xxiv.

12 Richard Sherr, "Chant in the Renaissance and Interactions With Polyphony," in *Plainsong in the Age of Polyphony*, ed. Thomas Forrest Kelly (Cambridge: Cambridge University Press, 1992), 178–208.

13 Leonard Ellinwood, rev. Paul Doe, *Thomas Tallis: English Sacred Music*, vol. 1, *Anthems*, Early English Church Music 12 (London: Stainer & Bell, 1971), 125.

14 Gaskin, *Music Copyists in Late Sixteenth-Century England*, 199; British Library, RM 24.d.2, rear flyleaf.

15 Robert Dowland, *A musicall banquet* (London, 1610), f. Ai r.

16 William Camden, *Britannia siue Florentissimorum regnorum. . . descriptio*, (London, 1586), f. A2r: "ut Britanniae antiquitatem, & suae antiquitati Britanniam restituerem."

17 John Earle, *Micro-cosmographie, or, A peece of the world discovered in essayes and characters* (London, 1628), f. Cv–C2r.

Chapter Sixteen

1 Philip Brett, "Edward Paston (1550–1630): A Norfolk Gentleman and his Musical Collection," *Transactions of the Cambridge Bibliographical Society* 4 (1964), 51–69, reprinted in *William Byrd and his Contemporaries: Essays and a Monograph*, ed. Joseph Kerman and Davitt Moroney (Berkeley and Los Angeles: University of California Press, 2007), 31–59.

2 Joseph Kerman, "The Missa *Puer natus est* by Thomas Tallis," in *Write All These Down: Essays on Music* (Berkeley and Los Angeles: University of California Press, 1994), 125–38; also in *Sundry Sorts of Music Books: Essays on the British Library Collections Presented to O. W. Neighbour on his 70th Birthday*, ed. Chris Banks, Arthur Searle and Malcolm Turner (London: British Library, 1993), 40–53.

3 Roger Bray, "Music and the Quadrivium in Early Tudor England," *Music and Letters* 76 (1995): 1–18.

4 Thurston Dart, "Cambrian Eupompus," *The Listener* 1359 (17 March 1955): 497.

5 David Humphreys, "Why Did Tallis Compose the *Missa Puer nobis natus est?*," *Musical Times* 157 (2016): 11; David Humphreys, "Tallis's *Suscipe quaeso*," *Early Music* 28 (2000): 508–9.

6 John Harley, *Thomas Tallis* (Farnham: Ashgate, 2015), 128–9; Benjamin Wardhaugh, *A Wealth of Numbers: An Anthology of 500 Years of Popular Mathematics Writing* (Princeton: Princeton University Press, 2012), 4; L. M. Eldredge, Kari Anne Rand Schmidt, and M. B. Smith, "Four Medieval Manuscripts with Mathematical Games," *Medium Ævum* 68 (1999): 209–17.

7 Tatiana String, "A Neglected Henrician Decorative Ceiling," *Antiquaries Journal* 76 (1996): 139–51.

8 Sally Dunkley, preface to *Thomas Tallis: Mass Puer natus est nobis* (Hereford: Cantus Firmus Music, 2015), 3–4.

9 Roger Bray, review of Ronald Woodley, *John Tucke: A Case Study in Early Tudor Music, Music and Letters* 75 (1994): 588–90.

10 British Library, Lansdowne MS 763, f. 52r–v.

11 Walter Odington, *Summa de speculatione musice*, ed. Edmund Coussemaker, in *Scriptorum de musica medii ævi, Nova Series* (Paris: Durand, 1864), 3:217: "secundum suas vocales."

12 Richard Culmer, *Cathedral Newes from Canterbury* (London, 1644), 21–2; David Skinner, "'Deliuer me from my deceytful ennemies': A Tallis Contrafactum in Time of War," *Early Music* 44 (2016): 246.

13 Heather Gilderdale Scott, "The Royal Window (c. 1485) at Canterbury Cathedral and the Magnificat Window (c. 1500) at Great Malvern Priory (Worcs.): Dynastic Rivalry in Late Medieval England?," in *Medieval Art, Architecture and Archaeology at Canterbury*, ed. Alixe Bovey, Conference Transactions of the British Archaeological Association no. 35 (Leeds: Maney Publishing, 2013), 228.

14 Hugh Benham, *John Taverner: His Life and Music* (Aldershot: Ashgate, 2003), 154–5.

15 John Milsom, "William Mundy's 'Vox patris caelestis' and the Accession of Mary Tudor," *Music and Letters* 91 (2010): 1–38.

16 John Milsom, "A New Tallis Contrafactum," *Musical Times* 123 (1982): 429–31.

17 Skinner, "Deliuer me from my deceytful ennemies," 237.

18 Roger Bowers, "The Liturgy of the Cathedral and its Music, c.1075–1642," in *A History of Canterbury Cathedral*, ed. Patrick Collinson, Nigel Ramsey, and Margaret Sparks (Oxford: Oxford University Press, 1995), 428.

19 Cambridge University Library MS Dd.5.14, f. 73v; John Harley, *Thomas Tallis*, 149 (transcription) and 150 (image).

20 Iain Fenlon and Hugh Keyte, "Memorialls of Great Skill: A Tale of Five Cities," *Early Music* 8 (1980): 329–34.

21 Davitt Moroney, "Alessandro Striggio's Mass in Forty and Sixty Parts," *Journal of the American Musicological Society* 60 (2007): 1–69.

22 David Butchart, "The Letters of Alessandro Striggio: An Edition with Translation and Commentary," *RMA Research Chronicle* 23 (1990): 27–8.

23 Moroney, "Alessandro Striggio's Mass," 33.

24 Bertram Schofield, "The Manuscripts of Tallis's Forty-Part Motet," *Musical Quarterly* 37 (1951): 176–83.

25 Denis Stevens, "A Songe of Fortie Partes, Made by Mr. Tallys," *Early Music* 10 (1982): 180; Moroney, "Alessandro Striggio's Mass," 59.

26 Suzanne Cole, *Thomas Tallis and his Music in Victorian England* (Woodbridge: Boydell, 2008), 111, 119, 117.

27 Moroney, "Alessandro Striggio's Mass," 53.

28 Ian Woodfield, " 'Music of Forty Several Parts': A Song for the Creation of Princes," *Performance Practice Review* 7 (1994): 58.

29 John Milsom, "The Nonsuch Music Library," in Chris Banks, Arthur Searle, and Malcolm Turner, eds., *Sundry Sorts of Music Books: Essays on the British Library Collections Presented to O. W. Neighbour on his 70th Birthday* (London: British Library, 1993), 168–9.

Chapter Seventeen

1 Andrew Ashbee and John Harley, *The Cheque Books of the Chapel Royal* (Aldershot: Ashgate, 2000), 1:22.

2 Bodleian Library, MS Rawlinson D318, f. 27v.

3 Ashbee and Harley, *Cheque Books*, 1:106.

4 Henry Oliver Lancaster, *Expectations of Life: A Study in the Demography, Statistics, and History of World Mortality* (New York: Springer, 1990), 8.

5 John Harley, *Thomas Tallis* (Farnham: Ashgate, 2015), 229–33; National Archives PROB 11/68/662 and PROB 11/74/51.

6 John Harley, *The World of William Byrd: Musicians, Merchants and Magnates* (Burlington: Ashgate, 2010), 213; Peter Phillips, "Sign of Contradiction: Tallis at 500," *Musical Times* 146 (2005): 9.

7 Fiona Kisby, *The Royal Household Chapel in Early-Tudor London, 1485–1547* (PhD thesis, Royal Holloway, 1996), 444, 449.

8 *Elizabethan Churchwardens' Accounts*, Publications of the Bedfordshire Historical Record Society 33 (Aspley Guise: Bedfordshire Historical Record Society, 1953), 70; *Henry IV, Part I*, 2.4.

9 Thurston Dart, "Two New Documents Relating to the Royal Music, 1584–1605," *Music & Letters* 45 (1964): 19–20; Edward Rimbault, ed., *The Old Cheque-book: Or Book of Remembrance, of the Chapel Royal* (London: Camden Society, 1872), 122.

10 Ian Payne, "A Tale of Two Counties: The Biography of Thomas Tallis (c.1505–85) Revisited," *Transactions of the Leicestershire Archaeological and Historical Society* 88 (2014): 85–100.

11 Payne, "A Tale of Two Counties," 97.

12 Payne, "A Tale of Two Counties," 98; Maidstone, Centre for Kentish Studies, PRC 17/29/226.

13 Data compiled by Janell K. Lovelace from the brass rubbing collection of the Ashmolean Museum; see also Herbert Haines, *A Manual of Monumental Brasses, comprising an introduction to the Study of these Memorials, and a list of those remaining in the British Isles* (Oxford: J. H. and J. parker, 1861), and Mill Stephenson, *A List of Monumental Brasses in the British Isles* (London: Headley, 1926).

14 David Pinto, "Magic and Mystery in Gibbons and Dowland," *Early Music* 33 (2005): 137.

15 *Registers of the English College at Valladolid, 1589–1862,* Catholic Record Society 30 (1930), 44: "q[uo]d non sit visus satis idoneus huic instituto."

16 Jeremy Smith, *Thomas East and Music Publishing in Renaissance England* (Oxford: Oxford University Press, 2003), 55–6.

17 Malcolm Rose, "The History and Significance of the Lodewijk Theewes Claviorgan," *Early Music* 32 (2004): 577–93.

18 John Bennett, "A Tallis Patron?," *RMA Research Chronicle* 21 (1988): 41–4.

19 Andrew Ashbee, *Records of English Court Music*, vol. 4, *1603–1625* (Aldershot: Scolar, 1991), 3.

20 Antony Buxton, *Domestic Culture in Early Modern England* (Woodbridge: Boydell, 2015), 171.

21 Buxton, *Domestic Culture*, 177.

22 Kerry McCarthy, "Tallis's Epitaph Revisited," *Early Music* 47 (2019): 57–64.

23 Cambridge University Library MS Dd.5.75, f. 12v.

24 Jeremy Smith, "Unlawful Song: Byrd, the Babington Plot and the Paget Choir," *Early Music* 38 (2010): 505–7.

25 Paul Doe, *Tallis* (Oxford: Oxford University Press, 1968): 58: "But whereas [Tallis's] anthems possess a certain freshness and functional merit, these mid-century secular pieces are very much a product of what C. S. Lewis called 'the drab age'."

26 Oxford, Christ Church, Mus. 984–88; facsimile ed. John Milsom, *The Dow Partbooks*, DIAMM Facsimiles 2 (Oxford: DIAMM, 2010): 36.

27 Philip Brett, ed., *Byrd Edition*, vol. 15, *Consort Songs for Voice and Viols* (London: Stainer & Bell, 1970), 114–18.

28 Robin Leaver, *The Work of John Marbeck* (Appleford: Sutton Courtenay, 1978), 25.

29 John Marbeck, *A concordance that is to saie, a worke wherein by the ordre of the letters of the A.B.C. ye maie redely finde any worde conteigned in the whole Bible* (London: Richard Grafton, 1550), f. a.ii; *The Book of Common Prayer with Musical Notes*, ed. Edward Rimbault (London: Novello, 1871), vi.

30 Philip Brett, ed., *Byrd Edition*, vol. 5, *Gradualia I (1605): The Marian Masses* (London: Stainer and Bell, 1989), xxxii and xxxvii: ". . . neque mea aetate, quam omnem in Musicis contrivi, indignum."

31 Magnus Williamson, ed., *John Sheppard*, vol. 3, *Hymns, Psalms, Antiphons, and Other Latin Polyphony*, Early English Church Music 54 (London: Stainer & Bell, 2012), xiv.

32 Williamson, ed., *John Sheppard*, 3:xi, fn. 1: "studiosus Musices, quatenus viginti annos ei facultati operam continuo navarerit multasque cantiones composuerit."

33 David Wulstan, "Where There's a Will: New Light on John Sheppard," *Musical Times* 135 (1994): 25–7.

34 John Harley, *William Byrd: Gentleman of the Chapel Royal* (Aldershot: Ashgate, 1999), 147.

General Index

For the benefit of digital users, indexed terms that span two pages (e.g., 52–53) may, on occasion, appear on only one of those pages.

Agricola, Alexander, 85
Antiphonale ad usum ecclesiae Sarum (1519–20), x–xi, 75–80, 83–86, 102, 175–77
Apel, Willi, 104–5
Apostles' Creed, 130–31
Archbishop Parker's Psalter, 108, 147–59, 163–64, 177, 207–8, 221
Arne, Thomas, 144–45
Arundel House, 192–93, 195
Aston, Hugh, 120–21
  Te matrem Dei laudamus, 16

Baker, Humfrey, 184–85
Baldwin, John, 48, 60, 121–22, 172, 173–82, 217
Bassano family of musicians, 40
Beaufort, Margaret, 42, 217
Bess of Hardwick, Countess of Shrewsbury, 67–68
Black, John, *Report upone quhan sall my sorifull siching slaik,* 110
Blackfriars, 82
Blitheman, William, 43
Blow, John, 144–45
Boleyn, Anne, 53–54, 61, 97–98, 106–7, 126, 155–56, 218–19
Book of Common Prayer, 49–50, 52, 76–77, 130, 137–38, 139–40, 143–44
Borne, John, 31
Bower, Richard, 42–43, 51
Brandon, Thomas, 4
Bristol, 125
Brown, William, 25
Bull, John, 104, 193–94, 200, 217
Bull, Thomas, 37, 121
Bury, Thomas, 42, 71–72, 202–3, 217, 222
Bynneman, Henry, 171
Byrd, John, 45–46
Byrd, Simon, 45–46
Byrd, Thomas, 47, 198, 200–1
Byrd, William, x, 24–25, 28–29, 34, 41, 43, 44–46, 82, 123–24, 162–72, 177, 197, 198, 199, 200–1, 203, 218

1575 printing monopoly shared with Tallis, 44–48, 51–52, 53–54, 55, 162, 171–72, 198, 200, 220
  Gradualia I (1605), 206–7
  Great Service, 144, 179, 182
  Lamentations of Jeremiah, 181
  Laudate pueri, 165–66
  Masses, 114, 117, 131
  My Lady Nevell's Book, 173
  O lux beata Trinitas, 172
  Psalms, Sonnets and Songs (1588), 82, 162–63
  Quomodo cantabimus, 169, 179
  Short Service, 144–45
  Tribue Domine, 167–68
  Ye sacred Muses, 205–6
"Byrd" (chorister at St. George's, Windsor, in 1548), 45–46, 60

Cabezón, Antonio de, 51–52, 191
Calvin, John, 119, 220
Cambridge, 34–35, 50, 94–95, 184–85, 219, 221
  King's College, 75–76, 90
  Peterhouse College, 113–14
  University Library, 184–85, 203
Camden, William, 182
Canterbury
  cathedral, ix, 25–26, 29, 31–38, 121–22, 191
  city waits, 4–5
  priory of St. Gregory, 3–4
Cantiones quae ab argumento sacrae vocantur (1575), xi, 44–46, 53–54, 61, 99, 147, 161–72, 174, 180–81, 197, 205, 223
Case, John, 151–52
Castiglione, Baldassare, 90
Catherine of Aragon, 10–11, 71, 220
Caustun, Thomas, 141, 157
Certain Notes (1560/1565), 147–48
Chapel Royal, ix, 15–17, 19, 32, 34, 37–38, 39–72, 80–81, 82, 85, 93, 94–95, 107–8, 125–26, 128–29, 134–35, 137–38, 141, 168, 169, 173–74, 175, 176–77, 185–86, 191–92, 197, 198–99, 201